ACCOUNTING
SUPER REVIEW®

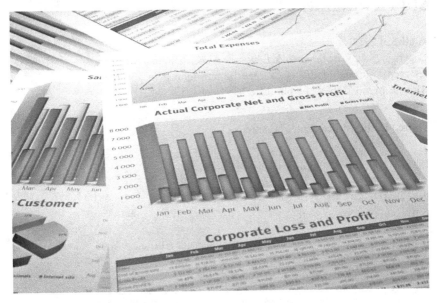

By the Staff of
Research & Education Association

Research & Education Association
Visit our website at: www.rea.com

Research & Education Association
61 Ethel Road West
Piscataway, New Jersey 08854
E-mail: info@rea.com

ACCOUNTING
SUPER REVIEW®

Published 2017

Copyright © 2000 by Research & Education Association, Inc. All rights reserved. No part of this book may be reproduced in any form without permission of the publisher.

Printed in the United States of America

Library of Congress Control Number 00-132726

ISBN-13: 978-0-87891-175-2
ISBN-10: 0-87891-175-8

SUPER REVIEW® and REA® are registered trademarks of Research & Education Association, Inc.

REA's *Accounting Super Review*®

Need help with Accounting? Want a quick review or refresher for class? This is the book for you!

REA's *Accounting Super Review*® gives you everything you need to know!

This *Super Review*® can be used as a supplement to your high school or college textbook, or as a handy guide for anyone who needs a fast review of the subject.

- **Comprehensive, yet concise coverage** – review covers the material that is typically taught in a beginning-level accounting course. Each topic is presented in a clear and easy-to-understand format.

- **Questions and answers for each topic** – let you practice what you've learned and increase your subject knowledge.

- **End-of-chapter quizzes** – gauge your understanding of the important information you need to know, so you'll be ready for any accounting question you encounter on your next quiz or test.

Whether you need a quick refresher on the subject, or are prepping for your next test, we think you'll agree that REA's *Super Review*® provides all you need to know!

Available Super Review® Titles

ARTS/HUMANITIES

Basic Music
Classical Mythology
History of Architecture
History of Greek Art

BUSINESS

Accounting
Macroeconomics
Microeconomics

COMPUTER SCIENCE

C++
Java

HISTORY

Canadian History
European History
United States History

LANGUAGES

English
French
French Verbs
Italian
Japanese for Beginners
Japanese Verbs
Latin
Spanish

MATHEMATICS

Algebra & Trigonometry
Basic Math & Pre-Algebra
Calculus
Geometry
Linear Algebra
Pre-Calculus
Statistics

SCIENCES

Anatomy & Physiology
Biology
Chemistry
Entomology
Geology
Microbiology
Organic Chemistry I & II
Physics

SOCIAL SCIENCES

Psychology I & II
Sociology

WRITING

College & University Writing

About Research & Education Association

Founded in 1959, Research & Education Association is dedicated to publishing the finest and most effective educational materials—including study guides and test preps—for students in middle school, high school, college, graduate school, and beyond.

Today, REA's wide-ranging catalog is a leading resource for teachers, students, and professionals. Visit *www.rea.com* to see a complete listing of all our titles.

Acknowledgments

We would like to thank Pam Weston, Publisher, for setting the quality standards for production integrity and managing the publication to completion; Larry B. Kling, Vice President, Editorial, for his supervision of revisions and overall direction; Claudia Petrilli, Graphic Designer, for designing our cover.

CONTENTS

Chapter   **Page**

1   **INTRODUCTION** 1

     1.1   Definition of Accounting 1
     1.2   Users of Accounting Information 1
     1.3   Generally Accepted Accounting Principles 2
     1.4   The Accounting Equation 3
     1.5   Expanding the Accounting Equation 3
     1.6   Transactions 4
     1.7   Accounting Statements 4

2   **THE ACCOUNTING CYCLE** 8

     2.1   Accounts 8
     2.2   Recording Transactions 9
     2.3   Account Balances 10

3   **ADJUSTING ENTRIES** 12

     3.1   Cash Basis of Accounting 12
     3.2   Accrual Basis of Accounting 12
     3.3   The Adjusting Process 14

     Quiz: Introduction—Adjusting Entries 17

4   **CLOSING ENTRIES** 20

     4.1   Definition and Purpose of Closing Entries 20
     4.2   Steps in Closing Entries 21
     4.3   An Extended Example 22

5   **THE WORKSHEET** 26

    5.1   The Worksheet 26
    5.2   Worksheet Procedures 26

6   **ACCOUNTING FOR A MERCHANDISING OPERATION** 37

    6.1   Gross Profit/Margin 37
    6.2   Perpetual and Periodic Accounting Systems 37
    6.3   Transportation Charges 41
    6.4   Merchandise Returns 42
    6.5   Merchandise Allowances 42
    6.6   Trade Discounts 43
    6.7   Sales Discounts 44
    6.8   Detailed Income Statement 44

    Quiz: Closing Entries—Accounting for a Merchandising Operation 50

7   **INTERNAL CONTROL AND SPECIALIZED JOURNALS** 54

    7.1   Types of Internal Control 54
    7.2   Personnel Controls 54
    7.3   Records Control 55
    7.4   Specialized Journals 56

8   **CASH** 64

    8.1   Definition of Cash 64
    8.2   Internal Control and Cash 64
    8.3   Bank Account Reconciliations 65
    8.4   Petty Cash 73

9 RECEIVABLES 78

9.1   Accounts Receivable 78
9.2   Uncollectible Accounts Receivable 81
9.3   Direct Write-Off Method of Accounting
      for Uncollectible Accounts 84
9.4   Notes Receivable 87
9.5   Discounting Notes Receivable 88
9.6   Dishonored Notes Receivable 91

Quiz: Internal Control and Specialized Journals—
       Receivables 92

10 INVENTORY 96

10.1   Introduction to Inventory Accounting 96
10.2   Periodic and Perpetual Accounting
       Systems 96
10.3   Inventory Methods 97
10.4   Comparison of Cost Methods 109
10.5   Lower-of-Cost-or-Market 110

11 PROPERTY, PLANT, AND EQUIPMENT 111

11.1   Property, Plant, and Equipment 111
11.2   Cost Basis for Property, Plant, and
       Equipment 111
11.3   Depreciation 112

12 OTHER LONG-TERM ASSETS 130

12.1   Introduction of Other
       Long-Term Assets 130
12.2   Leasing 132
12.3   Depletion 134
12.4   Intangible Assets 136

Quiz: Inventory—Other Long-Term Assets 147

viii

13 CURRENT LIABILITIES 150

13.1 Current Liabilities Defined 150
13.2 Accounts Payable 150
13.3 Notes Payable 151
13.4 Liability for Salaries and Wages 157
13.5 Warranties 164
13.6 Returnable Deposits 165

14 LONG-TERM LIABILITIES 168

14.1 Definitions 168
14.2 Pensions 168
14.3 Contingent Liabilities 171
14.4 Unearned Revenue (Deferrals) 172

Quiz: Current Liabilities—Long-Term
Liabilities 174

15 BONDS 178

15.1 Bonds Defined 178
15.2 Purchase of Bonds 178
15.3 Income on Bonds Receivable 180
15.4 Bonds Payable 183
15.5 Bond Issue Price 185
15.6 Bonds Sold at a Discount 185
15.7 Bonds Sold at a Premium 189
15.8 Effective Interest Method 199
15.9 Retirement of Bonds Payable 201

16 PARTNERSHIPS 203

16.1 Partnerships 203
16.2 Advantages and Disadvantages of a
Partnership 205
16.3 Accounting for Partnerships 205

16.4   Accounting for Investments
      in a Partnership 205
16.5   Partnership Income Division 206
16.6   Partnership Statements 213
16.7   Other Considerations 213

17 CORPORATIONS 214

17.1   Corporation Defined 214
17.2   Advantages of a Corporation 214
17.3   Disadvantages of a Corporation 215
17.4   Par Value Stock 215
17.5   No-Par Stock 217
17.6   Common Stock 219
17.7   Preferred Stock 220
17.8   Convertible Preferred Stock 221
17.9   Treasury Stock 222

Quiz: Bonds—Corporations 224

**18 CORPORATIONS: EARNINGS
AND DIVIDENDS** 228

18.1   Equity Section Structures 228
18.2   Corporate Income Taxes 229
18.3   Deferred Income Taxes 231
18.4   Unusual Items 234
18.5   Earnings Per Share 235
18.6   Retained Earnings Appropriations 235
18.7   Cash Dividends 237
18.8   Stock Dividends 240
18.9   Stock Splits 244
18.10 Effect of Treasury Stock 245

Quiz: Corporations: Earnings and Dividends 245

19 CONSOLIDATIONS 249

19.1 Parent and Subsidiary Company Relationships 249

19.2 Intercompany Eliminations 250

19.3 Preparation of Consolidated Financial Statements 250

19.4 Purchase Price Above Book Value 252

19.5 Purchase of Less Than 100 Percent of Subsidiary 255

19.6 Consolidated Income Statement 255

19.7 Pooling of Interest Method 255

20 STATEMENT OF CASH FLOWS 256

20.1 Purpose of Statement of Cash Flows 256

20.2 Preparation of the Statement of Cash Flows 257

21 FINANCIAL STATEMENT ANALYSIS 267

21.1 Comparative Financial Statements 267

21.2 Trend Analysis 267

21.3 Common-Size Financial Statements 268

21.4 Other Sources of Financial Information 290

Quiz: Consolidations—Financial Statement Analysis 290

CHAPTER 1

Introduction

1.1 Definition of Accounting

Accounting can be described as an information system that provides essential information about the financial activities of a business entity to various individuals or groups for their use in making informed decisions.

Accounting is primarily concerned with the design of the record-keeping system, the preparation of summarized reports based on the recorded data, and the interpretation of those reports.

1.2 Users of Accounting Information

Users of accounting information can be quite varied, depending on the type of decision under consideration. Accounting information might be used for decisions involving investments, to impose income taxes, or for regulatory or managerial decisions. The process of using accounting to provide information to users is illustrated in the chart on the following page.

As shown in this diagram, the first step is to identify user needs. A properly designed accounting system can then generate summarized reports (using recorded transaction data) to meet those needs for accounting information. Users can then use those reports to make informed business decisions.

CHART 1.2.1

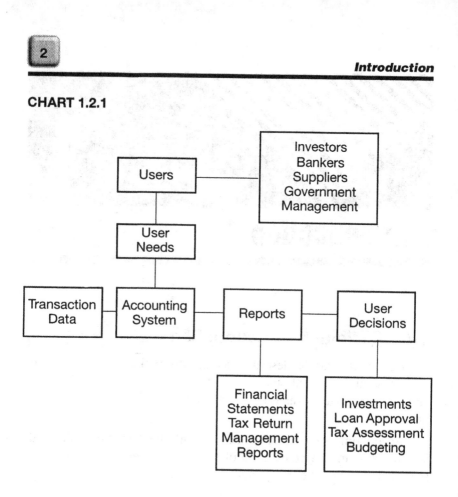

1.3 Generally Accepted Accounting Principles

This broad range of potential users has brought about the evolution of Generally Accepted Accounting Principles (GAAP) used in preparation of financial statements. Many of these principles have been formally established by standard-setting bodies such as the Financial Accounting Standards Board (FASB). Others have simply gained acceptance through widespread use. Adherence to GAAP provides a measure of consistency in preparation of financial statements.

1.4   The Accounting Equation

Assets are tangible or intangible properties owned by a business. The rights or claims to those assets are **equities**. Owners and creditors provide resources that enable a business to purchase assets and therefore are said to have equity in that business. For instance, an owner may start a business with $10,000 cash. This cash is used to buy equipment. The owner, who provided the funds for the equipment, has a claim to that equipment.

The relation between assets and equities is shown by the equation:

$$\text{Assets = Equities}$$

Equities can be subdivided into two categories: (1) **Liabilities:** (rights of creditors represented by debts of the business), and (2) **Owner's Equity:** (rights of the owner or owners.)

1.5   Expanding the Accounting Equation

Expanding the original equation by using the two categories of equities shown in Section 1.4 yields the **accounting equation:**

$$\text{Assets = Liabilities + Owner's Equity}$$

Creditors have preferential rights to the assets of a corporation. The residual claim of the owner or owners may be better understood by restating the accounting equation as:

$$\text{Assets - Liabilities = Owner's Equity}$$

The dollar totals of both sides of the accounting equation are always equal, since they are simply two views of the same business property. The list of assets provides a description of the various business properties, while the list of liabilities and equities indicates the funding source for those assets.

1.6   Transactions

A transaction can be defined as an occurrence or an event that must be recorded. Any business transaction can be stated in terms of the resulting change in the three basic elements of the accounting equation. The equality of the two sides of the accounting equation must be maintained upon completion of a transaction.

As an illustration, examine the result of a transaction to purchase land for $10,000 cash.

$$\text{Assets (+\$10,000 land} - \text{\$10,000 cash)} =$$
$$\text{Liabilities + Owner's Equity}$$

In this case, assets would be increased by $10,000 to reflect the land purchase and decreased by $10,000 to reflect cash paid. The net effect on assets is zero, so the accounting equation remains valid.

As another example, modify the transaction above to reflect the purchase of land by borrowing the $10,000 purchase price with a bank loan (also known as a note payable).

$$\text{Assets (+\$10,000 land)} =$$
$$\text{Liabilities (+\$10,000 note payable) + Owner's Equity}$$

In this case, assets and liabilities are each increased by $10,000. The accounting equation therefore remains in balance.

1.7   Accounting Statements

As defined in Section 1.1, one of the major concerns of accounting is the preparation of summarized reports of recorded data. The principal statements used to communicate summarized data are the income statement, the statement of owner's equity, and the balance sheet. A brief description of each statement follows:

INCOME STATEMENT:
A summary of the revenue and expenses of a business entity for a specific period of time, such as a month or a year. If total revenues for the period in question exceed total expenses, the result is net income (or net profit). If total expenses exceed total revenues, the result is a net loss.

STATEMENT OF OWNER'S EQUITY:

A summary of the changes in the owner's equity of a business entity for a specific period of time, such as a month or a year. In a corporation, the emphasis is on reports of changes in retained earnings (net income retained in the business). Those changes are reported in the retained earnings statement.

BALANCE SHEET:

A list of the assets, liabilities, and owner's equity of a business entity as of a specific date, usually at the close of the last day of a month or a year. Assets are usually listed first, followed by a list of liabilities and a section detailing owner's equity. Asset accounts (known as the left-hand side of the balance sheet) carry debit balances. Assets are usually listed with cash first, followed by accounts receivable, inventory, and other assets considered to be "current assets" (those easily converted to cash or expected to be converted to cash within one year). These are subtotaled and followed by a list of long-term assets such as land and equipment.

Liabilities are classified similarly. "Current liabilities" (those due within one year) are listed first, usually in the order of accounts payable, notes payable, and various other obligations such as salaries payable. These are subtotaled and followed by a listing of long-term liabilities (those due after one year). Liabilities and owner's equity (known as the right-hand side of the balance sheet) carry credit balances. Table 1.7.1 reflects the proper classification of accounts and balance sheet format.

TABLE 1.7.1

SAMPLE COMPANY
BALANCE SHEET
December 31, 20XX

Current Assets:

Cash
Accounts Receivable
Notes Receivable
Marketable Securities
Inventory
Prepaid Expenses
   Total Current Assets

Long-term Assets:

Land
Office Equipment
Plant and Equipment
  Total Property, Plant and
    Equipment
Total Long-term Assets

Other Assets:

Goodwill
Intangible Assets
  Total Other Assets

Total Assets

Current Liabilities:

Accounts Payable
Notes Payable
   (includes current portion
   of long-term debt)
Other Payables
  Total Current Liabilities

Long-term Liabilities:

Notes Payable
   (net of current portion)
Bonds Payable
  Total Long-term Liabilities

Total Liabilities

Owner's Equity:

Capital Stock
Retained Earnings
  Total Owner's Equity

**Total Liabilities and
  Owner's Equity**

STATEMENT OF CASH FLOWS:

The statement of cash flows is an important supplemental financial statement. This statement summarizes cash receipts and cash disbursements for a business during a given period of time, such as a month or a year. This statement supplements the income statement (which may be prepared on an accrual basis), providing users with information about an entity's ability (or inability) to meet its current cash obligations.

Problem Solving Example:

 Rumor has it that friends of the Samuels Corporation are raising money to be given as gifts to the corporation. Our client, the Samuels Corporation, suggests that we place these potential gifts in the Asset section of the Balance Sheet.

 After discussing these possible gifts with various corporation officers, we come to the conclusion that these gifts are not an absolute certainty. We decide not to add these amounts at the present time in the Asset section of the Samuels Corporation's Balance Sheet, or in the body of the Balance Sheet or as a footnote.

CHAPTER 2

The Accounting Cycle

2.1 Accounts

Transactions of a business are entered into **accounts**. The minimum parts of an account are:

Title – The name of items recorded in the account

Space for debits – Left side

Space for credits – Right side

In its simplest form, an account can be illustrated using a T format. A **T account** is shown in Example 2.1.1.

EXAMPLE 2.1.1

Account Title	
debits	credits

A complete set of accounts for a business is referred to as a **ledger**.

Debit is usually abbreviated Dt.

Credit is usually abbreviated Cr.

Debiting an account is often referred to as **charging** the account.

2.2 Recording Transactions

The first step in the accounting cycle is the execution of a **transaction**. Information pertaining to the transaction is then placed in a **document**. Utilizing the debit and credit scheme, the transaction is then recorded in the **journal**. Journalizing requires that the transaction is analyzed to determine which accounts are affected, whether the effect is an increase or decrease, and finally, if this increase or decrease is represented by a debit or credit. Example 2.2.1 illustrates a simple journal format.

EXAMPLE 2.2.1

On June 1, land costing $4,500 was purchased with cash.

Date	Account Name	Post	Debit	Credit
June 1	Land	51	4,500	
	Cash	1		4,500

The numbers in the post column are the account numbers. This number is recorded when the separate debits and credits are posted in the proper ledger accounts.

After a transaction is **journalized** (entered in the journal), the information is **posted** (recorded in the ledger). A simple ledger is illustrated in Example 2.2.2.

EXAMPLE 2.2.2

ACCOUNT Cash   **Account No. 1**

Date	Item	Post	Debit	Credit	Balance Debit	Balance Credit
June 1		1		4,500		4,500

ACCOUNT Land   **Account No. 51**

Date	Item	Post	Debit	Credit	Balance Debit	Balance Credit
June 1		51	4,500		4,500	

The flow of information in the recording process can be graphically illustrated as follows:

| Transaction takes place | Document prepared | Recorded in **Journal** | Posted in **Ledger** |

Problem Solving Example:

Q The Brown Manufacturing Corporation has the following balances in the following accounts: Checking Account Cash $5,000; Savings Account Cash $300; Petty Cash $100; Money Orders on Hand $500; Certified Checks on Hand $150; Bank Drafts on Hand $100; Postdated Checks on Hand $500; IOU's on Hand $50; Postage Stamps on Hand $37; Travel Advances to Employees $580; Change Fund $900. How much cash does Brown Manufacturing Corporation have on hand, and how should the other items be classified in the Balance Sheet?

A $7,050 cash, composed of: Checking Account Cash $5,000; Savings Account Cash $300; Petty Cash $100; Money Orders on Hand $500; Certified Checks on Hand $150; Bank Drafts on Hand $100; and Change Fund $900. Total $7,050.

Postdated checks are considered Accounts Receivable; IOU's are considered Accounts Receivable; Postage Stamps are considered Office Supplies; Travel Advances to employees that are taken out of employees' salaries are considered Receivables; Travel advances not taken out of employees' salaries are Prepaid Expenses.

2.3 Account Balances

The balance of an account is calculated by summing both sides individually and finding the difference between the totals for each side as shown in Example 2.3.1.

EXAMPLE 2.3.1

Accounts Receivable

450	250
1,000	300
700	800
2,150	400
	1,750

Balance is a $400 debit

The usual balance, and effect of debits and credits on groups of accounts, is shown in Table 2.3.1.

TABLE 2.3.1

	Usual Balance	Debit	Credit
Balance-sheet accounts:			
Assets	Debit	Increase	Decrease
Liabilities	Credit	Decrease	Increase
Owner's Equity	Credit	Decrease	Increase
Income-statement accounts:			
Revenue	Credit	Decrease	Increase
Expense	Debit	Increase	Decrease

CHAPTER 3

Adjusting Entries

3.1 Cash Basis of Accounting

Businesses may use either the cash basis or the accrual basis of accounting to report revenues and expenses. Using the cash basis of accounting, a business would report revenues only when cash is received and expenses only when cash is disbursed. Net income is the difference between cash receipts and disbursements. This method may be acceptable for some small businesses, but its use is generally discouraged.

3.2 Accrual Basis of Accounting

Businesses using the accrual basis of accounting report revenues in the period in which they are earned (even if the cash is received in the next accounting period). Under this basis, expenses are reported in the period in which they are incurred, not when cash is paid out.

As an example, assume that a business reports income and expenses on a monthly basis. Revenue from December sales would be reported as income during that month although cash for those sales may not be received until January (the next accounting period). Expenses are recognized monthly as they are incurred. Generally Accepted Accounting Principles require the use of the accrual basis so that revenues recognized during a given accounting period are **matched** with related expenses incurred in that same period. This process is facilitated by an adjusting process performed at the end of each accounting period.

Problem Solving Example:

Q When a firm's accounting system is on an accrual basis, which of the following adjustments must be made at the end of each accounting period?

    (A)   Accrued income receivable
    (B)   Prepaid expenses
    (C)   Unearned income
    (D)   Depreciation
    (E)   All of the above

A For income tax purposes, a business in which inventories are not a factor may report income on either a cash or accrual basis. Under the cash basis, revenues are considered earned at the time they are received in cash, and expenses are considered to be incurred at the time cash is disbursed in their payment. On the other hand, under the accrual basis of accounting, revenues are credited to the period in which they are earned, regardless of when payment is received. Also, expenses are charged to the period in which they are incurred, regardless of when cash is disbursed. As a result, a number of adjustments must be made at the end of each accounting period. Accrued income receivable (income that has been earned but not yet collected because payment is not due), prepaid expenses (expenses that have been paid for in advance of use), and unearned income (payment received for goods or services in advance of their delivery) must all be adjusted at the end of each accounting period.

In addition, depreciation is always adjusted at the end of each accounting period, regardless of the accounting system used. The correct answer is therefore (E).

3.3 The Adjusting Process

3.3.1 Adjustment of Prepaid Asset Accounts

Many accounts do not require adjustment at the end of an accounting period. Accounts that are usually updated upon each transaction, such as cash, accounts receivable, or accounts payable, will probably reflect the true existing balance at the end of a period. Some accounts, however, are not ordinarily updated except at the end of a period. Insurance premiums are usually paid in advance, creating a prepaid insurance account. These premiums are amortized (or used) in equal portions each day of the accounting period. Most businesses forego making daily entries to reflect this "usage" and simply adjust the balance at the end of the period by crediting prepaid insurance and debiting insurance expense as shown in the T accounts below. Assume that insurance premiums for six months total $600 and are paid on January 1. Each month's "usage" will be $100. At the end of January, the prepaid insurance and insurance expense accounts are adjusted to reflect the $100 charge by debiting insurance expense and crediting prepaid insurance.

EXAMPLE 3.3.1

Prepaid Insurance		Insurance Expense	
1/1 600	1/31 100	1/31 100	
1/31 500			

After the adjustment, the prepaid insurance account has a debit balance of $500 and insurance expense has a debit balance of $100.

3.3.2 Adjustment of Asset Accounts

Many businesses are unlikely to record the use of supplies each day, preferring to adjust the account at the end of the period. Supplies usage can be determined in this case by subtracting the amount of supplies on hand at the end of the period from supplies available during the period. To illustrate, assume a balance of $750 in supplies as of January 1. Five hundred dollars in supplies were purchased on January 20, so available supplies during the period are $1,250. A physical count on January 31 indicates a balance of $800. Supplies used during January must then be $450 ($1,250 − $800). The adjusting entry would be a debit to supplies expense and a credit to supplies of $450 each as shown in Example 3.3.2.

EXAMPLE 3.3.2

Supplies		Supplies Expense	
1/1 750	1/31 450	1/31 450	
1/20 500			
1/31 800			

After the adjustment, the supplies account reflects a debit balance of $800 and supplies expense reflects a balance of $450.

3.3.3   Adjustment of Plant Asset Accounts

Plant assets like equipment are not "used up" like supplies, but equipment does suffer a loss in usefulness over its lifetime. This loss is a business expense known as **depreciation**. The adjusting process for depreciation expense is similar to those previously discussed, with one notable difference. It is common practice to report plant assets at their original cost along with the amount of depreciation accumulated since their acquisition. As before, the amount of depreciation expense for the period is reflected as a debit to depreciation expense, but instead of crediting the asset account, a **contra-asset** account called accumulated depreciation is credited. To illustrate, equipment is purchased on January 1 for $12,000 with a useful life of 10 years. Depreciation expense is calculated at $100 per month since the equipment is assumed to have no residual value. The required adjusting entries are shown in Example 3.3.3.

EXAMPLE 3.3.3

Equipment		Accumulated Depreciation	
1/1 12,000			1/31 100
1/31 12,000			

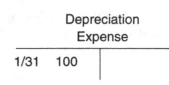

Depreciation Expense

1/31   100

After adjustment, the balance in the equipment account is unchanged. Depreciation expense is debited for $100 and accumulated depreciation is credited for $100. The depreciable balance of equipment is now $11,900 ($12,000 cost − $100 accumulated depreciation). This is the **book value** of the equipment.

3.3.4   Adjustment of Liability Accounts

Liabilities can also require adjustment. If an accounting period, for instance, should end between payment periods, it would be proper to record the amount of wages due at the end of the accounting period. Wage expense accumulates as a liability each day and can be referred to as an accrued expense. To illustrate, assume employee wages total $20,000 each biweekly pay period. In this case, the accounting period ends between payment dates. The adjusting entry will be a debit to wage expense and a credit to wages payable for the amount of wages accrued as of 1/31 ($10,000), as shown in Example 3.3.4.

EXAMPLE 3.3.4

Wage Expense		Wages Payable	
1/10 20,000			1/31 10,000
1/21 20,000			
1/31 10,000			
1/31 50,000			

After the adjustment, the balance in the wage expense account is $50,000 (the true amount of expense for the month), while wages payable reflects the amount of liability for wages owed as of January 31 ($10,000).

Quiz: Introduction – Adjusting Entries

1. Which of the following is correct?

    (A) Assets should be recorded at market value.

    (B) Assets should be recorded at cost.

    (C) Owner's Equity should be recorded at cost.

    (D) Owner's Equity should be recorded at market value.

2. Which of the following is NOT a good example of the accounting equation?

    (A) Assets + Liabilities = Owner's Equity

    (B) Assets – Liabilities = Owner's Equity

    (C) Owner's Equity + Liabilities = Assets

    (D) Assets – Owner's Equity = Liabilities

3. How does one expand the accounting equation?

    (A) By making the equation longer

    (B) By taking away various elements in the equation

    (C) By leaving the equation "as is"

    (D) By moving around various parts of the equation

4. Which of the following is NOT an accounting statement?

    (A) Journal

    (B) Balance Sheet

    (C) Income Statement

    (D) Statement of Owner's Equity

5. Which of the following is NOT a major section of the Sample Company's Balance Sheet?

   (A) Current Assets

   (B) Long-Term Assets

   (C) Expenses

   (D) Current Liabilities

6. Which of the following is NOT a part of an account?

   (A) Ledger   (C) Debit side

   (B) Title   (D) Credit side

7. An asset account usually has a

   (A) Credit balance.   (C) Both A and B.

   (B) Debit balance.   (D) None of the above

8. If an accountant is using the cash basis of accounting, how does he or she determine the net income at month's end?

   (A) By subtracting liabilities from assets

   (B) By subtracting expenses from revenues

   (C) By subtracting cash disbursements from cash receipts

   (D) None of the above

9. If an accountant is using the accrual basis of accounting, how does he or she determine the net income at month's end?

   (A) By subtracting liabilities from assets

   (B) By subtracting expenses from revenues

   (C) By subtracting cash disbursements from cash receipts

   (D) None of the above

10. What kinds of accounts are NOT adjusted at month's end?

    (A) Accumulated depreciation

    (B) Prepaid items

    (C) Accrued items

    (D) Cash items

ANSWER KEY

1.	(B)	6.	(A)
2.	(A)	7.	(B)
3.	(D)	8.	(C)
4.	(A)	9.	(B)
5.	(C)	10.	(D)

CHAPTER 4

Closing Entries

4.1 Definition and Purpose of Closing Entries

Closing entries are used to classify and summarize all **revenue** and **expense** accounts. Each expense and revenue account is completely cleared (leaving a zero balance) at the end of the accounting cycle. These accounts are temporary holding accounts whose balances should be transferred to an account that is permanent in nature. This would be the capital (retained earnings) account. The accumulation of new amounts of revenues and expenses begins at the start of each new accounting period.

These accounts are closed (transferred) to a summary account called **revenue and expense summary**. The revenue and expense summary account is then closed to the capital (retained earnings) account.

Ideally, closing should take place after an organization's busy period. At this time, inventories should be low and liquidity should be high. Drawing (dividends) accounts are also closed at the end of the accounting cycle.

The effect of closing entries is to bring to zero all accounts that affect the income statement. Accounts that are closed will not show any balances in the balance sheet.

4.2 Steps in Closing Entries

As in other parts of the recording process of the accounting cycle, the closing of accounts involves both the **recording** of entries in the journal and then the **posting** of the amounts and explanations in the ledger.

Revenue accounts normally have a credit balance and expense accounts normally have a debit balance. When closing accounts, an amount will be debited (revenue) or credited (expense) to the account to leave a zero balance. A like amount will be entered into the revenue and expense summary account.

The steps needed to close accounts and transfer amounts to the revenue and expense summary are summarized in Example 4.2.1.

TABLE 4.2.1

Type of Account	Entry in Account	Entry in Revenue and Expense Summary
Revenue	Debit	Credit
Expense	Credit	Debit

The entries to close the revenue and expense summary account will depend on whether the revenues were greater than expenses, or vice versa. This relationship is summarized in Table 4.2.2

TABLE 4.2.2

	Entry in Revenue and Expense Summary	Entry in Capital Account (Retained Earnings)
Revenues > Expenses	Debit	Credit
Expenses > Revenues	Credit	Debit

4.3   An Extended Example

The following information is available before the closing process is started:

Sales Revenue		Interest Revenue		Wages Expense	
	1/12 120		1/30 40	1/15 100	
	1/19 80			1/30 30	
	1/25 30				

Rent Expense		Revenue and Expense Summary		Capital (Retained Earnings)	
1/1 20					1/1 330
1/15 130					

4.3.1   Closing Revenue and Expense Accounts

The entries to close the revenue and expense accounts as of January 31 would be:

Date	Description	Debit	Credit
1/31	Sales Revenue	230	
	Revenue and Expense Summary		230
	Interest Revenue	40	
	Revenue and Expense Summary		40
	Revenue and Expense Summary	130	
	Wages Expense		130
	Revenue and Expense Summary	150	
	Rent Expense		150

These entries can be combined. If this was done the entry for both revenue accounts would be:

Date	Description	Debit	Credit
1/31	Sales Revenue	230	
	Interest Revenue	40	
	Revenue and Expense Summary		270

However, for purposes of this book, we will always make single entries. The accounts after the revenue and expense accounts are closed will be as follows:

Sales Revenue		Interest Revenue		Wages Expense	
1/31 230	1/12 120	1/31 40	1/30 40	1/15 100	1/31 130
	1/19 80			1/30 30	
	1/25 30				
230	230	40	40	130	130

Rent Expense		Revenue and Expense Summary		Capital (Retained Earnings)	
1/1 20	1/31 150	1/31 130	1/31 230		1/1 330
1/15 130		1/31 150	1/31 40		
150	150				

4.3.2 Closing the Revenue and Expense Summary

The entry to close the revenue and expense summary would be:

Date	Description	Debit	Credit
1/31	Capital (Retained Earnings)	10	
	Revenue and Expense Summary		10

After this last entry is made, this is the way the accounts will look:

Sales Revenue		Interest Revenue		Wages Expense	
1/31 230	1/12 120	1/31 40	1/30 40	1/15 100	1/31 130
	1/19 80			1/30 30	
	1/25 30				
230	230	40	40	130	130

Rent Expense		Revenue and Expense Summary		Capital (Retained Earnings)	
1/1 20	1/31 150	1/31 130	1/31 230	1/31 10	1/1 330
1/15 130		1/31 150	1/31 40		
150	150	280	270		Bal. 320

4.3.3   Effect on Capital (Retained Earnings)

As can be seen, the net effect of all the closing entries is to reduce Capital (Retained Earnings) by $10, from $330 to $320. This agrees with the following analysis:

Revenues:			Expenses:		
1/12	Sales Revenue	$120	1/1	Rent Expense	$20
1/19	Sales Revenue	80	1/15	Rent Expense	130
1/25	Sales Revenue	30	1/15	Wages Expense	100
1/30	Interest Revenue	40	1/30	Wages Expense	30
	Total Revenues	$270		Total Expenses	$280

Total Revenues	$270
Total Expenses	−280
Income	$ (10)

Since there was a loss, Capital (Retained Earnings) is reduced.

Problem Solving Example:

 The Income Statement for Brown Insurance Company for the month of December is as follows. From this information make the closing entries in General Journal form.

BROWN INSURANCE COMPANY
Income Statement
For the Month Ending December 31, 20XX

Commissions Earned		$4,000
Expenses:		
Advertising Expense	350	
Rent Expense	400	

Telephone Expense	130	
Salaries Expense	2,000	
Depreciation Expense: office equipment	30	
Total Expenses		2,910
Net Income		1,090

A

Commissions Earned	4,000	
Income Summary		4,000
Income Summary:	2,910	
Advertising Expense		350
Rent Expense		400
Telephone Expense		130
Salaries Expense		2,000
Depreciation Expense: office equipment		30
Income Summary	1,090	
Brown, Capital (Retained Earnings)		1,090

The Worksheet

CHAPTER 5

5.1 The Worksheet

At the end of an accounting period, a number of actions are necessary. A trial balance must be constructed, adjusting entries must be journalized and posted, closing entries must be journalized and posted, and financial statements must be prepared. To simplify these procedures and to aid in eliminating errors, a **worksheet** is used. A worksheet is a columnar sheet of paper designed to arrange accounting data required at the end of a period in a convenient and systematic manner. This worksheet, as shown in Example 5.2.1, contains five pairs of columns with each pair consisting of a debit and credit column.

5.2 Worksheet Procedures

The procedures for preparing a worksheet are as follows:

1. Ledger account balances at the end of the month are entered in the Trial Balance columns. The debit and credit columns are then totaled.

2. Required period-end adjustments are then entered in the Adjustments columns. As a cross reference, the debit and credit parts of each adjusting entry are keyed together by placing a key letter to the left of each amount.

EXAMPLE 5.2.1

SAMPLE COMPANY
Worksheet
For the month ended January 31, 20XX

	Trial Balance Debit	Trial Balance Credit	Adjustments Debit	Adjustments Credit	Adjusted Trial Balance Debit	Adjusted Trial Balance Credit	Income Statement Debit	Income Statement Credit	Balance Sheet Debit	Balance Sheet Credit
Cash	12000				12000				12000	
Accounts Receivable	25000				25000				25000	
Prepaid Insurance	600			(a) 100	500				500	
Office Supplies	1250			(b) 450	800				800	
Equipment	12000				12000				12000	
Accumulated Depreciation				(c) 100		100				100
Accounts Payable		10000				10000				10000
Wages Payable				(d) 10000		10000				10000
Capital Stock		5000				5000				5000
Retained Earnings		15850				15850				15850
Sales Revenue		60000				60000		60000		
Supplies Expense			(b) 450		450		450			
Insurance Expense			(a) 100		100		100			
Depreciation Expense			(c) 100		100		100			
Wage Expense	40000		(d) 10000		50000		50000			
Total	90850	90850	10650	10650	100950	100950	50650	60000	50300	40950
Net Income							9350			9350
Total							60000	60000	50300	50300

3. The adjusted account balances are then entered in the Adjusted Trial Balance columns. Each account balance in the first two columns is combined with any necessary adjusting entry through horizontal addition or subtraction.

4. Each account balance is then extended in the appropriate Balance Sheet or Income Statement column. Assets, liabilities, and owner's equity (or stockholder's equity if a corporation) accounts are balance sheet accounts. Revenue and expense accounts are income statement accounts. Each amount in the Adjusted Trial Balance columns is extended to only one of the four remaining columns.

5. The Balance Sheet and Income Statement accounts are then totaled. The difference between debit and credit columns will determine whether the result of the company's operations for the period is a profit or loss. If credits to income accounts exceed debits to expense accounts, the result is a net profit; if debits exceed credits, the result is a net loss. This amount is entered as a debit or credit as needed to balance the debit and credit columns of the income statement and balance sheet. The columns are then totaled. All of the paired debit and credit columns should total to equal amounts.

Using the example adjusting entries from Chapter 3, four adjustments are illustrated in Example 5.2.1. These adjusting entries are reflected in the Adjustments columns of the worksheet. The effects of these adjustments are then reflected in the Adjusted Trial Balance columns. As an example, note that Prepaid Insurance began with a balance of $600. A credit of $100 was applied to this account as a result of an adjusting entry, resulting in an adjusted balance of $500. Since Prepaid Insurance is an asset account, this amount is carried across to the debit column of the Balance Sheet section. The other part of this entry, reflected as a credit of $100 to Insurance Expense, is shown in the debit column of Adjustments. This amount is carried to an Adjusted Trial Balance and to the debit column of the Income Statement section. The other three adjustments reflected on this worksheet are handled similarly.

Problem Solving Example:

The unadjusted trial balance for Jones Hardware Store at the end of the current fiscal year is:

Jones Hardware Store Trial Balance Dec. 31, 20XX		
	Debit	Credit
Cash	$1,080	
Accounts receivable	4,300	
Inventory	22,100	
Furniture and equipment	34,000	
Accum. deprec. – Furniture; equip.		$15,600
Office supplies	850	
Accounts payable		6,020
Jones–capital account		15,970
Jones–withdrawal account	2,000	
Sales		37,000
Rent expense	1,000	
Utilities expense	480	
Insurance expense	600	
Salaries expense	7,800	
Advertising expense	200	
Interest expense	180	
	$74,590	$74,590

The following accounts are also found in the ledger:

> office supplies, prepaid insurance, depreciation expense, accrued salaries payable, cost of goods sold.

The following adjustments must be considered.

(a) Office supplies on hand total $320.

(b) An inventory was taken and $600 is left at the end of the fiscal year.

(c) Two months' rent, $800, has been prepaid in cash

(d) Sixty dollars of electricity and gas was consumed; the bill is due to be paid by the middle of next month.

(e) Three hundred dollars is owed to employees for work done the present period. It will also be paid in the middle of next month.

(f) At the beginning of the fiscal year, a $600 premium was paid for a three-year insurance policy. Two years of the policy are left at the end of the fiscal year.

(g) Furniture and equipment depreciation was $800 for the year.

Using a ten-column worksheet format,

(i) Record the trial balance and the adjustments.

(ii) Record the adjusted trial balance and the income statement.

(iii) On the same worksheet, prepare the balance sheet.

(iv) Prepare a formal income statement and the formal balance sheet.

 (i) Using the debit-credit format of the worksheet simplifies our task. The thing to remember is that for every debit, there must be a corresponding credit of the same amount. It remains for us to enter the adjustments in the proper accounts. The trial balance and adjustments are as follows:

| Accounts | Trial Balance | | Adjustments | |
	Debit	Credit	Debit	Credit
Cash	1,080			(c) 800
Accounts receivable	4,300			
Inventory	22,100			(b) 21,500
Furniture and equipment	34,000			
Accum. deprec. – Furniture; equipment		15,600		(g) 800

Prepaid insurance	600					(f)	200
Prepaid rent			(c)	800			
Accounts payable		6,020				(d)	60
Jones–capital account		15,970					
Jones–withdrawal							
account	2,000						
Sales		37,000					
Rent expense	1,000						
Utilities expense	480		(d)	60			
Insurance expense			(f)	200			
Salaries expense	7,800		(e)	300			
Advertising expense	200						
Supplies expense			(a)	530			
Interest expense	180						
Depreciation expense			(g)	800			
Office supplies	850					(a)	530
Accrued salaries							
payable						(e)	300
Cost of goods sold			(b)	21,500			
	74,590	74,590		24,190			24,190

Note that on the worksheet we add any additional accounts needed in making adjustments to the list of those already on the list.

(a) Office Supplies are an asset. At first we are told that we have $850 left in the account. But then we find that at the end of the year we only have $320 left in the account; the account has been decreased by $530. Therefore, we credit the asset $530 to show this decrease.

The purpose of expense accounts is to match any expenditure or decrease to the period in which it occurred, in order to determine, as precisely as possible, how much was spent in a period to generate that period's income. A decrease of $530 in Supplies for a period means that $530 was "spent" on supplies to help earn that period's income. Therefore, we have a $530 Supplies Expense which is debited, as it represents a decrease to the Capital account. (The Capital account can be increased or credited by a net profit. Therefore, anything, such as an expense which decreases the net profit, also decreases the Capital Account).

(b) If $600 of inventory are left, then $22,100 − $600 = $21,500 was deducted (credited) from the Inventory account. This also means that the cost of goods sold was $21,500 and this is debited to the Cost of Goods Sold account.

(c) Prepaid rent is an asset and is debited to the Prepaid Rent account. We can credit Cash for $800 to note the decrease in cash resulting from payment.

(d) Utilities expense is $60 and is debited to the Utilities Expense account. Since this is to be paid next month, $60 is credited to Accounts Payable.

(e) $300 is debited to the Salaries Expense account since services have been realized, and therefore should be matched to the period just ending. The same amount is credited to the liabilities account, Accrued Salaries Payable, since the salaries have not been paid yet.

(f) The $600 premium giving three years' protection is the same as three premiums, each worth $200 and each giving one year of protection. After one year, there is $400 left in the Prepaid Insurance since there was a decrease of $200. Since Prepaid Insurance is an asset, it is decreased by a credit. As has been already mentioned, expenses attributable to a particular period are debited to the expense accounts. Since $200 was "spent" on insurance during the period, there should be a debit to Insurance Expense. Next year when another $200 of the prepaid insurance is used up, an identical adjustment will have to be made on the balance sheet.

(g) Depreciation of an asset represents the asset's decline in value through time and is demonstrated by deducting a certain part of its original dollar cost each accounting period. In this example, the office furniture and equipment are considered to have declined in value by $800 in this period. The account Accumulated Depreciation is a contra-asset account; it shows how much value has been deducted from an asset's value so far. Since it represents a decrease in an asset, it is credited when additional depreciation is assigned to an asset.

Depreciation also represents which portion of the original cost of an asset was used during the period to add to a firm's productivity. It is therefore an expense and should be debited to the Depreciation Expense account.

(ii) Adjusted trial balance—To get the adjusted trial balance, in each account, either subtract or add the amount found in the adjustments debit-credit columns. For example, Accounts Receivable remains the same since no adjustments were made. The entry for Accounts Receivable would be unchanged in adjusted trial balance, namely, a debit of $4,300. For Inventory this is not the case. The adjustments require a credit (decrease) to the Inventory account. Subtract $21,500 from $22,100 to get a debit in the adjusted trial balance of $600.

For Utilities Expense, the corresponding adjustment is a debit and thus we should add $480 and $60 to obtain a utilities expense of $540 (debit) in the adjusted trial balance. Other entries are found in the same way, remembering that entries in debits have the opposite sign of credit entries. For example, if, before adjustment, there is some money in the Cash account, it is of course recorded as a debit and considered a positive amount. So, if there is an adjusting entry to this account in the credit column it represents an amount to be subtracted and is therefore a negative number.

The income statement column is prepared by just copying the sales, expense, and cost of goods sold figures of the adjusted trial balance to a corresponding worksheet format to find net income earned.

| | Adjusted Trial | | Income Statement | |
Accounts	Debit	Credit	Debit	Credit
Cash	280			
Accounts receivable	4,300			
Inventory	600			
Furniture and equipment	34,000			
Accum. deprec. – Furniture, equip.		16,400		
Accounts payable		6,080		

Jones-capital account withdrawal		15,970				
Jones-capital account	2,000					
Sales		37,000			37,000	
Rent expense	1,000			1,000		
Utilities expense	540			540		
Insurance expense	200			200		
Salaries expense	8,100			8,100		
Advertising expense	200			200		
Supplies expense	530			530		
Interest expense	180			180		
Depreciation expense	800			800		
Office supplies	320					
Prepaid insurance	400					
Prepaid rent	800					
Accrued salaries payable		300				
Cost of goods sold	21,500			21,500		
	75,750	75,750		33,050	37,000	
Net income				3,950		
				37,000	37,000	

	Balance Sheet	
Accounts	Debit	Credit
Cash	280	
Accounts receivable	4,300	
Inventory	600	
Furniture and equipment	34,000	
Accum. deprec. – Furniture equip.		16,400
Accounts payable		6,080
Jones–capital account		15,970
Jones–drawing account	2,000	

Sales		
Rent expense		
Utilities expense		
Insurance expense		
Salaries expense		
Advertising expense		
Supplies expense		
Interest expense		
Office supplies	320	
Prepaid insurance	400	
Prepaid rent	800	
Accrued salaries payable		300
Cost of goods sold		
Net Income		3,950
	42,700	42,700

(iii) The balance sheet, like the income statement, is just a matter of taking the proper entries of the adjusted trial balance and putting these in credit-debit format in the worksheet. We take only "balance sheet accounts" in this case, the assets, liabilities, and the owner's capital accounts. Under assets we have cash, accounts receivable, inventory, furniture and equipment, accumulated depreciation, office supplies, prepaid insurance, and prepaid rent. The liability accounts are Accounts Payable and Salaries Payable. As for the owner's equity account on the balance sheet, the drawing account and the net income determine the change in the equity account. So we add the net income to and subtract the amount of withdrawal from the "Jones–Capital" account. This is what will appear as the owner's capital on the balance sheet. The drawing and net income accounts do not appear separately on the balance sheet; we merely calculate their effect on the capital account and then just show what is left in the capital account.

(iv) A formal income statement and a balance sheet are prepared directly from the worksheet figures.

Jones Hardware Store
Income Statement

For Last Month of Current Fiscal Year

Sales _____		$37,000
less cost of goods sold _____		21,500
gross profit _____		15,500
Administrative expenses		
rent expense _____	$1,000	
utilities expense_____	540	
salaries expense _____	8,100	
insurance expense _____	200	
advertising expense _____	200	
supplies expense _____	530	
interest expense _____	180	
depreciation expense _____	800	11,550
Net income _____		3,950

Jones Hardware Store
Balance Sheet as of the End of Current Fiscal Year

Assets		Liabilities	
Current:			
Cash _____	280	Acc. payable _____	6,080
Accounts receivable_____	4,300	Salaries payable ____	300
Inventory _____	600	Total _____	6,380
Office supplies _____	320	Owner's equity	
Prepaid rent_____	800	Jones–capital _____	17,920
Prepaid insurance _____	400	Liab. + Equity _____	24,300
Total current assets	6,700		
Fixed:			
Furniture, equipment	34,000		
less accum. deprec.	16,400		
	17,600		
Total Assets	24,300		

CHAPTER 6

Accounting for a
Merchandising Operation

6.1 Gross Profit/Margin

Gross profit and **gross margin** are terms used interchangeably to denote the difference between the amount of sales and the **cost of goods sold**. The general format for the top part of the income statement is usually as shown in Example 6.1.1.

EXAMPLE 6.1.1

Sales	$300
Less Cost of Goods Sold	200
Gross Profit/Gross Margin	$100

6.2 Perpetual and Periodic Accounting Systems

There are two basic ways to set up inventory systems to process the flow of information about purchases and sales. These are known as perpetual and periodic accounting systems.

6.2.1 Entries Under Perpetual Accounting System

When utilizing **perpetual**, each purchase and sale transaction has a two-step entry. Sales entries directly affect the **cost of goods sold** account. Assuming that merchandise costing $350 was purchased, and one-half of that merchandise was sold for $300, the necessary entries are shown in Example 6.2.1.

EXAMPLE 6.2.1

To Record Purchase of Merchandise

Date	Description	Debit	Credit
	Merchandise Inventory	350	
	Cash or Accounts Payable		350

To Record Sales of Merchandise

Date	Description	Debit	Credit
	Cash (or some other asset)	300	
	Sales		300

If the merchandise is sold for cash, then cash would be debited. If instead, a promise to pay later was made, accounts or notes receivable would be debited.

Additionally, an entry is needed to adjust both inventory and cost of goods sold as shown in Example 6.2.2.

EXAMPLE 6.2.2

Date	Description	Debit	Credit
	Cost of Goods Sold ($350 × 1/2)	175	
	Inventory		175

Under this method, inventory should always be determinable by looking in the records. Even when using this method, a physical inventory should be taken at least once each accounting cycle to assure the accuracy of the records.

Problem Solving Examples:

 The Wilson Company records purchases at gross and uses a periodic inventory system. On August 1, the Wilson Company purchases $50,000 worth of inventory.

Make the entry that would appear on the books.

Year		($ in dollars)
August 1 Purchases	50,000	
Accounts Payable–Smith		50,000

Merchandise is coming into the company at cost price of $50,000, so the Cost Expense account Purchases is debited for $50,000. At this date (August 1), the Wilson Company is not yet paying cash, so it credits Accounts Payable for $50,000, and in the subsidiary ledger (Accounts Payable subsidiary ledger) it credits Smith, the company from which the merchandise was purchased.

The Wilson Company records purchases at gross and uses a periodic inventory system. On August 1, the Wilson Company purchases from the Smith Company $50,000 worth of inventory. Purchases is debited and Accounts Payable–Smith is credited for $50,000. On September 1, the Wilson Company gives the Smith Company a $50,000, 10-month note at 8% in payment of account.

Show the entry on the books of the Wilson Company.

Year	($ in dollars)
September 1 Accounts Payable–Smith	50,000
Notes Payable	50,000

On August 1, when the Wilson Company purchases the merchandise, it gave its oral promise to pay the $50,000 by crediting Accounts Payable–Smith for $50,000. On September 1, 2000, the Wilson Company receives back its oral promise to pay by debiting Accounts Payable–Smith for $50,000. It then gives the Smith Company a written promise to pay—it gives a note for $50,000—and credits the account Notes Payable on its books for $50,000.

6.2.2 Entries Under Periodic Accounting Systems

Using the transaction from the previous section, the entries under a periodic accounting system are shown in Example 6.2.3.

EXAMPLE 6.2.3

To Record Purchase of Merchandise

Date	Description	Debit	Credit
	Purchases	350	
	Cash or Accounts Payable		350

To Record Sale of Merchandise

	Cash (or some other asset)	300	
	Sales		300

Using this method, no entries are made to adjust the inventory and cost of goods sold upon sale. These adjustments are made at the end of the accounting period. Inventory will be debited for the ending inventory amount and credited with the amount of beginning inventory. This will leave as a balance the amount of the ending physical inventory.

The calculation to determine **cost of goods sold** is shown in Example 6.2.4.

EXAMPLE 6.2.4

Merchandise Inventory – Beginning of Year	$150
Add Purchases During the Year	350
Total Goods Available for Sale	$500
Deduct Merchandise Inventory – End of Year	325
Cost of Goods Sold	$175

Problem Solving Examples:

 The Bruce Company has completed making brooms which are still stored on the Bruce Company property. These brooms have not yet been sold as of year's end. Should they be included in Bruce Company's Year-End Inventory?

 Yes. They are part of the Finished Goods Inventory and should be included since they have not yet been sold.

 The Jones Company has purchased raw materials for use in the factory. The freight charges on these goods come to $100. Should this $100 be included in Inventory?

 No. They should be placed in Freight In, a cost account. This will be figured into the Cost of Goods Sold, but is separate from Inventory.

6.3 Transportation Charges

There are two types of transportation charges. Charges for transporting merchandise to the company are **freight in**. This will be an additional cost of acquiring the goods. Outward bound charges to transport goods the firm sold are **freight out**. These are shown as **shipping expense** (a form of selling expense).

F.O.B. destination means that shipping charges are free at the destination. The charges are borne by the seller.

F.O.B. shipping point means that the seller delivers the merchandise to the carrier. However, the purchaser bears the cost of the transportation charges.

6.4 Merchandise Returns

Nearly every business has some merchandise that is returned. This may be due to quality, color, or some other factor. The seller will call these **sales returns**, while the buyer calls them **purchase returns**. The journal entry to record a return on the seller's books is shown in Example 6.4.1.

EXAMPLE 6.4.1

Date	Description	Debit	Credit
	Sales Returns and Allowances Cash (or some other asset)	10	 10

Example 6.4.2 reflects the entry on the books of the buyer.

EXAMPLE 6.4.2

Date	Description	Debit	Credit
	Cash (or Accounts Payable) Purchase Returns and Allowances	10	 10

6.5 Merchandise Allowances

Subsequent to a sale, some merchandise can become subject to a reduced price. To the seller, this would be a **sales allowance** and to the buyer this would be a **purchase allowance**.

Entries to record merchandise allowances are identical to those for returns. Usually returns and allowances are grouped into the same account. It is important to keep them separate from sales so analysis can be done on the level of returns and allowances in relation to total sales and purchases.

6.6   Trade Discounts

Trade discounts are price concessions made to certain buyers where the actual price charged is less than the **list price**. No entries are required since sales are recorded at actual price, not the list price.

Problem Solving Examples:

 A calculator has a list price of $10.00 and the seller is offering a $4.00 trade discount. What is the percentage of the discount?

 The percentage of a trade discount is calculated as

$$\% \text{ of discount} = \frac{\text{Amount of discount (in dollars)}}{\text{List price}} \times 100\%$$

$$= \frac{\$4.00}{\$10.00} \times 100\%$$

$$= 40\%$$

 On December 10, Shepp's Store bought a set of camping hot plates from Wilderness Wholesalers for $56.65 minus a trade discount of 10%. The terms offered were 2/10, n/30. If Shepp's Store paid the bill on December 20, what was the amount paid?

 First, find the amount left to pay after the 10% trade discount is taken. Multiply $56.65 by .10, the decimal equivalent of 10%, to get $5.66 as the amount of the trade discount. Now, subtract $5.66 from the gross amount, $56.65, to get $50.99 as the amount left after the discount.

Any subsequent discounts will be deducted from this amount.

The term 2/10 mean that a 2% discount will be given if payment is made within ten days. Ten days from December 10, the date of purchase, is December 20. Since payment was made on December 20, the discount could be taken.

Discount: 2% of $50.99 = 0.02 × $50.99 = $1.02

This discount is deducted from $50.99 to get the amount of the payment:

$50.99 − $1.02 = $49.97

Shepp's Store paid Wilderness Wholesalers $49.97 on December 20. Had Shepp's Store waited one more day to pay, the discount would not have been in effect. The term n/30 tells us that $50.99, the price without the 2% discount, was due by January 9 (December 10 + 30 days).

6.7 Sales Discounts

Cash discounts are deductions allowed to customers to encourage them to pay their bills in a timely manner. These discounts are usually stated as: 2/10; n/30. This means a discount of 2% is available if paid within 10 days, but after that time, the customers must pay the full amount. Assume a sales discount was given for the $300 sale described above. If the customer paid within the ten days, the entry to record the receipt of the cash is shown in Example 6.7.1.

EXAMPLE 6.7.1

Date	Description	Debit	Credit
	Cash	294	
	Sales Discounts and Allowances	6	
	($300 × 2%)		
	Accounts Receivable		300

6.8 Detailed Income Statement

An income statement illustrating all of the items covered in this chapter follows in Example 6.8.1 (all numbers are assumed).

EXAMPLE 6.8.1

Gross Sales			$400
Less: Sales Returns and Allowances		20	
Sales Discounts		10	30
Net Sales			370
Cost of Goods Sold:			
Inventory January 1, 20XX		130	
Purchases		100	
Less: Purchase Returns	15		
Purchase Discounts	25	40	
Net Purchases		60	
Add: Freight In		25	
Cost of Merchandise Purchased		85	
Cost of Goods Available for Sale		215	
Deduct: Inventory January 31, 20XX		105	
Cost of Goods Sold			110
Gross Profit (or Margin)			260

Problem Solving Examples:

Q The Brown Company wishes to borrow money from the First National Bank and plans to submit the following Income Statement to the bank. Look it over and tell how it can be improved.

Income Statement

Sales		$700,000
Dividends		32,000
Gain on Recovery of Insurance from Fire Loss		40,000
Total Income		772,000
Less:		
Advertising Expense	20,000	
Cost of Goods Sold	400,000	
Salaries Expense	10,000	
Loss on Old Inventories	20,000	
Total		450,000
Income before Income Tax		$322,000
Income Tax		15,000
Net Income after Tax		$307,000

Suggestions for revision of this Income Statement:

1. The Income Statement needs a full heading, including the name of the company and the period of time that the statement includes.

2. The Gain on Recovery of Insurance from Fire Loss should be classified as an Extraordinary Item in a separate section of the Income Statement.

3. Cost of Goods Sold should be listed first.

4. Loss on Old Inventory might be classified at the bottom of the Income Statement as an Unusual Item.

Prepare a Multiple-Step Income Statement for the Michael Seed Company from the following information:

1.	Interest Expense on Bonds Payable	1,800
2.	Income Taxes	12,000
3.	Transportation In	2,700
4.	Sales	100,000
5.	Merchandise Inventory—Ending	16,000
6.	Merchandise Inventory—Beginning	15,000
7.	Depreciation of Sales Equipment	6,400
8.	Sales Commissions	7,000
9.	Transportation Out	2,700
10.	Rental Revenue	17,000
11.	Purchases	60,000
12.	Purchases Returns	5,800
13.	Depreciation of Office Equipment	3,900
14.	Officers' Salaries	4,000

A

MICHAEL SEED COMPANY
Income Statement
For Year Ending December 31, 20XX

Sales			$100,000
Cost of Goods Sold Section:			
Beginning Inventory		15,000	
Purchases	60,000		
Purchases Returns	5,800		
Net Purchases		54,200	
Transportation In		2,700	
Merchandise Available for Sale		71,900	
Ending Inventory		16,000	
Cost of Goods Sold			55,900
Gross Profit on Sales			44,100
Operating Expense Section:			
Selling Expenses:			
Transportation Out	2,700		
Sales Commissions	7,000		
Depreciation of Sales Equipment	6,400		
Total Selling Expense		16,100	
Administration Expenses:			
Officers' Salaries	4,000		
Depreciation of Office Equipment	3,900		
Total Admin. Expense		7,900	
Total Operating Expense		24,000	24,000
Operating Income			20,100
Other Income:			
Rental Revenue		17,000	
Other Expense:			
Interest Expense on Bonds Payable		1,800	15,200
Net Income before Income Taxes			35,300
Income Taxes			12,000
Net Income after Income Taxes			$23,300

Given below is information relating to the Ward Corporation for the year. Prepare a Multiple-Step Income Statement for the year. Assume that 70,000 shares of Common Stock are outstanding. Also prepare a separate Statement of Retained Earnings. Federal tax is at the 30% rate.

Retained Earnings, Dec. 31, 20XX	2,000,000
Dividends declared	100,000
Casualty loss (Extraordinary Item) before taxes	60,000
Depreciation expenses omitted by accident in 20XX	30,000
Write-off of inventory due to obsolescence	15,000
Interest Revenue	10,000
Dividend Revenue	20,000
Administrative Expenses	40,000
Selling Expenses	60,000
Cost of Goods Sold	800,000
Net Sales	1,000,000

WARD CORPORATION
Income Statement
For Year Ending December 31, 20XX

Net Sales		$1,000,000
Cost of Goods Sold		800,000
Gross Profit on Sales		200,000
Operating Expenses:		
Administrative Expenses	40,000	
Selling Expenses	60,000	
Total Operating Expenses		100,000
Operating Income		100,000
Other Revenue:		
Dividend Revenue	20,000	
Interest Revenue	10,000	
Total Other Revenue		30,000
Subtotal		130,000

Other Expenses:

Write-off of Obsolescent Inventory		15,000
Net Income before Tax and Extraordinary Item		115,000
Less Income Tax (30%)		34,500
Net Income before Extraordinary Item		80,500
Extraordinary Item:		
Casualty Loss	60,000	
Less applicable tax reduction (30%)	18,000	42,000
Net Income		$38,500

Per Share of Common Stock:
(70,000 shares of Common Stock are outstanding)

Income before Extraordinary Item	$1.15 per share
($80,500 divided by 70,000 shares)	
Less Extraordinary Item (net of tax)	
($42,000 divided by 70,000 shares)	.60 per share
Net Income	
($38,500 divided by 70,000 shares)	$ .55 per share

WARD CORPORATION
Retained Earnings Statement
For Year Ending December 31, 20XX

Retained Earnings, January 1, 20XX	$2,000,000
Depreciation Expense (net of tax)	
($30,000 less 30% or $9,000)	21,000
Adjusted Balance	1,979,000
Net Income (from Income Statement)	38,500
Subtotal	2,017,500
Dividend Declared	100,000
Retained Earnings, December 31, 20XX	$1,917,500

Quiz: Closing Entries – Merchandising Operation

1. What two steps are used in making closing entries?

    (A) Trial balance and balance sheet

    (B) Adjusted trial balance and income statement

    (C) Recording and posting

    (D) None of these

2. Into what account or accounts are closing entries eventually posted?

    (A) Income and expense accounts

    (B) Liability and asset accounts

    (C) Owner's Capital account or Retained Earnings account

    (D) Rent expense or rent income

3. What are the subsections of the worksheet?

    (A) Income and expense

    (B) Assets, liabilities, owner's equity, revenue, and expense

    (C) Retained earnings and income summary

    (D) Trial balance, adjustments, adjusted trial balance, income statement, and balance sheet

4. In a mercantile business how is the gross profit determined?

    (A) By adding the beginning inventory and ending inventory

    (B) By subtracting the ending inventory from the beginning inventory

(C) By subtracting the operating expenses from the sales

(D) By subtracting the cost of goods sold from the sales

5. Under the Perpetual Inventory system, what entry or entries need to be made when merchandise is sold?

(A) Debit cash or some other account and credit sales

(B) Debit cash or some other account and credit sales, and also debit cost of goods sold and credit inventory

(C) Debit cost of goods sold and credit inventory

(D) Debit inventory and credit cost of goods sold, and also debit cash and credit sales

6. Under the Periodic Inventory system, what entry or entries need to be made when merchandise is sold?

(A) Debit cash or some other account and credit sales

(B) Debit cash or some other account and credit sales, and also debit cost of goods sold and credit inventory

(C) Debit cost of goods sold and credit inventory

(D) Debit inventory and credit cost of goods sold, and also debit cash and credit sales

7. How do Freight In and Freight Out differ as to their locations in the Income Statement?

(A) Freight Out is under the Cost of Goods Sold section on the Income Statement, and Freight In is not located on the Income Statement.

(B) Freight In is not located on the Income Statement, and Freight Out is located in the Cost of Goods Sold section of the Income Statement.

(C) Freight In should be located in the Cost of Goods Sold section of the Income Statement while Freight Out should be located in the Operating Expenses section of the Income Statement.

    (D) None of these

8. What is the difference between Sales Returns and Purchases Returns?

    (A) Sales Returns are on the buyer's books while Purchases Returns are on the seller's books.

    (B) Sales Returns are on the seller's books while Purchases Returns are on the buyer's books.

    (C) Sales Returns are located on the balance sheet while Purchases Returns are not located on the balance sheet.

    (D) Purchases Returns are located on the balance sheet while Sales Returns are not located on the balance sheet.

9. How does a merchandise return differ from a merchandise allowance?

    (A) No difference—they are both the same.

    (B) If the goods are actually shipped back to the seller, it is a merchandise return; however, if the buyer keeps the merchandise and the seller lowers the price of the merchandise to the buyer, it is a merchandise allowance.

    (C) If the goods are actually shipped back to the buyer, it is a merchandise return; however, if the seller keeps the merchandise and the buyer lowers the price of the merchandise to the seller, it is a merchandise allowance.

    (D) None of these

10. A customer purchases a $100 item from the Brown Company and pays for it within the 10-day discount period. There is a 2% Sales Discount, so the Brown Company receives only $98. (2% of $100 = $2; $100 − $2 = $98.) How is this recorded on the books of the Brown Company?

   (A) Debit Cash $98 and credit Accounts Receivable $98

   (B) Debit Cash $98 and debit Sales Discount $2; and credit Accounts Receivable $100

   (C) Debit Cash $100 and credit Accounts Receivable $100

   (D) Debit Cash $100 and credit Accounts Payable $100

ANSWER KEY

1.	(C)	6.	(A)
2.	(C)	7.	(C)
3.	(D)	8.	(B)
4.	(D)	9.	(B)
5.	(B)	10.	(B)

CHAPTER 7

Internal Control and Specialized Journals

7.1 Types of Internal Control

Internal controls can be characterized as **internal administrative controls** or **internal accounting controls**. **Internal administrative controls** are those procedures and records that can assist management to reach business goals.

Internal accounting controls are those procedures and records that are concerned primarily with the **reliability** of financial records and reports, as well as safeguarding of assets.

7.2 Personnel Controls

An organization cannot function properly without **competent employees**. This process should begin with selection of employees who have the necessary skills and intelligence to perform the job assignment. All employees should then be provided with adequate training and supervision in order to accomplish their assigned tasks in the most efficient manner.

Employee responsibilities must be clearly defined. This encourages efficiency and helps to avoid employee confusion. Overlapping or ill-defined job responsibilities can sometimes lead to errors or irregularities.

Employees should be **rotated** to different jobs within an organization periodically. This procedure provides several benefits. First, employees gain a larger understanding of the overall organization. In addition, it can increase both the value of an employee as well as provide management with a good deal of flexibility since employees are familiar with more than one job. This process can also strengthen the organization since irregularities or deviations from standard operating policies will be discovered when employees are rotated. In fact, employee rotation may discourage irregular practices since the employee is aware that someone else will be reviewing their work very shortly.

7.3 Records Control

An employee given responsibility or custodianship of an asset should not be the employee charged with maintenance of records for that asset. As an example, it is good practice to avoid a situation where an employee responsible for maintaining payroll records can also sign payroll checks.

Proper control of an organization's assets cannot be maintained without **adequate** records. This requires careful design of an accounting information system to ensure that such information is available for management on a timely basis and that the information provided is accurate.

All general ledger accounts must be **reconciled** or compared with subsidiary ledgers at the end of each accounting period. Any differences between the two balances must be investigated and explained so that errors or irregularities can be identified and corrected. In addition, account records that involve physical assets such as inventory, equipment, or supplies should also be periodically reconciled with a physical count of those assets.

Periodic internal audits by organization employees may be used to discover errors or irregularities, to determine if policies and procedures are being followed, and to uncover inefficiency. As a final check and balance, an organization may use external auditors to review the existing system of internal control and make suggestions for improvement.

7.4   Specialized Journals

7.4.1   Purpose of Specialized Journals

Many organizations often incur the same kind of transaction, such as a sale of merchandise on credit, many times during any given day. To save time, a **specialized journal** is used for that kind of transaction *only*. The most common kinds of specialized journals are the sales journal, the purchases journal, the cash receipts journal, and the cash disbursements journal. The general journal is used to record those entries that do not fit in one of these specialized journals.

7.4.2   Sales Journal

The sales journal is used to record the sale of merchandise on credit *only*. This journal is illustrated in Example 7.4.1. In this example, several sales have been made on credit. Cash sales are recorded in the cash receipts journal, not the sales journal.

EXAMPLE 7.4.1

The Sample Company
Sales Journal

Date	Account Debited	Invoice No.	Ref.	Amount
Year				
Jan 2	John Jackson	222	X	1,000
6	Sally Jones	224	X	1,200
11	James Smith	225	X	900
				3,100
				(4) (80)

Each entry in the sales journal represents a debit to a customer's account. Charges to customer accounts should be posted daily and a check mark should be placed in the journal to indicate that this entry has been made.

Each entry in the sales journal also represents a credit to sales. Instead of posting a separate credit to Sales with each entry, in this example one entry is made to that account at the end of the month for the total amount of sales recorded in the sales journal.

In the illustrated example, sales on account totaled $3,100 for January. This amount is posted as a debit to Accounts Receivable and a credit to Sales as shown in Example 7.4.2.

EXAMPLE 7.4.2

The Sample Company
General Ledger

Accounts Receivable 4		Sales 80
Year		Year
Jan 31 3,100		Jan 31 3,100

Completion of this posting is noted in the sales journal by placing the account numbers of the two accounts below the total sales amount for the month.

Problem Solving Examples:

 This sales journal records only sales on credit. Where are cash sales recorded?

 In the Cash Receipts Journal.

 At the lower right-hand corner of the Sample Company Sales Journal is a "4" in parentheses. What does this refer to?

The "4" is the number of the Accounts Receivable account in the general ledger. It means that the total of $3,100 has been debited to this account.

 At the lower right-hand corner of the Sample Company Sales Journal is an "80" in parentheses. What does this refer to?

 The "80" is the number of the Sales account in the general ledger. It means that the total of $3,100 has been credited to this account.

7.4.3 Purchases Journal

Only purchases of merchandise on credit are recorded in the purchases journal. In this instance, the term merchandise refers to goods acquired for resale to customers. Merchandise purchased for cash is recorded in the cash disbursements journal. An example of the purchases journal is shown in Example 7.4.3.

EXAMPLE 7.4.3

The Sample Company
Purchases Journal

Date	Account Credited	Invoice Date	Ref.	Credit
Year		Year		
Jan 4	Jones Company	Jan 4	X	2,400
9	Smith Corporation	8	X	5,500
13	Atlantic Supply Co.	12	X	1,300
				9,200
				(21) (9)

Problem Solving Examples:

 This purchase journal records only purchases on credit. Where are cash purchases recorded?

 In the Cash Disbursements Journal.

 At the lower right-hand corner of the Sample Company Purchases Journal is a "21" in parentheses. What does this refer to?

 The "21" is the number of the Purchases account in the general ledger. It means that the total of $9,200 has been debited to this account.

 At the lower right-hand corner of the Sample Company Purchases Journal is a "9" in parentheses. What does this refer to?

 The "9" in parentheses is the number of the Accounts Payable account in the general ledger. It means that the total of $9,200 has been credited to this account.

Each entry in the purchases journal reflects a credit to a creditor's account and a debit to purchases. Total purchases for the month ($9,200) are recorded as a debit to purchases and a credit to accounts payable as shown in Example 7.4.4.

EXAMPLE 7.4.4

The Sample Company
General Ledger

Purchases		Accounts Payable	
Year		Year	
Jan 31 9,200		Jan 31 9,200	

Completion of this journal entry is noted in the purchases journal by placing the account numbers for the two accounts involved (21 for purchases and 9 for accounts payable) below the total amount of purchases for the month.

7.4.4 Cash Receipts Journal

All transactions involving the receipt of cash are recorded in the cash receipts journal. This journal is illustrated in Example 7.4.5. The cash receipts journal has three debit columns for cash, sales discounts, and other accounts as well as four credit columns for accounts receivable, sales, and other accounts.

The use of the debit columns for cash and sales discounts are self-explanatory. The debit column for other accounts may be used when cash is received in combination with some other asset.

The credit column for accounts receivable is used to record credits to customers' accounts as receivables are collected. The credit column for sales is used to accumulate cash sales during the month so that the total can be posted to the sales account. The credit column for other accounts may be used when a transaction may require credits to two different accounts.

The following transactions are recorded in the cash receipts journal shown in Example 7.4.5:

Year

Jan 2   Sold merchandise for cash in amount of $1,000.

Jan 11   Collected $1,200 from John Jackson for sale on
          January 4.

Jan 22   Sold land for $9,000 cash. Original cost of
          the land was $7,000.

At the end of the month, the journal columns for cash, sales discounts, accounts receivable, and sales are totaled and posted to the proper general ledger accounts. Completion of these entries is indicated by placing the corresponding general ledger account number below the column total. The totals of the other accounts columns are not posted since the individual items have already been posted. An X is placed below these columns to show that no posting is necessary.

EXAMPLE 7.4.5

Cash Receipts Journal

Date	Description	Post Ref.	Sundry Accts Credit	Sales Credit	Accts Rec. Credit	Sales Disc. Credit	Cash Debit
Year							
Jan 2	Sales			1,000			1,000
Jan 11	J. Jackson	101			1,200		1,200
Jan 22	Land	51	7,000				9,000
	Gain on						
	Land Sale	85	2,000				
				1,000	1,200		11,200
				(80)	(4)		(1)

7.4.5 Cash Disbursements Journal

All payments of cash are recorded in the cash disbursements journal. Like the cash receipts journal, the cash disbursements journal contains two credit columns for cash, purchase discounts, and other accounts as well as two debit columns for accounts payable, purchases, and other accounts. The following transactions are shown in Example 7.4.6:

Year

Jan 4   Paid $800 cash for merchandise.

Jan 7   Paid Jones Company for invoice of $2,400
            dated Jan 4 (less 2% discount)

Jan 9   Bought equipment for $6,000 cash.

EXAMPLE 7.4.6

Cash Disbursements Journal

Date	Ck No.	Description	Post Ref.	Sundry Accts Debit	Accts Pay. Debit	Pur. Dis. Credit	Cash Credit
Year							
Jan 4	1	Purchases	90	800			800
Jan 7	2	Jones Co.	201		2,352	48	2,400
Jan 9	3	Equipment	52	6,000			6,000
					2,352	48	9,200
				X	X	(60)	(91)	(4)

The columns for cash, purchases, discounts, accounts payable, and purchases are totaled at the end of each month and these amounts posted to the appropriate general ledger accounts. The completion of these entries is noted in the cash disbursements journal by placing the appropriate general ledger account number below the total of each column. Since items in the other accounts columns are posted individually, the totals of these columns are not posted. Accordingly, an X is placed below the total of these columns to indicate that the total was not posted.

7.4.6 Subsidiary Ledgers

The preceding sections have dealt with the use of specialized journals as information sources for entries to general ledger accounts such as cash, accounts receivable and payable, purchases, and sales. In some cases, a business may need more detailed information, such as individual customer receivable balances or the amount owed to a particular vendor. This is accomplished through the use of **subsidiary ledgers.**

For example, a business might maintain an accounts receivable ledger consisting of separate ledger accounts for each customer, arranged alphabetically or by account number. Each entry to the sales journal or to the cash receipts journal (if the transaction was a collection of a receivable) would be posted to the appropriate customer ledger so customer records would be constantly updated. At the end of the month, the total of the subsidiary ledger accounts should balance to the controlling account (the general ledger account). A similar process could be used for individual vendors (using the purchases and cash disbursements journals) or for any general ledger account that involves subsidiary accounts.

CHAPTER 8

Cash

8.1 Definition of Cash

In accounting, **cash** is paper money, coin, bank balances, or other media of exchange such as bank drafts, checks, or postal money orders. Postage stamps are a prepaid expense, not cash. I.O.U.'s are receivables.

In most cases, cash is a current asset. However, if there is some reason the funds are restricted, the amount of restricted cash would then be excluded from the Current Assets section of the balance sheet. This would be true of funds in an insolvent bank or compensating balances required by lending banks.

8.2 Internal Control and Cash

As noted in the previous chapter, internal control should be especially well organized with respect to cash. Because cash is so difficult to trace and easily stolen, special consideration should be given to this area of internal control.

As a result of the ease with which cash can be stolen, organizations that handle much currency like gaming establishments and bars are particularly vulnerable to **skimming**. Skimming involves the failure to report all cash receipts in order to evade income taxes. A few special controls for cash can assist the firm in controlling this very easily stolen resource. The following list will go a long way in assuring security of cash:

1. Establish a definite routine for handling of cash and separate duties so that collusion would be required to conceal a theft.

2. Anyone involved with receiving or disbursing cash should have no access to the accounting records for those transactions. Anyone involved with recording such transactions should have no access to the cash.

3. Deposit all receipts each day. No payments should be made from daily receipts.

4. All disbursements should be made with prenumbered checks. All checks (including spoiled) should be accounted for.

5. All bank accounts should be **reconciled** monthly.

6. A **petty cash** fund should be set up to make minor disbursements. It should be reconciled monthly.

8.3 Bank Account Reconciliations

Usually the major amount of the cash assets of a firm is in the form of deposits with banks or other financial institutions. Realize that a debit (asset) to the bank is a credit (liability) to you. Likewise, when the bank says a credit, this will be a debit on the firm's books. This reversal in accounting terms that occurs when dealing with bank accounts often causes problems.

When doing bank reconciliations, the best procedure is to work to the **true cash balance**. This will require certain adjustments to be made to the balance shown in the bank statement. There will also be some adjustments that must be made on the books of the depositor.

8.3.1 Adjustments to Bank Balance

Numerous items will require an adjustment to the balance shown in the bank statement. These include **deposits in transit, outstanding checks,** and **errors made by the bank**. In the case of each of these items, an adjustment must be made to bring the bank balance to the **true balance**. However, none of these items will require an entry in the books of the depositor. With the exception of errors, in due time, the bank will receive notice of the reconciling items in the normal course of business.

Deposits in transit are deposits that were made in the time period being accounted for, but for some reason the bank did not record them. This is usually the result of a deposit made late in the day or in the mail. This amount will be added to the **balance per bank**.

Outstanding checks are checks that have been written, but have not cleared the bank as of the date of the bank statement. This is usually the largest part of a bank reconciliation. These amounts must be subtracted from the balance per bank to arrive at the true cash amount.

Outstanding checks should be watched carefully. A continuing large amount of checks outstanding may indicate a problem in control of cash. As a good practice, all checks over six months old should be canceled and reissued. This happens when a check is lost, accidentally torn up, and for other such reasons.

Errors by the bank typically involve a problem with incorrectly recorded numbers or names. A deposit or check may be encoded incorrectly by the proof operator.

For example, if the customer number is incorrectly recorded, this will cause a deposit to be put into the wrong person's account. Both accounts (the one the check did go into and the one it was supposed to go into) are now incorrect. The account that erroneously received the deposit should subtract it from the balance per bank. The account that did not receive the expected deposit will need to add that amount to the balance per bank.

Should the error be in the encoding of the amount of a check, again the balance per bank will need to be adjusted accordingly. For instance, if a check for $23.50 was encoded by the bank in the amount of $25.30, the bank will show a balance that is understated by the differences, $25.30 − $23.50, or $1.80. Again, this will require the depositor to notify the bank of the error and to note the error in the reconciliation of the bank account. No entry is required in the books of the depositor.

8.3.2 Adjustments to Book Balance

Any items that require an adjustment to the depositor's book balance in a reconciliation will require entries to be recorded in the depositor's accounting records. Examples include **overdrafts, auto-**

matic deposits, **automatic loans**, and **monthly service charges**. A last and perhaps special instance is **returned checks**, also known as **not sufficient funds** (NSF).

Overdrafts arise when someone writes checks for more money than is in the account. Although banks dislike this action, many allow it in certain instances. Usually there will be an additional charge if an overdraft occurs. The correct action to take when this happens is to make a deposit to cover the overdraft and make an entry for any charges incurred. The proper entry to account for these charges is shown in Example 8.3.1.

EXAMPLE 8.3.1

Date	Description	Debit	Credit
	Bank Charges – Overdraft	10	
	Cash		10

Electronic wire transfers have made **automatic payroll bank deposits** fairly common. If this is not recorded, the depositor's books will be understated by the amount of the deposit. The proper entry to adjust for this is shown in Example 8.3.2.

EXAMPLE 8.3.2

Date	Description	Debit	Credit
	Cash	300	
	Payroll Income		300

Many banks allow for an **automatic loan** if the amount in a depositor's account goes below a specified level. The bank will have additional charges for this service. Assuming that the bank loaned a depositor $350 on automatic loan, the depositor would make the following entry shown in Example 8.3.3.

EXAMPLE 8.3.3

Date	Description	Debit	Credit
	Cash	350	
	Notes Payable – Bank		350

The interest on the loan would normally not be paid until the loan was paid off.

Many checking accounts have monthly **service charges** for maintaining the account records. Others have a varied list of charges depending on the level of activity in the account. This may take the form of a per check or per transaction charge. Check printing is often included as a charge to the account. Example 8.3.4 reflects the required entry.

EXAMPLE 8.3.4

Date	Description	Debit	Credit
	Bank Service Charges	15	
	Cash		15

The last type of adjustment to the depositor's books involves **NSF** or **returned checks**. Usually this action will require a multiple entry. This circumstance develops when a check a depositor submitted in a deposit is presented to the bank of the person who wrote the check, and the bank will not honor the check for lack of funds. This will require an entry as shown in Example 8.3.5 to the cash account of the depositor as well as an adjustment to some other asset, usually accounts receivable.

EXAMPLE 8.3.5

Date	Description	Debit	Credit
	Accounts Receivable – A. Brown	100	
	Cash in Bank		100

8.3.3 A Sample Reconciliation

Example 8.3.6 is a complete reconciliation that illustrates many of the adjustments discussed in the previous sections. The exact format is not important. It is, however, important that both the bank balance and book balance are adjusted to the **true balance**.

EXAMPLE 8.3.6

SAMPLE COMPANY
BANK RECONCILIATION
January 31, 20XX

Balance per bank		$3,134
Add: Deposit in transit (1/31)		1,215
Subtotal		4,349
Deductions:		
Outstanding Checks:		
No. 235	$ 120	
No. 334	65	
No. 736	230	
No. 880	330	745
True balance per bank		$3,604
Balance per books:		$7,159
Add: Automatic deposit not recorded		1,250
Subtotal		8,409
Deductions:		
NSF check	$4,780	
Bank service charges	25	4,805
True balance per books		$3,604

Problem Solving Example:

Martha Hanson received her bank statement at the end of the month. It showed that she had a bank balance of $5,000. But her check stub balance showed $6,000. She comes to her accountant and asks him or her to explain the discrepancy.

Along with the bank statement are 10 cancelled checks and several deposit slips, one debit memorandum for $100, one credit memorandum for $300, and one insufficient funds check for $3,600. Reconcile Martha's bank statement.

Reconciling a bank statement immediately upon receipt is important for every business or person. The bank usually gives the customer a 10-day grace period to find any bank mistakes. Also, if the customer has made a mistake, he or she should correct it on the books to prevent future checks bouncing. And usually when one check bounces, many checks bounce.

MARTHA HANSON
BANK RECONCILIATION
December 31, 20XX

Bank Balance		$5,000.00
Deposits in Transit ($400 and $200)	+	600.00
Subtotal		5,600.00
Outstanding Checks	−	3,000.00
Revised Balance		$2,600.00
Book Balance		$6,000.00
Plus Note Collected by Bank (credit memorandum)	+	300.00
Subtotal		$6,300.00
Less Service Charge of Bank	−	100.00
Subtotal		6,200.00
Insufficient Funds Check	−	3,600.00
Revised Balance		$2,600.00

The bank statement reconciliation is started with a three-line heading. The first line gives the name of the person or business. In this case, the name of the person is Martha Hanson. The second line gives the name of the statement—in this case, Bank Reconciliation. The third line gives the date.

The body of the reconciliation is in two parts: the bank part and the customer part. The bank part begins with the figure that the bank has on the bank statement, which, in this case, is $5,000. The next line is entitled Deposits in Transit. Some people use the term Unrecorded Deposits. These are deposits that the customer has made during the month that the bank, for some reason, has not recorded on its books. Usually, the deposits are the ones made at the end of the period and which the bank has not yet had time to place on its books. In this case, we have two deposits in transit: one for $400 and one for $200, or a total of $600. Deposits in transit are discovered by comparing the deposits recorded on the bank statement with the deposits recorded on the company books or on the personal check stubs. In this case, the two unrecorded deposits are on the check stubs of the customer but have not yet been placed or recorded on the books of the bank. When these two unrecorded deposits are placed on the bank books, they will be added to the amount that the customer has deposited in the bank; so the $600 (total of $400 and $200) is added to the bank balance in the reconciliation.

The next step is to compute the total dollar value of the outstanding checks. Outstanding checks are those checks that have been written but have not come back through the bank and been mailed to the customer along with the bank statement. The outstanding checks are determined as follows: take the individual canceled checks that have been returned with the bank statement and compare these with the checks recorded in the Cash Payments Journal or in the check stubs. Usually, a check mark is made in the Cash Payments Journal or in the check stubs for each canceled check. After this has been accomplished, the written check amounts that do not have check marks beside them are the outstanding checks, or the checks that have not yet been returned to the customer by the bank. These checks are then added up, and the total dollar value of these outstanding checks is subtracted in the bank reconciliation. The reason that they are subtracted is that when they finally do come through the bank, the bank will subtract their face value from the amount the customer has in the bank.

In the case of Martha Hanson, she had outstanding checks amounting to $3,000; so $3,000 is subtracted from her bank balance in the reconciliation report.

This gives Martha Hanson a revised balance of $2,600.

The next step is to look at Martha's book balance. This is either the balance of her cash journal or the running balance in her check stubs. We begin with her book balance of $6,000. Along with the bank statement, Martha has received a Credit Memorandum from the bank. This is a slip of paper mentioning that the bank is crediting Martha's account for $300 because one of her notes was collected by the bank from a customer. Many times, when a customer cannot or will not pay, or is slow to pay, a businessperson will send the Note Receivable to the bank and ask the bank to collect it. This often encourages the debtor to pay promptly because most persons want to keep their bank credit in good shape. So let us say that some time ago, Martha Hanson gave a customer's note to the bank for collection. The bank has collected the $300 note and placed the $300 in Martha Hanson's account. Toward the bottom of the reconciliation, we add $300 to Martha's bank balance. In one way, banks keep books opposite to the way other businesses keep books. To banks, the customers are creditors because the banks owe the customers the money deposited in the banks. These customer-creditors are liabilities to the bank, and so customer accounts have credit balances. When these balances increase, the bank credits the account. On the contrary, when the accounts decrease, the bank debits the account. So a bank credit memorandum shows an increase in the customer's account and a bank debit memorandum shows a decrease in the customer's account. In the case of the note collected by the bank, it is a credit memorandum and a $300 increase in the customer's bank balance is recorded in the Reconciliation.

But there is also a debit memorandum. This is a service charge or several service charges from the bank for services that the bank has rendered to the customer (depositor). In this case, all the service charges for the period add up to $100; so in the reconciliation $100 is subtracted from the balance.

Along with the bank statement is a debtor's insufficient funds check for $3,600. An insufficient funds check is also called a "bounced check." Let us say that one of Martha Hanson's customers (debtors) owed her $3,600, and he gave her his check for that amount. She then deposited the $3,600 check in her bank account and the bank gave her credit for it. Later it was discovered that the customer did not have this much money in his personal bank account; so the bank returned or bounced the check, sending it back to Martha Hanson and debiting or deducting $3,600 from her account in the bank. Since this is a decrease in Martha's balance, we deduct the $3,600 from her bank balance in the bank reconciliation. This brings Martha's account down to $2,600 Revised Balance, which is the same as the $2,600 revised balance in the first half of the Reconciliation. This makes the Reconciliation balance, and Martha revises her books to show the amount of $2,600, or she revises her check stub running balance to show this amount.

If this procedure does not show a balance, her next step is to go over the bank statement and try to find a mistake in the bank's figures. Of course, if she finds a mistake in the bank's figures, she should phone the bank immediately.

8.4   Petty Cash

To avoid much red tape and many small insignificant checks, most organizations use a **petty cash fund** to take care of minor disbursements. This fund is usually set up on an **imprest** basis. That means the fund is set up with a certain amount of cash and all minor payments are made from the cash. The entry to set up the fund is shown in Example 8.4.1.

EXAMPLE 8.4.1

Date	Description	Debit	Credit
	Petty Cash	200	
	Cash in Bank		200

When there is a need to replenish the petty cash fund, a debit is made to each of the individual expenses paid from the fund, and a credit is made to Cash in Bank for the total amount to replenish the fund. Example 8.4.2 illustrates such an entry.

EXAMPLE 8.4.2

Date	Description	Debit	Credit
	Postage	23	
	Advertising	59	
	Office Supplies	29	
	Delivery Expenses	37	
	Cash in Bank		148

The only time another entry would be made to petty cash would be when the account is closed or the amount in it is adjusted to a new level.

Problem Solving Example:

 How do you get internal control of Petty Cash?

 By using the Imprest System. When the owner begins to set up a Petty Cash System, he or she decides how much should be in the Petty Cash drawer. Let us say he decides on $100. He writes a check, taking $100 out of his regular bank account and placing this $100 in his Petty Cash drawer, probably part of his cash register in the store. At the same time, he makes the following entry in his books:

Year		($ in dollars)
January 2	Petty Cash	100
	Cash in Bank	100

Petty Cash is one of the Cash accounts. It has a debit balance, and it is a current asset, just as the Cash account is a current asset. Petty Cash is debited, because this amount is placed in the Petty Cash drawer. Cash in Bank or just Cash is credited because this amount has been taken out of the owner's account in the bank.

The Petty Cash account will appear as follows on the owner's books.

Petty Cash		
Year		
January 2	100	

The Imprest System means that the $100 debit in the Petty Cash account is impressed in the account. It stays there and never leaves. (Of course, if the owner later decided to change the amount of money in the account, or perhaps do away with the account entirely, he or she could do this.) But usually the $100 will stay permanently in the account. This is one of the reasons the boss has **internal control** over the account.

The owner also has **Petty Cash Vouchers** printed. They could appear as follows:

Brookings Clothing Store
Petty Cash Voucher

Amount _____

ACCOUNT DEBITED _____

Date _____

Signature of Recipient of Cash _____

Signature of Manager _____

The use of the Petty Cash Vouchers is another means of internal control for the manager. When paying Petty Cash amounts from the Petty Cash drawer, each clerk must fill out a Petty Cash Voucher and have both the recipient and the manager sign the voucher. The clerk then files the completed voucher in the Petty Cash drawer. At any time, the manager can open the drawer, and the amounts of the vouchers plus the amount of Cash in the drawer should add up to the $100.

If the year is coming to an end, or if the Petty Cash drawer cash is running low, the manager can replenish the Petty Cash as follows:

Let us say that only $5 remains in the Petty Cash drawer and that the Petty Cash Vouchers add up to $95. The owner takes the vouchers out of the drawer and puts them in various piles, depending on the types of expenses or assets purchased with the Petty Cash. He then adds up the vouchers in each pile and makes an entry in his journal similar to the following:

Year		($ in dollars)	
February 15	Office Supplies Expense	46.50	
	Store Supplies Expense	30.00	
	Stamps	18.50	
	Cash in Bank		95.00
	To replenish the Petty Cash fund		

The vouchers are then filed in a file drawer; a check is written for $95; and $95 is taken out of the regular Cash bank account and placed in the Petty Cash drawer along with the $5 that is still in the drawer, making a total of $100 cash.

It will be noted that the various expense and asset accounts are debited because the Brookings Clothing Store got the use of them. Cash in Bank is credited, because $95 is taken out of the firm's regular Cash account. Petty Cash is not touched. It is imprest and remains the same. This Imprest System, plus the use of vouchers, gives the owner internal control and prevents customers and employees from stealing from the Petty Cash fund.

Let us say the owner wishes to increase the Petty Cash fund from $100 to $150. He would make the following entry:

Year		($ in dollars)
March 1	Petty Cash	50
	Cash in Bank	50
	To increase Petty Cash	

After this entry has been made, the Petty Cash account in the ledger would appear as follows:

Petty Cash		
Year		
January 2	100.00	
Year		
March 1	50.00	
	150.00	

Let us say that in later years the owner decided to lower the amount of Cash in the Petty Cash drawer from $150 to $75. This could be accomplished by the following entry:

Year	($ in dollars)
September 1 Cash in Bank	75.00
Petty Cash	75.00
To decrease Petty Cash	

After this entry has been made, the Petty Cash account in the ledger would appear as follows:

Petty Cash

Year		Year	
January 2	100.00	September 1	75.00
Year			
March 1	50.00		
	150.00		
Balance	75.00		

CHAPTER 9

Receivables

9.1 Accounts Receivable

Accounts receivable arise when a business makes sales on credit. In such cases, the sales agreement calls for payment within a certain time period and may offer a discount for payment before the due date. Whether a general journal or a specialized journal such as the sales journal is used, the journal entries for a credit sale and subsequent collection would be as shown in Example 9.1.1.

EXAMPLE 9.1.1

To Record the Sale of Merchandise on Account to John Doe

The Sample Company
General Journal

Date	Acct. No.	Description	Debit	Credit
20XX Jan. 4	4	Accounts Receivable: John Doe	1,000	
	80	Sales		1,000

To Record the Collection of Accounts Receivable from John Doe

Jan 9	1	Cash	1,000	
	4	Accounts Receivable:		
		John Doe		1,000

If a discount of 2% for payment within 10 days had been offered to John Doe, the entry of January 9 would be as shown in Example 9.1.2.

EXAMPLE 9.1.2

To Record the Collection of a $1,000 Sale Made to John Doe on January 4 less 2% discount

The Sample Company
General Journal

Date	Acct. No.	Description	Debit	Credit
20XX				
Jan 9	1	Cash	980	
	81	Sales Discounts	20	
	4	Accounts Receivable:		
		John Doe		1,000

A business may allow the return of merchandise by the customer for credit against their account. This is accomplished through the use of the sales returns and allowances account. For example, if the customer in the previous example, John Doe, returned merchandise for $100 credit prior to payment, accounts receivable would be adjusted through the entry shown in Example 9.1.3.

EXAMPLE 9.1.3

The Sample Company
General Journal

Date	Acct. No.	Description	Debit	Credit
20XX				
Jan 7	82	Sales Returns and Allowances	100	
	4	Accounts Receivable: John Doe		100

Problem Solving Example:

 The Swisher Furniture Company was short of cash and long on accounts receivable. They needed $600,000 cash to pay their debts and to have enough working capital to continue operating their business. After discussing their financial problems with the bank, they were advised that the bank would lend them this large amount of money, $600,000, if they would make a specific assignment of $800,000 of their Accounts Receivable to the bank; and the going interest rate is 9%. This was done; and the Swisher Furniture Company received the $600,000 loan from the bank. Two weeks later, the Swisher Furniture Company received $200,000 payment from customers and turned this money over to the bank. What entries should be made on Swisher Furniture Company books?

Year		($ in dollars)	
July 15	Cash	200,000	
	Accounts Receivable Assigned		200,000
	Cash received from customers		
15	Notes Payable	200,000	
	Cash		200,000

In the first entry, $200,000 cash was received from customers; so the account Cash was debited for that amount. The Asset account, Accounts Receivable Assigned, was credited for $200,000, bringing its balance down to $600,000.

In the second entry, the $200,000 received from customers was immediately turned over to the bank in partial payment of the note; so Notes Payable is debited for $200,000 because we now owe less on the note; and Cash is credited for $200,000 because we are paying the bank that amount.

9.2 Uncollectible Accounts Receivable

Uncollectible accounts receivable are the accounts receivable that a company cannot collect. When the conclusion is reached that a receivable is not collectible, that amount is **written off**, or removed from the company's books. Since that sale was originally recorded as revenue, this action has the effect of reducing income.

9.2.1 Allowance Method of Accounting for Uncollectible Accounts

This method is also known as the reserve method because it provides in advance for uncollectible receivables. This provision for uncollectibility is made through an adjusting entry performed at the end of a fiscal period and serves two purposes. It reduces the value of receivables to the amount of cash expected to be received and allocates the expected expense associated with this reduction to the current fiscal period.

The amount of provision to be established can be calculated several different ways. One method involves the careful examination of each customer's account to determine the probability of collection. Those deemed questionable as to collectibility are then totaled and that amount will be used as the provision amount. A simpler method involves a percentage estimate of uncollectible accounts based on outstanding receivables. Many businesses have found that the percentage of uncollectible accounts varies little from year to year and therefore feel comfortable making provisions based on this historical figure.

Once the provision amount is established, that figure will be debited to **uncollectible accounts expense** (or **bad debts expense**) and credited to **allowance for doubtful accounts**. For example, assume that The Sample Company has outstanding accounts receivable totaling $100,000 as of December 31. After examination of the individual accounts, management believes all but $5,000 is likely to be collected. The adjusting entry to reflect the provision for uncollectible accounts is shown in Example 9.2.1.

EXAMPLE 9.2.1

The Sample Company
General Journal

Date	Acct. No.	Description	Debit	Credit
20XX Dec 31	95	Uncollectible Accounts Expense	5,000	
	5	Allowance for Doubtful Accounts		5,000

The debit balance of $100,000 in outstanding accounts receivable represents total claims against customers. The net realizable value of those receivables (the amount expected to be collected) is $95,000. The amount of accounts receivable reported on the financial statement is generally the net realizable value, accompanied by a notation as to the amount of allowance for uncollectible accounts.

9.2.2 Write-Offs to the Allowance Account

When an account is determined to be uncollectible, that amount is charged against the allowance for uncollectible accounts. As an example, the account of Mary Smith, which has a balance of $200, is deemed to be uncollectible on May 13. The entry to reflect this action is shown in Example 9.2.2.

EXAMPLE 9.2.2

To Record Write-off of Uncollectible Account

The Sample Company
General Journal

Date	Acct. No.	Description	Debit	Credit
20XX May 13	5	Allowance for Doubtful Accounts	200	
	4	Accounts Receivable: Mary Smith		200

An account that has been written off may later be collected. In such an instance, the account should be reinstated through an entry just the reverse of that used to write-off the account. To illustrate, should the account written off in Example 9.2.2 be subsequently collected, an entry to reinstate that account is shown in Example 9.2.3.

EXAMPLE 9.2.3

The Sample Company
General Journal

Date	Acct. No.	Description	Debit	Credit
20XX Jul 20	4	Accounts Receivable: Mary Smith	200	
	5	Allowance for Doubtful Accounts		200

9.3 Direct Write-Off Method of Accounting for Uncollectible Accounts

The allowance method of accounting for uncollectible accounts is preferred, since it allows the matching of uncollectible accounts expenses with the associated revenues. There may be situations, however, where the direct write-off method may be used. There may be situations where it is not feasible to estimate the amount of uncollectible accounts or the amount may not be material. In such cases, a business may choose to adopt the direct write-off method. Under this method, an allowance account or an adjusting entry at the end of the fiscal period is not needed. When an account is deemed to be uncollectible, an entry to reflect that decision is made as shown in Example 9.3.1.

EXAMPLE 9.3.1

To Write-Off Uncollectible Account

The Sample Company
General Journal

Date	Acct. No.	Description	Debit	Credit
20XX June 6	95	Uncollectible Accounts Expense	25	
	4	Accounts Receivable: Mary Smith		25

Subsequent recovery of an account that has been written off would require an entry to reinstate that account. The entry would be performed in reverse manner from the entry shown in Example 9.3.1.

Problem Solving Examples:

 The Jacobson Clothing Store sells to many of their customers on account. Most of the customers pay promptly, but a few are slow to pay, and even fewer never pay. How does Jacobson Clothing Store handle bad debts at the end of the year, at the time they discover that the particular customer won't pay, and at a later date when the customer surprises them and finally pays his or her debt after the company has written it off?

Let us assume that in one year, customer Raymond Harrison has purchased $800 worth of clothing, for which he has not paid, as the year ends. What entry is made on the books of the Jacobson Clothing Store at year's end? At a later date when we hear Harrison has gone bankrupt? And at an even later date when Harrison comes into the store unexpectedly and pays us?

20XX	($ in dollars)
December 31 (No entry)	

In the Direct Write-Off method of accounting for bad debts, there is no Allowance for Doubtful Accounts. The business makes no year-end entries and does not have to guess how much is going to be lost.

On March 31, in the following year, we hear that Raymond Harrison has gone bankrupt and it looks as if we will not get paid the $800 he owes us on account. So we make the following entry:

20XX		($ in dollars)	
March 31	Bad Debts Expense	800	
	Accounts Receivable–Raymond Harrison		800

As can be seen in the entry above, Bad Debts Expense is debited for $800 only when we learn that we will probably never receive the money because the customer has gone bankrupt. The Internal Revenue

Service favors this method because we don't subtract the loss until we are sure that we have actually lost the money. Accounts Receivable–Raymond Harrison is credited, and this closes out the Harrison account on our books. Although Harrison really still owes us the money, it looks as if we will never collect it; so we write him off. We mark his account **bankrupt** so that in later years we will never sell him any more clothing on account.

Theoretically, the accounting profession does not favor this method because we sold Harrison the merchandise in the one year but did not debit Bad Debts Expense until the next year when Harrison went bankrupt. So the Bad Debts Expense is subtracted in the Income Statement of the wrong year.

Let us say that in the following September (after the year ended with no payment), Harrison receives a great deal of money from his rich uncle and comes into our store and pays us the $800. How do we handle this on our books?

Our books are not set up for this occasion; so it takes two entries to handle the matter, as follows:

20XX		($ in dollars)
September 14	Accounts Receivable–Harrison	800	
	Bad Debts Expense		800
	To reinstate the account		
14	Cash	800	
	Accounts Receivable–Harrison		800
	To show the receipt of cash		

The first of these two entries is called "Reinstating the Account." It turns around the entry of March 31. Accounts Receivable–Harrison is debited so that the account of Harrison is no longer closed. It is open again and Harrison owes us the money according to the books. Bad Debts Expense is credited for $800; so this does away with the Bad Debts Expense and Harrison is no longer a bad debt.

The second of these two entries debits Cash for $800 because we are receiving the money from Harrison. We credit Accounts Receivable–Harrison to show that Harrison no longer owes us money and we cancel his debt. As we write him off, we could write-off the word "bankrupt" to show that the man pays his debts.

 What are the two methods of handling bad debts in the business world? Which method is best and why?

 The two methods by which accountants handle bad debts in the business world are as follows:

1. The Direct Write-Off Method
2. The Allowance Method

The Direct Write-Off Method is favored by the Internal Revenue Service. In fact, it is the only method the IRS will accept at the present time. This is because the account, Bad Debts Expense, is not debited until the time when it appears that the debt will never be collected, such as the time when a customer goes bankrupt or leaves the area and it looks as if he or she will never repay the debt.

The Allowance Method is favored by accountants because the account, Bad Debts Expense, is debited at the end of each month or each year for the amount that the owner thinks he or she will lose in bad debts. Accountants favor the Allowance Method because Bad Debts Expense is deducted in the year when the merchandise was sold, not in the year when the customer goes bankrupt. By deducting the Bad Debts Expense in the year in which the merchandise was sold, one subtracts the proper Expenses from the proper Revenue to get the proper Net Income for the year.

9.4 Notes Receivable

Notes receivable arise when customers or others obligate themselves to a business through a formal contract to repay the face amount of a loan at a specific date with interest calculated at a specific rate. For example, assume that Paul Johnson borrows $5,000 from The Sample Company on April 4. The terms of the note require repayment within 60 days. Interest is to be calculated at 12%. The entry to reflect this transaction and subsequent payment of the loan is shown in Example 9.4.1.

EXAMPLE 9.4.1

To Reflect Loan to Paul Johnson of $5,000 for 60 Days at 12%

The Sample Company
General Journal

Date	Acct. No.	Description	Debit	Credit
20XX April 4	7	Notes Receivable: Paul Johnson	5,000	
	1	Cash		5,000

To Record Payment of Note Receivable

May 4	1	Cash	5,100	
	7	Notes Receivable: Paul Johnson		5,000
	86	Interest Income		100

9.5 Discounting Notes Receivable

A business may not wish to wait until a note receivable matures before receiving cash. In such a case, it may **discount** or sell a note receivable to a bank. The bank obviously will not pay the full maturity value of the note and will calculate a discount based on an agreed percentage. Using the note receivable shown in Example 9.4.1, assume that The Sample Company needs the cash immediately and discounts the note to its bank on April 6. The bank charges a discount rate of 14%. The discount value of the note is calculated in Example 9.5.1.

EXAMPLE 9.5.1

Face value of the note	$5,000
Interest on note – 60 days @ 12%	100
Maturity value	5,100
Discount period April 6 to June 3: 58 days	
Discount on maturity value: 58 days @ 14%	115
Proceeds	$4,985

The journal entry to record this transaction is shown in Example 9.5.2.

EXAMPLE 9.5.2

The Sample Company
General Journal

Date	Acct. No.	Description	Debit	Credit
20XX April 6	1	Cash	4,985	
	96	Interest Expense	15	
	7	Notes Receivable		5,000

In this case, the proceeds received from discounting were less than the face value of the note. Had the proceeds exceeded the face value of the note receivable, the difference would have been interest income, instead of interest expense.

Problem Solving Example:

The Swisher Furniture Company is short of cash and long on accounts receivable. In fact, they need $600,000 cash to pay their debts and to have enough working capital to continue. After discussing their financial problems with the bank, they are advised that the bank will lend them this large amount of money, $600,000, if they will make a specific assignment of $800,000 of their accounts receivable to the bank. The company agrees upon this. The interest rate is nine percent. What entry or entries are made on the Swisher Furniture Company books on July 1, when the money is borrowed?

20XX		($ in dollars)	
July 1	Cash	600,000	
	Discount on Notes Payable	4,500	
	Notes Payable		604,500
1	Accounts Receivable Assigned	800,000	
	Accounts Receivable		800,000

In the first entry, Cash is debited for $600,000 on the books of the Swisher Furniture Company as the company receives the $600,000 loan from the bank. The Contra-Liability account, Discount on Notes Payable, is debited for one month's interest, computed as follows: $600,000 × 9% = $54,000; $54,000 divided by 12 months = $4,500. Thus, the Discount on Notes Payable is debited for $4,500. Notes Payable is credited for the $604,500 total, and that is also the face value of the note. ($600,000 + $4,500 = $604,500.)

Since a large amount of money is being borrowed, the bank has insisted on a specific assignment of accounts receivable. And the assignment ($800,000) is quite a bit higher than the amount borrowed ($600,000). To show the assignment, an Asset account entitled Accounts Receivable Assigned is set up and debited for $800,000. Accounts Receivable is credited for $800,000. Let us assume that before the assignment the Swisher Furniture Company had accounts receivable totaling $900,000. If this is true, the Accounts Receivable account and the Accounts Receivable Assigned account would appear as follows on the books of the Swisher Company:

Accounts Receivable

Balance	6/30/XX	900,000	7/1/XX	800,000
		100,000		

Accounts Receivable Assigned

7/1/XX	800,000	

As can be seen from looking at the two above accounts, on June 30 the Accounts Receivable account had a debit balance of $900,000. With the borrowing of $600,000 from the bank, the Swisher Furniture Company assigned $800,000 of its Accounts Receivable to the bank; thereafter, the balance of Accounts Receivable (unassigned) is $100,000. The second Asset account, Accounts Receivable Assigned, shows the $800,000 balance.

9.6 Dishonored Notes Receivable

When a customer fails to pay a note receivable on the due date, the note is **dishonored** and is no longer considered a valid asset of the company. In such cases, the face amount of the note receivable may be charged against an allowance account similar to that used for uncollectible accounts receivable. Any interest income that has been accrued and recorded as interest receivable would then be written off. As an alternative, the face amount of the note plus accrued interest may be converted to an account receivable and handled according to established procedures for that type of account.

Quiz: Internal Control and Specialized Journals – Receivables

1. Accurate record control can be handled in a business by all the following except which one?

    (A) Comparing the general journal with the balance sheet

    (B) Reconciliation of subsidiary records with general ledgers

    (C) Internal audits

    (D) External audits

2. Which of the following is NOT a specialized journal?

    (A) Cash Receipts Journal

    (B) General Journal

    (C) Cash Payments Journal

    (D) Sales Journal

3. When goods are sold for $200 and payment is immediately received, what entry is made on the books of the seller?

    (A) Debit Cash $200 and credit Accounts Receivable $200

    (B) Debit Cash $196 and debit Sales Discount $4, and credit Accounts Receivable $200

    (C) Debit Cash $200 and credit Sales $200

    (D) Debit Accounts Receivable $200 and credit Sales $200

4. When goods are sold for $200 and goods are paid for within the discount period and the discount rate is 2%, what is the amount of the discount?

   (A) $2   (C) $4

   (B) $3   (D) None of these

5. What entry is made when an account is written off for lack of payment, under the Direct Write-Off Method?

   (A) Debit Allowance for Doubtful Accounts and credit Accounts Receivable

   (B) Debit Bad Debts Expense and credit Accounts Receivable

   (C) Debit Bad Debts Expense and credit Allowance for Doubtful Accounts

   (D) Debit Allowance for Doubtful Accounts and credit Bad Debt Expense

6. What entry is made when an account is written off for lack of payment, and the Allowance Method is used?

   (A) Debit Allowance for Doubtful Accounts and credit Accounts Receivable

   (B) Debit Loss and credit Accounts Receivable

   (C) Debit Bad Debts Expense and credit Allowance for Doubtful Accounts

   (D) Debit Allowance for Doubtful Accounts and credit Bad Debts Expense

7. If we make a sale, and at the time of the sale the note is received from a customer for the dollar amount of the sale, what entry is made on the books of the seller?

   (A) Debit Notes Receivable and credit Cash

(B) Debit Cash and debit Sales Discount and credit Accounts Receivable

(C) Debit Notes Receivable and credit Accounts Receivable

(D) Debit Cash and credit Sales

8. The proceeds of a note are

(A) the amount that the person receives from the bank when he or she discounts a customer's note.

(B) the amount which has been borrowed.

(C) the dollar value of the interest on the note.

(D) the interest rate on the note.

9. The maturity value of a note receivable is

(A) the face value of the note.

(B) the interest rate of the note.

(C) the dollar value of the interest on the note.

(D) the face value of the note plus interest.

10. What happens when a customer dishonors a note receivable?

(A) The customer pays the note.

(B) The customer pays the interest but not the principal.

(C) The customer fails to pay the note receivable when it becomes due.

(D) The customer takes out a new note when the old note becomes due.

ANSWER KEY

1.	(A)	6.	(A)
2.	(B)	7.	(A)
3.	(A)	8.	(A)
4.	(C)	9.	(D)
5.	(B)	10.	(C)

CHAPTER 10

Inventory

10.1 Introduction to Inventory Accounting

In the United States, four inventory methods have gained wide acceptance and are considered generally accepted. These methods are **FIFO, LIFO, weighted average,** and **specific identification.**

The Internal Revenue Service (IRS) requires that any businesses which resell merchandise inventory must keep accounting records on the accrual basis. The **consistency** convention requires that businesses not change inventory methods often.

Use of an inventory method does not mean that the physical flow of goods follows the cost flow. The methods are used to better approximate current economic conditions of the costs involved. Hence, even if an organization is using **LIFO** for inventory costing, the actual flow of physical goods could be on a **FIFO** basis.

10.2 Periodic and Perpetual Accounting Systems

There are two main accounting systems, **periodic** and **perpetual,** for keeping track of inventory. Refer to Chapter 6 for further elaboration on this topic.

10.3 Inventory Methods

Table 10.3.1 provides information to be used to demonstrate the various inventory methods.

TABLE 10.3.1

THE SAMPLE COMPANY
INVENTORY RECORDS

Date	Action	Units	Cost per Unit	Total Amount	Balance (in Units)
1-1	Balance	15	$10	$150	15
1-7	Purchased	30	11	330	45
1-10	Purchased	20	12	240	65
1-15	Sold	10	–	–	55
1-25	Sold	10	–	–	45
1-30	Sold	15	–	–	30
Total				$720	

When calculating inventory and cost of goods sold, there are two truths that will always hold. The total goods available for sale is equal to the sum of the ending inventory and the cost of goods sold. Using the data above, that means that ending inventory, plus the cost of goods sold, will be equal to $720. Likewise, the sum of the units in ending inventory and the units in cost of goods sold will total 65. By checking these numbers each time ending inventory and cost of goods sold is calculated, minor arithmetic errors can be quickly identified.

10.3.1 FIFO

The **first-in, first-out** inventory method assumes that costs are charged against revenue in the order in which they were incurred. Thus, the most recent costs are assumed to still be in inventory.

Using the data given above, the results of using FIFO are shown in Example 10.3.1.

EXAMPLE 10.3.1

CALCULATIONS USING FIFO

Ending Inventory			Cost of Goods Sold				
Date Pur.	Cost	Total	Date Pur.	Date Sold	Cost	Total	
1-10:	20x$12@	= $240	1-1:	1-15	10x$10@	= $100	
1-7:	10x$11@	= 110	1-1:	1-25	5x$10@	= 50	
			1-7:	1-25	5x$11@	= 55	
			1-7:	1-30	15x$11@	= 165	
Total	30	$350	Total		35	$370	

As can be seen from the example, total units is equal to 65 (30 in ending inventory and 35 in cost of goods sold). Also, the sum of the ending inventory and cost of goods sold is equal to $720; $350 + $370 = $720.

Problem Solving Example:

The Brown Company sells one product. Presented below is information for the year for this company.

1/1/20XX	Beginning Inventory	50 units @ $5	=	$250
3/10/20XX	Sale	10 units @ $8		
3/25/20XX	Purchase	80 units @ $6	=	480
5/10/20XX	Sale	100 units @ $9		
8/7/20XX	Purchase	15 units @ $7	=	105

What is the dollar value of the ending inventory using the **periodic inventory method** (first-in, first-out method)?

What is the dollar value of the ending inventory using the **perpetual inventory method**, using the first-in, first-out computation?

A   In using the periodic inventory method, only the beginning inventory and the purchases are considered, not the sales. Following is the information about the beginning inventory and purchases, leaving out the sales:

1/1/20XX	Beginning Inventory	50 units @ $5	=	$250
3/25/20XX	Purchase	80 units @ $6	=	$480
8/7/20XX	Purchase	15 units @ $7	=	$105
Total units available for sale and				
their dollar value:		145		$835
Number of units sold		−110		
Number of units unsold				
(in Ending Inventory)		35		

As seen from the computations immediately above, there is the beginning inventory of 50 units, the March purchase of 80 units, and the August purchase of 15 units. These add up to a total of 145 units available for sale. From the information in the question, we see that the March sale was 10 units and the May sale was 100 units, or a total of 110 units. Next, we subtract the 110 units sold from the 145 units available for sale to get 35 units in the ending inventory.

The next step is to ascertain the dollar value of the ending inventory of 35 units, using the first-in, first-out computation. In the first-in, first-out method, the units in the beginning inventory and early purchases are sold first. This means that the ending inventory is made up of the later purchases. In order, then, to determine the dollar value of the ending inventory by the first-in, first-out computation, one must **start at the bottom** of the table and work up until one reaches the 35 units in the ending inventory. This is done as follows:

Determining the Dollar Value of the Ending Inventory Using the First-In, First-Out Method

Units from the 8/7/20XX			
purchase	15 units @ $7	=	$105
Some units from the			
3/25/20XX purchase	20 units @ $6	=	$120
Ending inventory (FIFO)	35 units		$225

Working backwards up the previous table until 35 units of ending inventory are reached, we start with the August 7 purchase of 15 units @ $7 = $105. Then we move up to the March 25 purchase. Subtracting 15 units of the August 7 purchase from the 35 units of the ending inventory, we discover that we need 20 more units. These are all taken from the March 25 purchase at $6. So we multiply the 20 units additional that are needed by the $6 per unit in the March 25 inventory, to get $120. Next, we add the $105 and the $120 to get $225, which is the dollar value of the 35 units in the ending inventory, using the first-in, first-out method.

The **perpetual inventory method** differs from the **periodic inventory method** of computing the dollar value of ending inventory in that under the perpetual inventory method, every time there is a sale, the units in the sale are subtracted from the units on hand, and a new dollar value of inventory is computed. Under the periodic inventory method, on the other hand, the units sold are not subtracted from the units available until the end of the fiscal period.

The computation of the dollar value of the ending inventory using the perpetual inventory method and using the first-in, first-out computation follows:

Perpetual Inventory Method
First-In, First-Out Computation

Date	In	Out	Balance
1/1/20XX			50 units @ $5 = $250
3/10/20XX		10 units @ $5 = $50	40 units @ $5 = $200
3/25/20XX	80 units @ $6 = $480		80 units @ $6 = $480
5/10/20XX		40 units @ $5 = $200	
		60 units @ $6 = $360	20 units @ $6 = $120
8/7/20XX	15 units @ $7 = $105		15 units @ $7 = $105

The Perpetual Inventory item is kept in a computer data base or on a storage card similar to the one above, with Date, In, Out, and Balance. On January 1, this item consisted of 50 units at $5 = $250. On March 10, 10 units were sold. These were units purchased at $5 per unit, and all these figures are at cost, not at sales price. Thus, 10 units are going out of inventory at a cost of $5 per unit, or $50. Subtracting the 10 units from the 50 units previously on hand, the balance is 40 units at $5, or $200.

On March 25, 80 units more are purchased, but this time at a higher price—$6 per unit, making it a cost of $480 (80 units × $6 = $480). This is added to the balance. The previous balance had been 40 units at $5 = $200. Now to this we add 80 units at $6 = $480.

On May 10, 100 units are sold. Since this is the first-in, first-out method, the 40 units purchased at $5 per unit will be sold first. Therefore, under the Out column, there are 40 units @ $5 = $200.

We still need 60 more units to make the 100 units being sold (100 − 40 = 60). The only units we still have left are those previously purchased at $6 per unit, so we take out 60 units at $6 = $360. All of this is subtracted from the previous inventory, so all that is left in the Balance column is 20 units @ $6 = $120.

On August 7, 15 units of the same item are purchased at $7 = $105. This is then added to the balance. So the balance at year's end is as follows:

20 units @ $6 = $120
15 units @ $7 = $105
35 units $225

Thus, the dollar value of the 35 units in the ending inventory as of December 31 is $225 under the perpetual inventory method using first-in, first-out computation.

What is the dollar value of the Cost of Goods Sold, using the perpetual inventory method and using the first-in, first-out computation?

Total units available for sale and their dollar value	145 units	$835
Less: Ending Inventory, Perpetual Inventory Method,		
FIFO Computation	− 35 units	−$225
Cost of Goods Sold	110 units	$610

Thus, the Cost of Goods Sold is $610, using the perpetual inventory method and the first-in, first-out computation.

10.3.2 LIFO

The **last-in, first-out** inventory method assumes that costs are charged against revenue in the **reverse** order in which they were incurred. Thus, the oldest costs are assumed to still be in inventory.

Using the data given in Table 10.3.1 and Example 10.3.1, the results of using LIFO are shown in Example 10.3.2.

EXAMPLE 10.3.2

CALCULATIONS USING LIFO

Ending Inventory			Cost of Goods Sold				
Date Pur.	Cost	Total	Date Pur.	Date Sold	Cost		Total
1-1:	15×$10@	= $150	1-15:	1-20	10×$12@	=	$120
1-7:	15×$11@	= 165	1-15:	1-25	10×$12@	=	120
			1-7:	1-30	15×$11@	=	165
Total	30	$315	Total		35		$405

As can be seen from the example, total units is equal to 65 (30 in ending inventory and 35 in cost of goods sold). Also, the sum of the ending inventory and cost of goods sold is equal to $720; $315 + $405 = $720.

LIFO is allowed for income tax reporting purposes. However, the IRS requires that if LIFO is used for income tax purposes, it must also be used for financial reporting purposes.

Problem Solving Example:

The Brown Company sells one product. Presented on the next page is information for the year for this company. Compute the dollar value of the ending inventory using the LIFO method. Number of units sold during the year:

Beginning Inventory and Purchases

1/1/20XX	Beginning Inventory	50 units @ $5	=	$250
3/25/20XX	Purchase	80 units @ $6	=	$480
8/7/20XX	Purchase	15 units @ $7	=	$105
Total units available for sale and their dollar value		145 units		$835

What is the dollar value of the Cost of Goods Sold using the periodic inventory method and using last-in, first-out computations?

What is the dollar value of the ending inventory using the perpetual inventory method and using the last-in, first-out computation?

A As seen from the computations immediately above, there is the beginning inventory of 50 units, the March purchase of 80 units, and the August purchase of 15 units. These add up to a total of 145 units available for sale. From the information in the question, we determine to compute the number of units in the ending inventory (unsold). As seen above, there are 145 units available for sale, and of these, 110 units were sold. There are, therefore, 35 units unsold in the ending inventory (145 units – 110 units = 35 units).

The next step is to ascertain the dollar value of the ending inventory of 35 units using the last-in, first out computation. In the LIFO computation, the last units purchased are sold first. This means that the ending inventory is derived from the earliest purchased units. So in order to compute the dollar value of the ending inventory by the last-in first-out computation, we need to start **at the top** of the above table and work down until we reach the 35 unsold units in the ending inventory, as follows:

1/1/20XX	Ending Inventory at Beginning Inventory Price	35 units @ $5 =	$175

There are 50 units in the beginning inventory that were purchased at $5 per unit. But in this computation we are interested in only 35 of these units that have still been unsold at year's end. So we multiply the 35 units by the $5 price to get $175, the dollar value of the ending inventory.

The dollar value of the Cost of Goods Sold, using the periodic inventory method and using last-in, first-out computations, is determined as follows:

Total units available for sale and their dollar value	145 units	$835
Less Ending Inventory (LIFO)	35 units	– 175
Cost of Goods Sold (LIFO)	105 units	$660

As previously computed, there were 145 units available for sale at $835 cost. These available units are either sold during the year or else they remain in the ending inventory unsold. The ending inventory of 35 units was computed, using the last-in, first-out computations, to be $175. Therefore, we subtract the $175 value of the unsold units from the $835 value of the units available for sale to get the $660 value of the units sold. Since we have kept cost prices separate from selling prices, and this is the cost price, we can call the $660 the Cost of Goods Sold, LIFO method.

The dollar value of the ending inventory using the perpetual inventory method and using the last-in, first-out computation is determined as follows:

The perpetual inventory method differs from the periodic inventory method of computing the dollar value of ending inventory in that under the perpetual inventory method, every time there is a sale, the units in the sale are subtracted from the units on hand, and a new dollar value of inventory is computed. Under the periodic inventory method, on the other hand, the units sold are not subtracted from the units available until the end of the fiscal period.

The computation of the dollar value of the ending inventory using the perpetual inventory method and using the last-in, first-out computation follows:

Perpetual Inventory Method
Last-In, First-Out Computation

Date	In	Out	Balance
1/1/20XX			50 units @ $5 = $250
3/10/20XX		10 units @ $5 = $50.00	40 units @ $5 = $200
3/25/20XX	80 units @ $6 = $480		80 units @ $6 = $480
5/10/20XX		80 units @ $6 = $480	
		20 units @ $5 = $100	20 units @ $5 = $100
8/7/20XX	15 units @ $7 = $105		15 units @ $7 = $105

The Perpetual Inventory item is kept in a computer data base or on a storage card similar to the one above, with Date, In, Out, and Balance. On January 1, this item consisted of 50 units at $5 = $250. On March 10, 10 units were sold. These were units purchased at $5 per unit, and all these figures are at cost, not at sales price. Thus, 10 units are going out of inventory at a cost of $5 per unit, or $50. Subtracting the 10 units from the 50 units previously on hand, the balance is 40 units at $5 or $200.

On March 25, 80 units more are purchased, but this time at a higher price—$6 per unit, making it a cost of $480 (80 units × $6 = $480). This is added to the balance. The previous balance had been 40 units at $5 = $200. Now to this we add 80 units at $6 = $480.

On May 10, 100 units are sold. Since this is the last-in, first-out method, the 80 units purchased on March 25 will be sold first. These 80 units were purchased at $6 per unit for $480 (80 × $6 = $480). But 100 units are leaving, so we will need another 20 units (100 − 80 = 20). These 20 units will have to come from the original inventory which was purchased at $5 per unit, for a total of $100 (20 × $5 = $100).

After the 100 units have gone out, there are only 20 units left in inventory, and these will be at the price of $5 per unit, or a value of $100 (20 × $5 = $100).

On August 7, 15 more units of the item are purchased at $7 per unit for a value of $105 (15 × $7 = $105). There are, then, the following entries in the inventory at year's end:

20 units @ $5 = $100
15 units @ $7 = $105
35            $205

Thus, the dollar value of the ending inventory using the perpetual inventory method and the last-in, first-out computation is 35 units for $205.

10.3.3 Weighted Average

The **weighted average method** is also sometimes called the **average cost method**. This method assumes that the same cost per unit is charged to units remaining in inventory as was charged to units that have been sold during the period. The calculations for this method are much simpler than those for FIFO and LIFO.

Using the same data from Table 10.3.1 and Examples 10.3.1 and 10.3.2, we find that the total cost of $720 divided by the total units of 65 gives a unit cost of $11.0769. Then the calculations for ending inventory and cost of goods sold are:

Ending inventory   = 30 units × $11.0769   = $332.31
Cost of goods sold   = 35 units × $11.0769   =   387.69
Total   65 $720.00

As can be seen from the example, total units is equal to 65 (30 in ending inventory and 35 in cost of goods sold). Also, the sum of the ending inventory and cost of goods sold is equal to $720; $332.31 + $387.69 = $720.

Problem Solving Example:

Beginning Inventory and Purchases

1/1/20XX	Beginning Inventory	50 units @ $5	=	$250
3/25/20XX	Purchase	80 units @ $6	=	$480
8/7/20XX	Purchase	15 units @ $7	=	$105
Total units available for sale and their dollar value		145 units		$835

Compute the dollar value of the ending inventory by the periodic inventory method using the **average cost** computation. What is the dollar value of the Cost of Goods Sold using the periodic inventory method, using the **average cost** method? What is the dollar value of the ending inventory using the perpetual inventory method and using the average cost computation, sometimes called the moving cost computation (moving average computation)?

 We have 145 units available for sale at a total cost of $835. The first step in computing the dollar value of the ending inventory by the average cost computation is to divide the $835 total cost by the 145 units to get $5.758620689 average cost per unit.

The second step is to multiply the $5.758620689 average cost per unit by the 35 units in the ending inventory to get $201.5517241, the dollar value of the ending inventory by the average cost computation. This will, of course, be rounded off to $201.55.

Step 1: Divide $835 by the 145 units = $5.758620689

Step 2: $5.758620689 × 35 = $201.55

As previously computed, there were 145 units available for sale at $835 cost. Of these available units, during the first year they are either sold or else they remain in the ending inventory unsold. The ending inventory of 35 units was computed, using the **average cost** computation, to be $201.55. Therefore, we subtract the $201.55 value of the unsold units in the ending inventory from the $835 value of the units sold. Since we have kept cost prices separate from selling prices, and this is the cost price, we can call the $633.45 ($835 – $201.55 = $633.45) the Cost of Goods Sold, **average cost** computation.

The perpetual inventory method differs from the periodic inventory method of computing the dollar value of ending inventory in that under the perpetual inventory method, every time there is a sale, the units in the sale are subtracted from the units on hand, and a new dollar value of inventory is computed. Under the periodic inventory method, on the other hand, the units sold are not subtracted from the units available until the end of the fiscal period.

The computation of the dollar value of the ending inventory using the perpetual inventory method and using the average cost computation (moving average computation) follows:

Perpetual Inventory Method
Moving Average Computation

Date	In	Out	Balance
1/1/20XX			50 units @ $5 = $250
3/10/20XX		10 units @ $5 = $50	40 units @ $5 = $200
3/25/20XX	80 units @ $6 = $480		120 units @ $5.67 = $680
5/10/20XX		100 units @ $5.67 = $567	20 units @ $5.67 = $113
8/7/20XX	15 units @ $7 = $105		35 units @ $6.2285 = $218

On the first day of the year, there were 50 units on hand that had been purchased for $5 per unit, totaling $250 (50 × $5 = $250). On March 10, 10 of these units were sold, leaving a balance of 40 units on hand which were previously purchased for $5, totaling $200 (40 × $5 = $200).

On March 25, 80 more units of the item were purchased at $6 per unit for $480. Adding the previous balance of 40 units to the new purchase of 80 units, we now have 120 units in the new balance. Adding the $200 cost value of the previous balance to the $480 cost of the new purchase, we now have up to $680, the cost price of the merchandise on hand at the end of the day, March 25. In order to get the unit cost, we divide the total cost of the inventory, $680, by the number of units in the inventory, 120, to get $5.67 per unit. This is the moving average.

On May 10, we sell 100 units and multiply this figure by the moving average per unit of $5.67, to get $567, the cost of the inventory moving out. This leaves 20 units in the inventory at the end of May 10, (120 units − 100 units = 20 units). These 20 units have a cost of $5.67 per unit, or $113 (20 × $5.67 = $113).

On August 7, 15 more units are purchased at $7 per unit for a total cost of $105 (15 × $7 = $105). The 20 units in the previous inventory are added to the 15 units newly purchased to give an ending inventory of 35 units. The previous dollar value of the inventory was $113, and this is added to the purchase price of $105 to get a total ending inventory of $218 ($113 + $105 = $218).

Thus, the ending inventory using the perpetual inventory method and the moving average computation is $218.

10.3.4 Specific Identification

When using **specific identification,** it is assumed that there is a linkage of costs with the physical units of inventory. In this case the calculations would rely upon a direct tracing of which units were sold and which are still in inventory. Then their respective costs would be assigned. This is the only method discussed in this chapter that does trace the actual physical flow of goods.

10.3.5 Replacement Cost

All of the methods discussed so far deal with **historical costs.** Within the accounting establishment, there is strong support for using the concept of **replacement cost.** This is sometimes referred to as **next-in, first-out,** or **NIFO.**

Currently, replacement cost is not allowed within **generally accepted accounting principles** or GAAP.

10.4 Comparison of Cost Methods

Remembering that the sum of ending inventory and cost of goods sold is equal to the total cost of goods available for sale, it is clear that a difference in ending inventory will have a like effect on cost of goods sold. Different methods will likewise produce different net income amounts.

In times of inflation (rising costs), using LIFO will reduce net income as the highest costs are charged to revenue first. FIFO, on the other hand, will have the highest net income. This is because under FIFO the lowest costs are charged to revenue first.

In times of deflation (declining costs), the reverse would be true. The high inflation rates during the 1960s and 1970s greatly increased the usage of LIFO.

At the same time, weighted average net income will always be between LIFO and FIFO unless the economy has shifted from inflation to deflation or vice versa.

10.5 Lower-of-Cost-or-Market

The **conservatism convention** basically says that accountants should use the worst estimate in terms of net income. Hence, an alternative method of valuing inventories is **lower-of-cost-or-market**. This would mandate that if the value of inventory is more than what it would cost to buy new like inventory, the inventory should be written down to market value. The loss in value would be charged to income.

If at a later date the value of the inventory (market price) increases, the inventory would be written up to whichever is lower, current value or what it originally cost. It can never be written up above original cost.

The lower-of-cost-or-market can be applied in one of three ways. It could be applied to each item in the inventory, to major categories or classes of goods, or to the inventory as a whole.

CHAPTER 11

Property, Plant, and Equipment

11.1 Property, Plant, and Equipment

Property, plant, and equipment describes assets such as land, buildings, machinery, tools, or furniture which are used in the course of business. These assets are tangible in nature and are not held for resale. Often these assets are referred to as **plant assets** or **fixed assets**. Assets acquired for resale in the normal course of business cannot be characterized as property, plant, and equipment regardless of type or length of time held. Land held for speculation should be considered an investment.

11.2 Cost Basis for Property, Plant, and Equipment

All costs necessary to purchase equipment and make it ready for use are included in its cost basis. Costs such as sales tax, transportation charges, insurance on the asset while in transit, and installation costs, should be added to the cost basis of the associated asset. If the asset is purchased secondhand, expenses for repair or new parts should be added to the purchase price.

Costs such as architect's fees, surveys, insurance during construction, and interest on loans to finance construction of a building, should be included in the cost basis for a building. Appropriate costs that may be added to the cost basis for land include broker's commissions, survey fees, title fees, as well as the cost of removing unwanted buildings.

Problem Solving Examples:

 When buying land, should land be recorded on the books at appraisal price or at cost price?

 At cost price. The cost price is definitely determinable while the appraisal price is an estimate.

 When buying real estate, there are closing costs which usually include attorneys' fees, title fees, recording fees at the courthouse, grading land, filling and clearing land, and improving land. Should these costs be debited to Land or to some other account such as Attorneys' Fees?

 They should be debited to Land because they add value to the land and probably the land would not have been purchased without the idea of grading, clearing, or making other improvements.

11.3 Depreciation

Property, plant, and equipment, with the exception of land, suffers a decline in usefulness over time due to physical wear and tear or technical obsolescence. This decrease in usefulness is known as **depreciation**. Each asset has an estimated useful life, which is used to calculate the amount of depreciation expense for each period. If the asset is deemed to have no value at the end of its useful life, depreciation expense will be calculated to reduce the **book value** (cost less accumulated depreciation) to zero at the end of the asset's useful life. If the asset is expected to have some minimal or residual value at the end of its useful life, depreciation expense should be calculated to reduce the book value of an asset to its residual value at the end of its useful life. Depreciation can be calculated several different ways, such as **straight-line**, **sum-of-the-years-digits**, **declining balance**, and **units-of-production**.

11.3.1 Straight-Line Method of Depreciation

The **straight-line** method of calculating depreciation is very popular due to its simplicity and because it can provide a reasonable allocation of costs to periodic revenue when usage is relatively the same from period to period. To illustrate, assume that the initial cost of an asset is $70,000, its estimated useful life is 10 years, and its residual value is $10,000. Annual depreciation would be calculated as shown in Example 11.3.1

EXAMPLE 11.3.1

Depreciable cost:

$70,000 initial cost – $10,000 residual value = $60,000

Annual depreciation:

$$\frac{\text{Depreciable cost}}{\text{Estimated life}} = \frac{\$60,000}{10 \text{ years}} = \$6,000 \text{ per year}$$

Problem Solving Example:

The Total Manufacturing Corporation has just built a new factory on land previously owned by the corporation. The cost of the building itself was $50,000. Appraisers calculate that the building should last 20 years and have no residual value at the end of that time. What method of depreciation should be used?

The straight-line method of depreciation.

A factory building depreciates greatly over a period of time, and the straight-line method allows the same amount of depreciation each year. On the contrary, the unit-of-output method of depreciation is best for factory machinery, as is the working-hour method of depreciation, because these methods increase the depreciation as the asset is used more fully in a particular year. On the other hand, the sum-of-years-digits method of depreciation and the double-declining-balance method of depreciation are best to depreciate assets that lose value the most in the beginning years of use, such as business cars and trucks.

Therefore, the straight-line method of depreciation is best for depreciating a business building. Set up a depreciation table for this asset for the period of 20 years and then explain the depreciation table.

Since the residual or scrap value is zero, the cost price of the building ($50,000) is the same price as the book value of the building ($50,000). The first column of the table on the next page represents the year, but the first line begins with year zero, and shows the $50,000 book value at the beginning of the year, immediately after the building was constructed. The Depreciation column shows the yearly depreciation of $2,500, computed as follows: $50,000 cost divided by 20 years use = $2,500 yearly depreciation according to the straight-line method. The accumulated depreciation is the sum of all the depreciation in the previous years and in the present year. At the date construction was completed, there was not yet any depreciation to accumulate; so the entry is zero. At the end of the first year, the depreciation was $2,500; so the accumulated depreciation was also $2,500.

Each year thereafter, the Accumulated Depreciation column increases by $2,500, the steady amount of the annual depreciation according to the straight-line method. The right-most column is the Book Value column. At the time of purchase, the book value ($50,000) is the same as the construction cost of the building ($50,000). Each year, the book value drops by the amount of the annual depreciation ($2,500) until, at the end of the 20th year, the book value is zero since there is no residual (scrap) value. On the other hand, at the end of the 20th year, the Accumulated Depreciation column shows a balance of $50,000, the total of all the depreciation that has accumulated over the 20 years at $2,500 per year.

TABLE 11.3.1

The Total Manufacturing Company
Depreciation Schedule for New Factory Building

Year	Accumulated Depreciation	Depreciation	Book Value
0	$ 0	$ 0	$ 50,000
1	2,500	2,500	47,500
2	2,500	5,000	45,000
3	2,500	7,500	42,500
4	2,500	10,000	40,000
5	2,500	12,500	37,500
6	2,500	15,000	35,000
7	2,500	17,500	32,500
8	2,500	20,000	30,000
9	2,500	22,500	27,500
10	2,500	25,000	25,000
11	2,500	27,500	22,500
12	2,500	30,000	20,000
13	2,500	32,500	17,500
14	2,500	35,000	15,000
15	2,500	37,500	12,500
16	2,500	40,000	10,000
17	2,500	42,500	7,500
18	2,500	45,000	5,000
19	2,500	47,500	2,500
20	2,500	50,000	0

11.3.2 Sum-of-the-Years-Digits Method of Depreciation

The **sum-of-the-years-digits** method of depreciation is an **accelerated** method of calculating depreciation in that it provides a declining depreciation charge over the life of an asset. The annual rate of depreciation is calculated by dividing the number of years left in the asset's useful life by the sum of the digits representing the years of estimated life. Using the information from Example 11.3.1, depreciation using the sum-of-the-years-digits method is shown in Example 11.3.2.

EXAMPLE 11.3.2

Depreciable cost = $60,000

Sum of the years of estimated life =
1 + 2 + 3 + 4 + 5 + 6 + 7 + 8 + 9 + 10 = 55

Year	Rate	Annual Depreciation	Accumulated Depreciation	Book Value
1	10/55	10,909	10,909	59,091
2	9/55	9,818	20,727	49,273
3	8/55	8,727	29,454	40,546
4	7/55	7,636	37,090	32,910
5	6/55	6,545	43,635	26,365
6	5/55	5,455	49,090	20,910
7	4/55	4,364	53,454	16,546
8	3/55	3,273	56,727	13,273
9	2/55	2,182	58,909	11,091
10	1/55	1,091	60,000	10,000

11.3.3 Declining Balance Method of Depreciation

Like sum-of-the-years-digits, the **declining balance** method of depreciation is an accelerated method of depreciation, providing a declining periodic depreciation charge over the estimated life of an asset. A common technique is to use the straight-line depreciation rate (from 11.3.1), doubling it (**double-declining-balance method**) for application to the cost of the asset less accumulated depreciation (book value). The residual value is **not** considered in calculating annual depreciation (although the asset should not be depreciated below its estimated residual value). Using the information from previous examples, the double-declining-balance method of depreciation is illustrated in Example 11.3.3.

EXAMPLE 11.3.3

Depreciation rate:

Straight-line rate is 10% per year (10 years estimated life)

10% x 2 = 20% per year for double-declining-balance rate

Cost = $70,000   Residual value = $10,000

Year	Rate	Annual Depreciation	Accumulated Depreciation	Book Value
1	20%	14,000	14,000	56,000
2	20%	11,200	25,200	44,800
3	20%	8,960	34,160	35,840
4	20%	7,168	41,328	28,672
5	20%	5,734	47,062	22,938
6	20%	4,588	51,650	18,350
7	20%	3,670	55,320	14,680
8	20%	2,936	58,256	11,744
9	20%	1,744	60,000	10,000

Since the asset cannot be depreciated below its residual value, depreciation in year 9 is limited to $1,744 instead of the calculated value of $2,349. This depreciates the asset to its residual value of $10,000. No further calculations are needed.

Problem Solving Example:

The Hamlin Car Rental Agency purchased a fleet of five rental cars for a total price of $100,000. It is estimated that after using these cars for a period of four years, there will be no residual value. Since these business cars depreciate the most rapidly during their first year of use, it has been decided to use the sum-of-years-digits method to depreciate these cars. Set up a depreciation schedule for these cars and explain the schedule.

A The first step is to deduct the residual value from the cost in order to determine the amount to be depreciated. Since, in this case, there is no residual value, the amount to be depreciated ($100,000) is the same as the cost price of the fleet ($100,000).

The next step is to determine the fraction to multiply by the total amount to be depreciated. The denominator of the fraction is determined by the length of estimated life of the asset (in this case, the length of life of the fleet of cars—four years). This is done by adding the length of life (four years) plus the length of life less one (three years) plus the length of life less two (two years) and so on, as follows in this case: $4 + 3 + 2 + 1 = 10$. Thus, the denominator of the fraction is 10. The numerator of the first year's fraction is the length of life (estimated) of the asset (in this case, four years). The numerator for the second year is the length of life of the asset less one (three years). The numerator for the third year is the length of life of the asset less two (two years). The numerator for the fourth year is the length of life of the asset less three (one year) as follows:

Fraction for the first year of asset life:	⁴⁄₁₀
Fraction for the second year of asset life:	³⁄₁₀
Fraction for the third year of asset life:	²⁄₁₀
Fraction for the fourth year of asset life:	¹⁄₁₀

Each of these fractions are multiplied by the **amount to be depreciated**, which in this case (since there is no residual value) is the cost price of the fleet of rental cars ($100,000). The depreciation schedule follows:

TABLE 11.3.2

Hamlin Car Rental Agency
Depreciation Schedule for Fleet of Five Cars
Purchased January 2, 20XX

Sum-of-the-Years-Digits Method of Depreciation

Year	Fraction	Amount to be Depreciated	Yearly Depreciation	Accumulated Depreciation	Book Value
					$100,000
1	4/10 × $100,000	$40,000	$40,000	60,000
2	3/10 × $100,000	30,000	70,000	30,000
3	2/10 × $100,000	20,000	90,000	10,000
4	1/10 × $100,000	10,000	100,000	0

At the beginning of the first year, the five business cars are purchased for $100,000. These must be business cars, since personal cars cannot legally be depreciated.

During the first year, 4/10 of the amount to be depreciated is used as the yearly depreciation: in this case, $40,000. Since there was no previously accumulated depreciation, this yearly depreciation figure of $40,000 is also entered as the balance of the Accumulated Depreciation account at the end of the first year. The book value has dropped to $60,000 ($100,000 original cost less $40,000 first-year depreciation = $60,000 book value as of December 31).

During the second year, 3/10 of the amount to be depreciated is used as the yearly depreciation: in this case, $30,000. Since the previous balance of the Accumulated Depreciation account was $40,000, this second year's depreciation amount of $30,000 is added to the $40,000 to make a running balance at the end of the second year in the Accumulated Depreciation account of $70,000. In the final Book Value column, the book value has dropped to $30,000 ($100,000 cost price less $70,000 balance in the Accumulated Depreciation account = $30,000 book value at the end of second year).

During the third year, 2/10 of the amount to be depreciated ($100,000) is used as the yearly depreciation: in this case, $20,000.

Since the previous balance of the Accumulated Depreciation account was $70,000, this third year's depreciation amount of $20,000 is added to the $70,000 to make a running balance at the end of the third year in the Accumulated Depreciation account of $90,000. In the final Book Value column, the book value has dropped to $10,000 ($100,000 cost price less $90,000 balance in the Accumulated Depreciation account = $10,000 book value at the end of the third year).

During the fourth year, 1/10 of the amount to be depreciated ($100,000) is used as the yearly depreciation: in this case, $10,000. Since the previous balance of the Accumulated Depreciation account was $90,000, this fourth year's depreciation amount of $10,000 is added to the $90,000 to make a running balance at the end of the fourth year in the Accumulated Depreciation account of $100,000. This final balance of $100,000 is equal to the purchase price of the fleet of trucks; so this shows that in the four years, the entire cost of the fleet of trucks has been depreciated. In the final Book Value column, the book value has dropped to 0 ($100,000 cost price less $100,000 accumulated depreciation = 0).

It has been decided instead to use the double-declining-balance method to depreciate these cars. Set up a depreciation schedule for these cars and explain the schedule.

The first step is to divide the number of years of expected life of the asset into 100 (the 100 standing for 100%). Thus, 100 divided by 4 is 25 (or 25%). The law allows the accountant to double this figure. There is no good reason for this except that this is a legal way of allowing more depreciation during the first year of use. (Thus, doubling 25% we get 50%.) ($25\% \times 2 = 50$.) Each year the balance (previous balance or declining balance) is used as the basis and multiplied by 50% to get the next year's depreciation as follows in the upcoming table:

TABLE 11.3.3

Hamlin Car Rental Agency
Depreciation Schedule for Fleet of Five Cars
Purchased January 2, 20XX

Double-Declining-Balance Method of Depreciation

Year	Previously Determined Percentage	Previous Balance	Yearly Depreciation	Accumulated Depreciation	Book Value
					$100,000
1	50% x	$100,000	$50,000	$50,000	50,000
2	50% x	50,000	25,000	75,000	25,000
3	50% x	25,000	12,500	87,500	12,500
4	50% x	12,500	6,250	93,750	6,250
5	50% x	6,250	3,125	96,875	3,125

At the beginning of the first year, the five business cars are purchased for $100,000. These must be business cars, since personal cars cannot legally be depreciated.

The percentage to be used in the double-declining-balance method for four years of depreciation is 50% ($100,000 purchase price divided by four years = 25) (25 × 2 = 50).

In the double-declining-balance method, the first year the 50% is multiplied by the original cost (in this case, $100,000), giving a first year's depreciation of $50,000. Since the Accumulated Depreciation account had no previous balance, this first-year's depreciation of $50,000 also becomes the balance of the Accumulated Depreciation account ($50,000). For the book value at the end of the first year, the $50,000 balance in the Accumulated Depreciation account is subtracted from the previous balance in the Book Value column (in this case the original purchase price of $100,000) to get $50,000.

During the second year of use, we multiply the 50% by the book value of the previous year (in this case $50,000) to get the yearly depreciation for the second year ($25,000) ($50,000 × 50% = $25,000). Then the $25,000 depreciation for the second year is added to the previous balance in the Accumulated Depreciation column ($50,000) to get $75,000 for the balance in the Accumulated Depreciation column at the end of the second year ($25,000 + $50,000 = $75,000). In order to determine the book value at the end of the second year, we subtract the second year's depreciation of $25,000 from the previous book value balance of $50,000 to get $25,000—the new book value at the end of the second year of use.

During the third year of use, we multiply the 50% by the book value of the previous year (in this case $25,000) to get the yearly depreciation for the third year ($12,500) ($25,000 × 50% = $12,500). Then the $12,500 depreciation for the third year is added to the previous balance in the Accumulated Depreciation column ($75,000) to get $87,500 for the balance in the Accumulated Depreciation column at the end of the third year ($12,500 + $75,000 = $87,500). In order to determine the book value at the end of the third year, we subtract the third year's depreciation of $12,500 from the previous book value balance of $25,000 to get $12,500, the new book value at the end of the third year of use.

During the fourth year of use, we multiply the 50% by the book value of the previous year (in this case $12,500) to get the yearly depreciation for the fourth year ($6,250) ($12,500 × 50% = $6,250). Then the $6,250 for the fourth year is added to the previous balance in the Accumulated Depreciation column ($87,500) to get $93,750 for the balance in the Accumulated Depreciation column at the end of the fourth year ($6,250 + $87,500 = $93,750). In order to determine the book value at the end of the fourth year, we subtract the fourth year's depreciation of $6,250 from the previous book value balance of $12,500 to get $6,250—the new book value at the end of the fourth year of use.

Deducting 50% of the previous year's depreciation each year will never get the depreciation down to zero. The table goes on for a fifth year; and, certainly, if the rental cars are still usable the fifth year, it would be legal to depreciate them $6,250 as the table shows. However, if the cars are no longer serviceable, the book value figure could be debited as a loss in the year the cars are junked.

11.3.4 Units-of-Production Method

In some cases, a more equitable allocation of cost would involve dividing an asset's cost by estimated units of output rather than estimated life. For example, a business might calculate depreciation for a truck based on mileage instead of estimated life. This calculation divides the depreciable cost of the truck (initial cost – residual value) by the estimated useful life of the truck to obtain a depreciation rate per mile. To illustrate, a truck with an initial cost of $20,000 and a residual value of $5,000 has an estimated useful life of 100,000 miles. The truck has been driven 25,000 miles during this accounting period. The calculation of the depreciation rate and the annual depreciation figure are shown in Example 11.3.4.

EXAMPLE 11.3.4

$$\frac{\$20,000 \text{ cost} - \$5,000 \text{ (depreciable cost of the truck)}}{100,000 \text{ miles (estimated useful life)}} = \$0.15 \text{ depreciation per mile}$$

25,000 miles (current period usage) × $0.15 = $3,750

Depreciation for this accounting period is $3,750.

Problem Solving Example:

The James Broom Works manufactures and sells brooms. On January 2, the James Broom Works purchased and installed a broom-making machine at a cost of $11,000. From past experience with this type of asset, it was estimated that the machine would be able to produce 100,000 brooms during its lifetime and would have a residual or scrap value of $1,000 at the end of that time. Show a depreciation table for this machine and explain the table.

The broom-making machine was purchased for $11,000 and it was estimated that its residual value would be $1,000;

therefore, the amount to be depreciated is $10,000 ($11,000 – $1,000 = $10,000). From past experience, it is estimated that the broom-making machine will be able to produce 100,000 brooms during its lifetime.

The next step is to compute the amount of depreciation per broom manufactured. This is done by dividing the amount to be depreciated ($10,000) by the estimated number of brooms the machine would be able to produce during its lifetime (100,000), getting $.10 depreciation per broom. ($10,000 divided by 100,000 brooms = $.10 depreciation per broom.)

TABLE 11.3.4

James Broom Works
Depreciation Schedule for Broom-Making Machine
Purchased January 2, 20XX

Year	Number of Brooms Produced	Depreciation Amount per Broom	Depreciation Amount for the Year	Accumulated Depreciation	Book Value
					$11,000
1	20,000	$.10	$2,000	$2,000	9,000
2	14,000	.10	1,400	3,400	7,600
3	3,000	.10	300	3,700	7,300
4	8,500	.10	850	4,550	6,450
5	10,000	.10	1,000	5,550	5,450
6	15,000	.10	1,500	7,050	3,950
7	7,000	.10	700	7,750	3,250
8	18,000	.10	1,800	9,550	1,450
9	1,000	.10	100	9,650	1,350
10	3,500	.10	350	10,000	1,000
Totals	100,000			$10,000	

Looking at the above table, we see that at the time of purchase, on January 2, the book value of the machine is the same as the purchase price of the machine—that is, $11,000.

At the end of the first year, the machine had produced 20,000 brooms; so we multiply the 20,000 brooms by the $.10 depreciation per broom (previously computed) to get $2,000 depreciation for the year. Since there had been no previously accumulated depreciation, the Accumulated Depreciation column also has a figure of $2,000 for the first year's depreciation. Finally, the Book Value column shows $9,000, the cost price of $11,000 less the first year's depreciation of $2,000. This means that the machine is probably worth around $9,000 at the end of the first year. However, it does not mean that the machine could necessarily be sold for $9,000 at the end of the first year. It might be sold for more or less than $9,000, or perhaps for $9,000. The book value is merely an estimated figure, as is the depreciation. However, the estimated depreciation figure of $2,000 for the first year can be legally deducted as an expense on the Income Statement for depreciation purposes.

At the end of the second year, the machine has been used to manufacture 14,000 more brooms; so we multiply the 14,000 brooms by the previously computed depreciation amount of $.10 per broom to get $1,400 depreciation for that year.

The $1,400 is added to the $2,000 previously accumulated depreciation to get a balance of $3,400 Accumulated Depreciation. Finally, the Book Value column shows $7,600, which is the cost price of $11,000 less the Accumulated Depreciation of $3,400. This means that the machine is probably worth around $7,600 at the end of the second year. However, it does not mean that the machine could necessarily be sold for $7,600 at that time. It might be sold for more or less than $7,600, or perhaps for $7,600. The book value is merely an estimated figure, as is the depreciation. However, the estimated depreciation figure of $1,400 for the second year can be legally deducted as an expense on the Income Statement for depreciation and for income tax purposes.

At the end of the third year, the machine has been used to manufacture 3,000 more brooms; so we multiply the 3,000 brooms by the previously computed depreciation amount of $.10 per broom to get $300 depreciation for that year. The $300 is added to the $3,400 previously accumulated depreciation to get a balance of $3,700 accumulated depreciation. Finally, the Book Value column shows $7,300, which is the cost price of $11,000 less the accumulated depreciation of $3,700. This means that the machine is probably worth around $7,300 at the end of the third year. However, it does not mean that the machine could necessarily be sold for $7,300 at that time. It might be sold for more or less than $7,300, or perhaps for $7,300. The book value is merely an estimated figure as is the depreciation. However, the estimated depreciation figure of $300 for the third year can be legally deducted as an expense on the Income Statement for income tax purposes.

At the end of the fourth year, the machine has been used to manufacture 8,500 more brooms; so we multiply the 8,500 brooms by the previously computed depreciation amount of $.10 per broom to get $850 depreciation for that year. The $850 is added to the $3,700 previously accumulated depreciation to get a balance of $4,550 accumulated depreciation. Finally, the Book Value column shows $6,450, which is the cost price of $11,000 less the accumulated depreciation of $4,550. This means that the machine is probably worth around $6,450 at the end of the fourth year. However, it does not mean that the machine could necessarily be sold for $6,450 at that time. It might be sold for more or less than $6,450, or perhaps for $6,450. The book value is merely an estimated figure, as is the depreciation. However, the estimated depreciation figure of $850 for the fourth year can be legally deducted as an expense on the Income Statement for income tax purposes.

At the end of the fifth year, the machine has been used to manufacture 10,000 more brooms; so we multiply the 10,000 brooms by the previously computed depreciation amount of $.10 per broom to get $1,000 depreciation for that year. The $1,000 is added to the $4,550 previously accumulated depreciation to get a balance of $5,550 accumulated depreciation. Finally, the Book Value column shows $5,450, which is the cost price of $11,000 less the accumulated depreciation of $5,550. This means that the machine is probably worth around $5,450 at the end of the fifth year. However, it does not mean that the machine could necessarily be sold for $5,450 at that time. It might be sold for more or less than $5,450, or perhaps for $5,450. The book value is merely an estimated figure, as is the depreciation. However, the estimated depreciation figure of $1,000 for the fifth year can be legally deducted as an expense on the Income Statement for income tax purposes.

At the end of the sixth year, the machine has been used to manufacture 15,000 more brooms; so we multiply the 15,000 brooms by the previously computed depreciation amount of $.10 per broom to get $1,500 depreciation for that year. The $1,500 is added to the $5,550 previously accumulated depreciation to get a balance of $7,050 accumulated depreciation. Finally, the Book Value column shows $3,950, which is the cost price of $11,000 less the accumulated depreciation of $7,050. This means that the machine is probably worth around $3,950 at the end of the sixth year. However, it does not mean that the machine could necessarily be sold for $3,950 at that time. It might be sold for more or less than $3,950, or perhaps for $3,950. The book value is merely an estimated figure, as is the depreciation. However, the estimated depreciation figure of $1,500 for the sixth year can be legally deducted as an expense on the Income Statement for income tax purposes.

At the end of the seventh year, the machine has been used to manufacture 7,000 more brooms; so we multiply the 7,000 brooms by the previously computed depreciation amount of $.10 per broom to get $700 depreciation for that year. The $700 is added to the $7,050 previously accumulated depreciation to get a balance of $7,750 accumulated depreciation. Finally, the Book Value column shows $3,250, which is the cost price of $11,000 less the accumulated depreciation of $7,750. This means that the machine is probably worth around $3,250 at the end of the seventh year. However, it does not mean that the machine could necessarily be sold for $3,250 at that time. It might be sold for more or less than $3,250, or perhaps for $3,250. The book value is merely an estimated figure, as is the depreciation. However, the estimated depreciation figure of $700 for the seventh year can be legally deducted as an expense on the Income Statement for income tax purposes.

At the end of the eighth year, the machine has been used to manufacture 18,000 more brooms; so we multiply the 18,000 brooms by the previously computed depreciation amount of $.10 per broom to get $1,800 depreciation for that year. The $1,800 is added to the $7,750 previously accumulated depreciation to get a balance of $9,550 accumulated depreciation. Finally, the Book Value column shows $1,450, which is the cost price of $11,000 less the accumulated depreciation of $9,550. This means that the machine is probably worth around $1,450 at the end of the eighth year. However, it does not mean that the machine could necessarily be sold for $1,450 at that time. It might be sold for more or less than $1,450, or perhaps for $1,450. The book value is merely an estimated figure, as is the depreciation. However, the estimated depreciation figure of $1,800 for the eighth year can be legally deducted as an expense on the Income Statement for income tax purposes.

At the end of the ninth year, the machine has been used to manufacture 1,000 more brooms; so we multiply the 1,000 brooms by the previously computed depreciation amount of $.10 per broom to get $100 depreciation for that year. The $100 is added to the $9,550 previously accumulated depreciation to get a balance of $9,650 accumulated depreciation. Finally, the Book Value column shows $1,350, which is the cost price of $11,000 less the accumulated depreciation of $9,650. This means that the machine is probably worth around $1,350 at the end of the ninth year. However, it does not mean that the machine could necessarily be sold for $1,350 at that time. It might be sold for more or less than $1,350, or perhaps for $1,350. The book value is merely an estimated figure, as is the depreciation. However, the estimated depreciation figure of $100 for the ninth year can be legally deducted as an expense on the Income Statement for income tax purposes.

At the end of the tenth year, the machine has been used to manufacture 3,500 more brooms; so we multiply the 3,500 brooms by the previously computed depreciation amount of $.10 per broom to get $350 depreciation for that year. The $350 is added to the $9,650 previously accumulated depreciation to get a balance of $10,000 accumulated depreciation. This $10,000 is the total amount to be depreciated, which is the $11,000 cost of the machine less the $1,000 residual value of the machine ($11,000 − $1,000 = $10,000). The balance of the accumulated depreciation account is $10,000 at the end of the tenth year, in this case, December 31; and all the allowed depreciation has been accumulated. Finally, the Book Value column shows $1,000, which is the cost price of $11,000 less the accumulated depreciation of $10,000.

This means that the machine is probably worth around $1,000 at the end of the tenth year. However, it does not mean that the machine could necessarily be sold for $1,000 at that time. It might be sold for more or less than $1,000, or perhaps for $1,000. The book value is merely an estimated figure, as is the depreciation. However, the estimated depreciation figure of $350 for the tenth year can be legally deducted as an expense on the Income Statement for income tax purposes. The book value at the end of the tenth year shows $1,000, which is the same amount as the estimated scrap value ($1,000). The depreciation is at an end for this machine. Looking at the column entitled, "Number of Brooms Produced," we add up all the figures in that column and derive a total of 100,000 brooms, which is the total number of brooms that we originally estimated could be produced during the life of the machine.

But what if the machine is still in working order and can produce more brooms? The accountant here has two options: he or she can stop depreciating, or he or she can continue depreciating the remaining scrap value. If the accountant chooses the former option, there will be no more depreciation expense for the following year (in this case, the eleventh year). If the accountant chooses the latter option, he can still depreciate the remaining $1,000, in this case 10,000 brooms. (10,000 brooms times $.10 depreciation per broom = $1,000.) If the latter option is chosen and the extra $1,000 is depreciated, the book value of the machine drops to zero and the accountant can show no loss when the machine is finally scrapped. (On the other hand, if the accountant chooses the former option and does not depreciate the extra $1,000, this $1,000 could be debited as a Loss Expense when the machine is finally discarded.)

CHAPTER 12

Other Long-Term Assets

12.1 Introduction of Other Long-Term Assets

In addition to plant, property, and equipment, there are numerous other **long-term assets** (in use more than one year) that will usually be found at the bottom of the asset side of the balance sheet. In this chapter we will review the most important of these assets. These will include **leaseholds, leasehold improvements, patents, copyrights,** and **goodwill**.

Although long-term assets that are not plant, property, and equipment (PPE) are not depreciated, many of them do lose value like PPE. We will also review the use of **depletion** of natural resources, as well as the **amortization** of **intangible assets**.

Problem Solving Examples:

 Sometimes land is purchased from a purchaser who has a mortgage on the property, and the new purchaser assumes this mortgage, or takes it over. Should the costs of assuming this mortgage be debited to the Land account or to some other account?

 The costs of assuming a mortgage should be debited to the Land account, since the mortgage is on the land. However, if the mortgage is on the building, the Building account should be debited.

Why is it so important to differentiate between land and building in making the journal entries? Aren't land and building purchased at the same time and usually for one total price?

Land and building are usually purchased at the same time and usually for one total price. However, an assessor (usually a local banker or real estate agent) who knows the value of local property should look over the land and building and determine what portion of the purchase price is allocable to the land and what portion of the purchase price is allocable to the building. The assessor should put this in writing and the purchaser should keep this information on file for tax purposes.

How does the separation of the Land account from the Building account affect the taxes of the entrepreneur?

Building is depreciable and land is not depreciable. In an adjusting entry at the end of each year, Depreciation Expense is debited and Accumulated Depreciation is credited for the amount of the yearly depreciation, as follows:

20XX		($ in dollars)
December 31	Depreciation Expense	500
	Accumulated Depreciation—Building	500

This Depreciation Expense is listed in the Income Statement as one of the expenses; and it effectively cuts down on the net income for the year, legally, and this cuts down on the income tax. On the other hand, if the amount is debited to the Land account, there is no way it can be depreciated legally. But doesn't land depreciate? Isn't there water and wind erosion that decreases the value of land? This may be, but it isn't taken into account legally. The only way to cut taxes because of any possible wind or water erosion to land would be if the land is later sold at a loss (which is an Expense account); and, at that time, the loss could be deducted from revenue to show a lower net income and would thus result in a lower income tax that year.

12.2 Leasing

There are two basic types of leases in the world of accounting. They are **operating leases** and **capital leases**. Financial Accounting Standards Board (FASB) Statement No. 13 very specifically spells out what conditions need to be met in order to be one kind or the other.

Problem Solving Example:

The Rayburn Land Management Corporation leased an apartment to Mr. and Mrs. James Brown on January 2, for a period of five years at $25,000 per year. The cost of the apartment as of this date is $150,000 to the Lessor, the Rayburn Land Management Corporation. The Lessor agrees to pay insurance, maintenance costs, and taxes. The apartment reverts to the Rayburn Land Management Corporation at the end of the lease period. The lease does not give Mr. and Mrs. James Brown the choice of renewing the lease at the end of the five-year lease period. The present value of an annuity due in advance of five payments of $25,000 each at the present 12% interest rate is $100,933.72. (Present value of five payments of $25,000 in advance at 12% (3.037349 + 1.000000) × $25,000 = $100,933.72.)

There is no agreement to transfer ownership from the Rayburn Land Management Corporation to Mr. and Mrs. James Brown at the end of the lease. The economic life of the apartment is estimated by assessors to be at least 10 years. Is this agreement an operating lease or a capital lease, and why?

This is an operating lease, not a capital lease. A capital lease must contain at least one of the following stipulations, according to the Financial Accounting Standards Board:

1.   The lease transfers ownership to the Lessee at term's end.

2.   The lease contains a bargain purchase option.

3. The lease term is equal to 75% or more of the estimated economic life of the leased property.

4. The present value of the minimum lease payments is equal to 90% or more of the fair value of the leased property to the Lessor.

Looking at the first rule, the lease in this problem does not transfer ownership to the Lessee at the end of the term; therefore, the first rule does not apply in this case. The lease does not contain a bargain purchase option; therefore, the second rule does not apply in this case. (A bargain purchase option means that at the end of the lease period the Lessee is able to buy the apartment at a reasonable price. No such agreement is contained here.)

Looking at the third rule, the lease term should be 75% of the economic life of the property being leased. In the case of this apartment, the lease term is five years, and the estimated economic life of the apartment is ten years, so the lease term is only 50% of the economic life of the property (5 divided by 10 = 50%).

Looking at the fourth rule, the present value of lease payments is 90% of the fair value. The cost of the apartment to the Lessor is $150,000, and the fair present value of the five $25,000 yearly payments, paid in advance, is $100,933.72. Thus, the present value ($100,933.72) is 67.289% of the total cost ($150,000). ($100,933.72 divided by $150,000 = 67.289%.) For the fourth rule to be valid, the present value of the lease payments must be 90% of the fair value. But it is only 67.289%. Therefore, the fourth rule is not valid either. Thus, none of the rules apply, so this is an operating lease rather than a capital lease.

12.2.1 Capital Leases

Leases that have one or more of the following provisions are defined as **capital leases**:

1. The lease transfers ownership of the leased asset to the Lessee at the end of the lease term.

2. The lease contains an option for a bargain purchase of the leased asset by the Lessee.

3. The lease term extends over most of the economic life of the leased asset.

4. The lease requires rental payments which approximate the fair market value of the leased asset.

The capital lease is accounted for as a purchase of the asset. Consequently, when the lease is executed, the Lessee will debit a fixed asset account for the fair market value of the asset and would set up a long-term lease liability.

12.2.2 Operating Leases

Operating leases are all other leases that do not meet one or more of the above conditions to be a capital lease. Operating leases are accounted for by recognizing rent expense as the leased asset used.

12.2.3 Leasehold and Leasehold Improvements

A **leasehold** is the right to use, for a certain amount of time (more than one year), a fixed asset. This is usually a building or part of a building. A **leasehold improvement** would be any improvement made to the leasehold that may not be removed when the lease expires. Examples include new walls, central air conditioning, or new fixtures.

Leaseholds and leasehold improvements are accounted for in the same manner as depreciation. However, straight-line is used as accelerated methods are not allowed for income tax purposes. This systematic write-off is called **amortization**.

When the life of the fixed asset is longer than the life of the lease, the amortization will be for the life of the lease.

12.3 Depletion

Accounting for the use of natural resources such as timber, oil, and metal ores is known as **depletion**. The costs for these natural resources is accounted for as fixed assets. Then the period cost (depletion) is based on the relationship of the total amount of the natural resource to the amount removed during the period.

For example, assume that a forest has been purchased to be used to provide timber for a lumber mill. The cost of purchasing this asset was $150,000. There are a total 1,500 acres of timber. During the current accounting period, 100 acres of timber were cut. The journal entry for this period is given in Example 12.3.1.

EXAMPLE 12.3.1

To Record the First Period Depletion of Timber

The Sample Company
General Journal

Date	Acct. No.	Description	Debit	Credit
20XX Apr 30	24 10	Depletion Expense – Timber Accumulated Depletion – Timber	10,000	10,000

The calculation to arrive at the $10,000 figure is:

100 acres/1,500 acres = 1/15; 1/15 × $150,000 = $10,000

Problem Solving Example:

The Promer Oil Company purchased 100 acres of Utah land because their officials said oil drilling prospects appeared excellent in that location. The cost of the land was $30,000. The costs of searching the land for the proper drilling location and actually drilling the oil well were $30,000. Intangible development costs such as erecting the oil well itself were $3,000. This is a total of $63,000. Engineers estimated that there were approximately 1,000,000 gallons of oil in the field. During the first year, 10,000 gallons of oil were extracted. The $63,000 cost is divided by the 1,000,000 approximate gallons of oil in the field to get $.063 depletion per gallon. During the first year, 10,000 gallons of oil were extracted from the ground; and during the second year, 60,000 gallons of oil were extracted from the ground.

What depletion entry will Promer Oil Company make on its books at the end of the second year and how will the Accumulated Depletion account look at the end of the second year?

20XX			($ in dollars)
December 31	Depletion Expense	3,780	
	Accumulated Depletion		3,780

At the end of the second year of oil extraction, on December 31, Depletion Expense is debited for $3,780 and Accumulated Depletion is credited for $3,780. This figure is computed by multiplying the $.063 depletion per gallon previously computed by the 60,000 gallons extracted from the ground during the year ($.063 × 60,000 gallons = $3,780).

Accumulated Depletion

	12/31 (Year 1)	630
	12/31 (Year 2)	3,780
		4,410

The depletion in the first year was $630; the depletion in the second year was $3,780; so the accumulated depletion at the end of the second year is $4,410 ($630 + $3,780 = $4,410).

12.4 Intangible Assets

In the operations of a company, there are often long-term assets that are not held for sale and do not have physical qualities. These are called **intangible assets**.

There are two major concerns in accounting for intangibles. The first problem is to determine the initial costs of the asset. Then there is the need to recognize the period of expiration of these costs. This is usually done by a process called **amortization.** Following are several types of intangible assets.

Problem Solving Example:

 The Luscious Chocolate Company is thinking of going out of business. Its competitor, the Brown Candy Company, likes the name "Luscious," and offers the Luscious Chocolate Company $3,000 for its name. This is agreeable, and the name is purchased by the Brown Candy Company for $3,000.

What entry should be made on the books of the Brown Candy Company at this time?

20XX	($ in dollars)	
January 2 Trade Name	3,000	
Cash		3,000

The trade name "Luscious" is an intangible asset, and it should be recorded on the books of the Brown Candy Company because the Brown Candy Company had to make an outlay of $3,000 for the name. Evidently the Brown Candy Company thought this payment was worthwhile and would eventually help the Brown Candy Company's business. The Trade Name account would be listed among the Intangible Assets on the Brown Candy Company Balance Sheet.

What would the entry be on December 31, to amortize this intangible asset?

20XX	($ in dollars)	
December 31 Amortization Expense	75	
Trade Name		75

A trademark or trade name, as long as reapplication to the U.S. Patent Office is made every 20 years, can be used indefinitely by the company owning it. However, accounting practice requires that it be written off over a maximum period of 40 years, or over its useful life if less than 40 years. Assume that Brown Candy Company decides to amortize this intangible asset over 40 years. They divide the $3,000 cost by 40 years to get $75 amortization or write-off per year. Thus, they debit Amortization Expense for $75, cutting down their net income by that amount, and credit the intangible asset account, Trade Name, by that amount. Therefore, at the end of 40 years, the Trade Name account will be down to zero.

The officers of the Brown Candy Company think that the benefits of using Luscious on their candy will only last five years. If they then divide the $3,000 cost of the intangible asset by five years to get $600, the Amortization entry would then be as follows:

20XX		($ in dollars)
December 31	Amortization Expense	600
	Trade Name	600

This latter choice by debiting the Amortization Expense account by $600 would greatly (and legally) cut down their net profit and their income tax.

12.4.1 Patents

Patents are rights granted exclusively to a person or company to produce and sell a particular invention. These rights are granted for 17 years by the federal government. The costs of the patent should be debited to an asset account and then written off in a systematic manner. Unless another method can be shown to be more appropriate, straight-line amortization should be used.

If the expected useful economic life of the patent is less than 17 years, then the shorter length of time will be used for the amortization process. A contract account (such as accumulated amortization) is usually not utilized with intangibles. Amortization is written off directly to the asset.

Consider a patent that cost $300,000 to develop. It is expected that the economic life of the patent will be ten years. The entry for the first full year of amortization would be as shown in Example 12.4.1.

EXAMPLE 12.4.1

To Record the Yearly Amortization of the Patent.

The Sample Company
General Journal

Date	Acct. No.	Description	Debit	Credit
20XX Dec. 31	23	Amortization Expense – Patents	30,000	
	11	Patents		30,000

Each succeeding year would have a similar entry recorded. Most intangible assets have a zero residual value.

Problem Solving Examples:

The March Manufacturing Company several years ago bought a patent on a cereal-making machine. In touring the plant of the Staver Cereal Company, it was noticed that a similar machine to that patented by the March Manufacturing Company was being used, and that this machine had not been purchased from the March Manufacturing Company. After intensive discussion, the disagreement could not be peacefully settled, so it was taken to court where the March Manufacturing Company sued the Staver Cereal Company for patent infringement.

The March Manufacturing Company won the suit and the Staver Cereal Company promised to quit using the machine and not use anything connected with the patent until the patent's rights had run out. However, $5,000 in extra legal fees were still to be paid by the March Manufacturing Company.

How will this $5,000 payment be recorded on the March Manufacturing Company books?

20XX	($ in dollars)
January 2 Patents	5,000
Cash	5,000

According to regulations of the Financial Accounting Standards Board, extra costs of a successful patent infringement suit should be debited to the Intangible Asset account, Patents, and amortized. In this case, Patents was debited for the $5,000 extra costs and Cash was credited.

How will the Patent account be amortized?

20XX	($ in dollars)
December 31 Amortization Expense	1,000
Patents	1,000

According to accounting rules and customs, patents are amortized over periods not exceeding 40 years and not less than five years, with the most appropriate time period the amount of time that the asset will be useful to the business. Since a successful patent infringement suit will probably be useful to the business for only a minimum length of time, it is best to amortize this asset over the minimum allowable period of years—in this case, five years.

The extra legal expenses debited to Patents were $5,000, divided by the five minimum years to get $1,000 depreciation each year. The $1,000 amortization expense each year will cut down the net income on the books by that amount and will lower the March Manufacturing Company's income tax. Also, the Patent account will be completely amortized, as far as these legal expenses are concerned, in the minimum of five years.

Q The Long Computer Software Company developed new computer software programs costing $3,000,000. They plan to use these programs exclusively within the company.

How should this be handled on the books?

A

20XX		($ in dollars)
January 2	Software Development Expense	3,000,000
	Cash	3,000,000

Since the Long Computer Software Company plans not to sell or lease this software, but to use it only within the company, it is perfectly legal and within the accounting rules to expense it in the year developed.

Instead of using the programs exclusively within the company, the software is the type that would be of interest to other firms and useful to them. The Long Computer Software Company plans to sell and/or lease this software.

How should this be handled on the books of the Long Computer Software Company?

20XX		($ in dollars)
January 2	Computer Software	3,000,000
	Cash	3,000,000

"Computer Software" is an Intangible Asset that is debited for the complete cost of $3,000,000. Cash is credited, since this amount was spent for developing the computer software.

12.4.2 Copyrights

Copyrights are the exclusive rights granted to publish and sell books, artistic compositions, and musical compositions. These rights are granted by the federal government and extend to 50 years past the author's death. Copyrights are recorded at the price paid for them. They are usually amortized over very short periods—usually two to three years. The accounting for copyrights would be identical to that for patents.

Problem Solving Example:

 Arthur Rutherford wrote many songs during his lifetime, the most famous of which was "Old Pete." He copyrighted each of these songs through the Library of Congress which gave him exclusive use of these songs and exclusive right to allow others to publish these songs or to sell these songs during his lifetime and 50 years thereafter. He died at the age of 76 and left these songs to his son, Ned. The Star Book Corporation has wished for a long time to publish all of Rutherford's songs in one book and sell them to the public. They finally prevailed upon Ned Rutherford to sell the copyright for a sum of $500 on January 2, ten years after his father's death. At that time the Star Book Corporation debited the account, Copyright to Arthur Rutherford's Songs, $500, and credited Cash $500.

What amortization entry will be made at the end of the year on the Star Book Corporation's accounts?

20XX		($ in dollars)
December 31	Amortization Expense	12.50
	Copyright to Arthur	
	Rutherford's Songs	12.50

United States laws dealing with copyrights are somewhat different from United States laws regarding patents, though they are both intangible assets. The Constitution gives the federal government control of patents to encourage invention. This national control also carries over to copyrights, though there are different rules. For instance, the United States Patent Office controls and issues patents for inventions, while the Library of Congress issues copyrights. Also, patents last for 17 years and can be renewed, whereas copyrights last for 50 years after the author's death and cannot be renewed.

Patents cover inventions, while copyrights cover original writings such as books, articles, architectural plans, musical scores, paintings, and sculptures. In the case of either patents or copyrights, infringers can be sued by the person or firm holding the patent or copyright.

In this case the Star Book Corporation purchased the exclusive right to publish and sell all of Arthur Rutherford's songs for the duration of the copyright. The copyright law allows copyright holders the exclusive right to their works for their life plus 50 years. Since Arthur Rutherford died and the copyright was not purchased until 10 years after his death, the copyright privilege had only 40 more years left (50 years after death less 10 years already elapsed = 40 more years).

Over what period shall the Star Book Corporation amortize this $500 purchase?

Since the exclusive right to the copyright will last for the Star Book Corporation only 40 more years, and since the Financial Accounting Standards Board recommends that copyrights be amortized over a period of not more than 40 years, then the term of 40 years seems to be the proper amortization time. Divide 40 years into the $500 purchase price to derive $12.50 per year amortization. Thus, the Amortization Expense account is debited for $12.50 and the Intangible Asset account, Copyright to Arthur Rutherford's Songs is credited for $12.50. If this entry is made at the end of each year for 40 years, the account Copyright to Arthur Rutherford's Songs will be written off entirely to expense.

However, the amortization period need not be this long. It could be written off in as few as five years if it is believed that the benefits will only last this long. If this is the case, we would divide five years into the $500 cost of the copyright to get $100 yearly amortization, and the entry would be as follows:

20XX		($ in dollars)
December 31	Amortization Expense	100
	Copyright to Arthur	
	Rutherford's Songs	100

If this entry were made at the end of each year for a period of five years, the total $500 balance of the Copyright account would have gradually been written off to expense.

The officers of the Star Book Corporation may decide upon an intermediate date, such as 20 years. Divide the 20 years into the $500 cost of the Copyright to get a yearly amortization of $25, and the entry would be as follows:

20XX		($ in dollars)
December 31	Amortization Expense	25
	Copyright to Arthur	
	Rutherford's Songs	25

If this entry were made at the end of each year for a period of 20 years, the total $500 balance of the Copyright account would have gradually been written off to expense.

12.4.3 Franchises

Franchises are rights and privileges granted to sell a service or product in a specified manner. These rights are usually granted by a distributor or manufacturer. Examples would be major sports teams or fast-food restaurants. The accounting for franchises will be handled the same way as for patents and copyrights.

Problem Solving Example:

Q The Brown Drug Store has decided to become the Rexall Drug Store for Central City, the town in which it is located. There is no other Rexall store in Central City, and the national Rexall chain has agreed to have the Brown Drug Store represent them in the area. The Brown Drug Store is to change its name to the Brown Rexall Drug

Store, buy all its drugs from the Rexall chain, and make the Rexall chain a one-time payment of $5,000 for the privilege of using their name. The Brown Drug Store feels that this contract will improve its business.

What entry will the Brown Rexall Drug Store make on its books on the date that the contract is signed and the money paid?

20XX		($ in dollars)
January 2	Franchise	5,000
	Cash	5,000

The Brown Rexall Drug Store is purchasing an intangible asset so it debits Franchise for $5,000. It is paying cash, so it credits Cash for $5,000.

What entry will be made on the books of the Brown Rexall Drug Store on December 31 to amortize this Intangible Asset?

20XX		($ in dollars)
December 31	Amortization Expense	500
	Franchise	500

The owner of the Brown Rexall Drug Store has decided to amortize the franchise over a period of 10 years. Since the franchise cost is $5,000, the Amortization entry will be for $500 ($5,000 divided by 10 = $500). Amortization Expense will be debited for $500, and this expense will effectively cut down the net income of the business for the year by that amount. The intangible asset, Franchise, will be credited for $500.

How will the Franchise account appear on the books of the Brown Rexall Drug Store at the end of the year after the amortization entry has been made?

Franchise

1/2/20XX	5,000	12/31/20XX	500
	4,500		

On January 2, when the franchise agreement was signed and the $5,000 paid by the Brown Rexall Drug Store to the Rexall Company, the intangible asset, Franchise, was debited for $5,000. On December 31, after the amortization entry was made, the account, Franchise, was credited for $500, thus leaving a balance in the Franchise account at the end of the year of $4,500 ($5,000 – $500 = $4,500).

Each year the Franchise account will be amortized another $500, so at the end of 10 years, the Franchise account will be completely written off and will have a balance of zero.

12.4.4 Goodwill

When a company or part of a company is purchased, it is not uncommon for the purchaser to pay more than the sum of the fair market value for the individual assets minus the liabilities. This excess is called **goodwill**. It is often attributed to good management, good location, outstanding reputation, or other such factors.

This cost is treated as an intangible asset and amortized over the expected economic life of the goodwill. However, this life cannot exceed 40 years and it cannot be written off all in one lump sum.

Quiz: Inventory – Other Long-Term Assets

1. The specific identification inventory method is

    (A) first-in, first-out.

    (B) last-in, first-out.

    (C) average cost.

    (D) None of these

2. Which accounting method is usually used for extremely valuable inventory such as paintings?

    (A) Specific identification

    (B) Last-in, first-out

    (C) Average cost

    (D) First-in, first-out

3. The cost of the inventory on hand is deducted at the time of each sale in the

    (A) periodic inventory method.

    (B) perpetual inventory method.

    (C) margin inventory method.

    (D) None of the above

4. Which one of the following methods of inventory computation are used most in the United States?

    (A) First-in, first-out

    (B) Specific identification

    (C) Last-in, first-out

    (D) Weighted average

5. Which inventory method would show lower profits and thus cut down on a business' income taxes during inflationary times?

   (A) FIFO

   (B) LIFO

   (C) Specific identification

   (D) Weighted average

6. If a firm is using the lower of cost or market method of accounting for inventory, and if the value of the inventory is more than it would cost to buy new inventory,

   (A) the old inventory should be written up to market value.

   (B) the old inventory should be written down to market value.

   (C) no entry should be made.

   (D) the old inventory should be written above market value.

7. What subheading in the Balance Sheet is used for the assets used in the business but does not include current assets or inventory or land used for speculation?

   (A) Property, Plant, and Equipment

   (B) Retained Earnings

   (C) Current Assets

   (D) Common Stock

8. Which of the following is NOT a major type of depreciation?

   (A) Sum-of-years-digits   (C) Temporary

   (B) Straight-line   (D) Declining balance

9. Leasing is the

   (A) loaning of property.

   (B) rental of property.

   (C) purchase or sale of property.

   (D) None of these

10. How does depletion differ from depreciation?

   (A) There is no difference.

   (B) Depletion is the writing off of the value of wasting assets such as timber, oil wells, and gas wells; whereas depreciation is the writing down of the value of fixed assets such as buildings and machinery.

   (C) Depletion is the writing down of the value of fixed assets such as buildings and machinery; whereas depreciation is the writing off of the value of wasting assets such as timber, oil wells, and gas wells.

   (D) None of these

ANSWER KEY

1.	(D)	6.	(B)
2.	(A)	7.	(A)
3.	(B)	8.	(C)
4.	(A)	9.	(B)
5.	(B)	10.	(B)

CHAPTER 13

Current Liabilities

13.1 Current Liabilities Defined

Current liabilities are those obligations that must be paid within one year. This includes the portion of long-term debt that is due and payable within one year. Common types of current liabilities include accounts payable, notes payable, accrued liabilities for wages or interest, as well as estimated liabilities such as income taxes.

13.2 Accounts Payable

Accounts payable arise when a business purchases inventory or equipment on a credit basis. An example of the journal entry to reflect the purchase of inventory on credit is shown in Example 13.2.1.

EXAMPLE 13.2.1

The Sample Company
General Journal

Date	Description	Debit	Credit
	Purchases	10,000	
	Accounts Payable		10,000

The use of the Purchases account is limited strictly to purchases of **inventory** on credit. Purchases of other items would be reflected as affecting those accounts directly. As an example, if equipment were purchased on account, the journal entry to reflect that is shown in Example 13.2.2.

EXAMPLE 13.2.2

The Sample Company
General Journal

Date	Description	Debit	Credit
	Equipment	5,000	
	Accounts Payable		5,000

Payment of those payables are recorded as a debit to accounts payable and a credit to cash as shown in Example 13.2.3.

EXAMPLE 13.2.3

The Sample Company
General Journal

Date	Description	Debit	Credit
	Accounts Payable	5,000	
	Cash		5,000

13.3 Notes Payable

Notes payable occur when a business borrows money. Business transactions such as the purchase of real estate or equipment, as well as a temporary need for additional working capital, may necessitate such borrowings. As an example, assume that on March 15, Smith Corporation borrows $100,000 from its bank for 90 days. Interest is payable at maturity and accrues at a rate of 12%. The journal entry to record this transaction is shown in Example 13.3.1.

EXAMPLE 13.3.1

Smith Corporation
General Journal

Date	Description	Debit	Credit
20XX Mar. 15	Cash	100,000	
	Notes Payable		100,000

On June 15, Smith Corporation repaid the loan plus $3,000 interest ($100,000 × 12% × 90/360). In this instance, a 360-day year is used for interest calculation. The journal entry to record this transaction is shown in Example 13.3.2.

EXAMPLE 13.3.2

Smith Corporation
General Journal

Date	Description	Debit	Credit
20XX June 15	Notes Payable	100,000	
	Interest Expense	3,000	
	Cash		103,000

Problem Solving Examples:

The Wilson Company records purchases at gross and uses a periodic inventory system. On August 1, the Wilson Company purchases from the Smith Company $50,000 worth of inventory. Purchases is debited and Accounts Payable–Smith is credited for $50,000. On September 1, the Wilson Company gives the Smith Company a $50,000, 10-month note at 8% in payment of the account.

Show the entry on the books of the Wilson Company.

A

20XX		($ in dollars)
September 1 Accounts Payable–Smith	50,000	
Notes Payable		50,000

On August 1, when the Wilson Company purchased the merchandise, it gave its oral promise to pay the $50,000 by crediting Accounts Payable–Smith for $50,000. On September 1, the Wilson Company receives back its oral promise to pay by debiting Accounts Payable–Smith for $50,000. It then gives the Smith Company a written promise to pay—it gives a note for $50,000—and credits the Notes Payable account on its books for $50,000.

Q The board of directors of the Sanson Corporation has decided to construct a new factory building on a piece of land that they already own. The factory building will cost $100,000. The company has not been able to borrow this money on a long-term basis but has received a short-term loan from the bank for $100,000 at six percent for six months. At the end of each six-month period, the company plans to pay both the principal and interest on the note and continue renewing the note for a period of 10 years.

What entry should be made on the books of the Sanson Corporation when the money is borrowed, and how should this note appear in the Balance Sheet at year's end?

A

20XX		($ in dollars)
December 31 Cash	100,000	
Notes Payable		100,000

The amount of $100,000 is being received by the Sanson Corporation, so Cash is debited for $100,000 on December 31, the date the money was borrowed from the bank. Notes Payable is credited for $100,000 since this note was given to the bank at that time.

The note should be listed under Current Liabilities on the Balance Sheet of the Sanson Corporation on December 31. Even though the corporation plans to continue renewing the note every six months for the next 10 years, the bank might not, in the future, agree to this. Thus, the note must be listed as a Current Liability, even though this weakens the Balance Sheet.

 The Wilson Company records purchases at gross and uses a periodic inventory system. On August 1, the Wilson Company purchases from the Smith Company $50,000 worth of inventory. Purchases is debited and Accounts Payable–Smith is credited for $50,000. On September 1, the Wilson Company gives the Smith Company a $50,000, 10-month note at 8% in payment of the account. It debits Accounts Payable–Smith for $50,000 and credits Notes Payable for $50,000.

On December 31, what adjusting entry should be made on the Wilson Company books to show accrual of interest?

20XX	($ in dollars)	
December 31 Interest Expense	1,333	
Interest Payable		1,333

The note is for $50,000 at 8%. This is $4,000 interest per year ($50,000 × 8% = $4,000). The note was written on September 1, and it is now December 31, or four months later (the months of September, October, November, and December). Since there are 12 months in a year, 1/3 of a year has passed (4/12 = 1/3). The interest accrued or built up for these four months is $1,333 ($4,000 interest per year × 1/3 of a year elapsed = $1,333).

Interest Expense is debited for $1,333. This expense can be subtracted from the Gross Income in the Income Statement to cut down the net income by that amount and the income tax also. Since the Wilson Company is not paying any cash at this time, the Current Liability account Interest Payable is credited for the $1,333.

What entry will be made on the maturity date when the Wilson Company pays the Smith Company both the principal and the interest?

20XX		($ in dollars)	
July 1	Interest Payable	1,333	
	Interest Expense	2,000	
	Cash		3,333
July 1	Notes Payable	50,000	
	Cash		50,000

On December 31, the adjusting entry credited Interest Payable for $1,333 for interest accrued during the months of September, October, November, and December. Now this account is closed out by an entry debiting Interest Payable for $1,333. Interest Expense is debited for $2,000 for the months of January, February, March, April, May, and June of the following year ($50,000 × 8% × 1/2 year = $2,000).

The Cash account is credited for $3,333, which is the total interest for 10 months ($50,000 × 8% × 10/12 of a year = $3,333).

In the second entry the Wilson Company receives back its note marked "Paid" so it debits Notes Payable for $50,000. It pays the principal of $50,000 so credits Cash for $50,000.

How will the Current Liabilities appear on the Balance Sheet of the Wilson Company on December 31?

Wilson Company
Partial Balance Sheet
December 31, 20XX

Current Liabilities:

Notes Payable	50,000
Interest Payable	1,333

On November 1, the Wilson Company borrowed $40,000 from the First National Bank of Central City at 10% for one year and signed a non-interest-bearing note for $44,000.

What entry will they make on their books at this time?

20XX		($ in dollars)	
November 1	Cash	40,000	
	Discount on Notes Payable	4,000	
	Notes Payable		44,000

The Wilson Company receives $40,000 from the First National Bank, so the Wilson Company debits Cash on its books for $40,000. The Wilson Company gives the bank a note, the face value of which is $44,000, so it credits Notes Payable for $44,000. The difference between the $44,000 and the $40,000 is $4,000 ($44,000 − $40,000 = $4,000). This $4,000 is debited to a Contra-Liability account entitled Discount on Notes Payable.

What entry will Wilson Company make on its books to record accrued interest on December 31?

20XX		($ in dollars)	
December 31	Interest Expense	667	
	Discount on Notes Payable		667

The interest accrued on the note payable (built up on the note payable) is $667 for the two months of November and December. The money was borrowed on November 1, and two months have since elapsed. It is now December 31, and interest has to be computed on the

note for those two months at 10%. This amounts to $667 ($40,000 ×
10% × 2/12 = $667).

Thus, Interest Expense is debited for the $667. This is an expense
account and will serve to cut down the net income for the year for the
Wilson Company by that amount. The money was being used by the
Wilson Company during November and December, and the expense of
borrowing that money is one of the company's expenses for the year.
The account, Discount on Notes Payable, is credited for the $667.

On December 31, the Wilson Company debited Interest Expense
for $667 and credited Discount on Notes Payable for $667.

How will the Current Liabilities section of the Wilson Company
Balance Sheet appear at December 31?

Wilson Company
Partial Balance Sheet
December 31, 20XX

Current Liabilities:

Notes Payable	44,000	
Less: Discount on Notes Payable	3,333	
		40,667

The notes payable is listed at the face value of the note—$44,000.
The balance of the Discount on Notes Payable account at year's end is
$3,333 ($4,000 – $667 = $3,333). This brings up the net amount owed
by the Wilson Company at year's end to $40,667. Thus, if the Wilson
Company wished to pay the note at this time, December 31, it would
owe the bank $40,667.

13.4 Liability for Salaries and Wages

Employees are rarely paid on a daily basis. Instead, a business
accrues liability for payroll between pay dates (usually biweekly). The
gross amount of **wages** is relatively easy to calculate, consisting of
hours worked multiplied by the hourly wage. **Salaries** are paid

biweekly or monthly based on some present annual amount. Employers are also responsible for withholding a portion of gross pay for social security (FICA) and federal income taxes. In addition, the employer may withhold state and municipal income taxes (if applicable). Example 13.4.1 reflects the journal entry necessary to record payroll expense and liabilities as of January 15 (the end of the payroll period).

EXAMPLE 13.4.1

The Sample Company
General Journal

Date	Description	Debit	Credit
20XX			
Jan. 15	Sales Salaries Expense	10,000	
	Office Wages Expense	5,000	
	FICA Tax Payable		1,050
	Liability for Income Tax		
	Withheld		2,500
	Accrued Payroll		11,450

In this example, although the business has incurred $15,000 in total salary and wages expenses, only $11,450 is actually paid out to employees. The remainder will be submitted to the appropriate government agencies at regular intervals. Other withholdings, such as union dues, would be handled similarly.

Problem Solving Example:

The Henry Smith Company began business on January 2. They immediately hired five employees. The employment contracts stated that the employees would get two weeks' paid vacation each year, beginning with the second year of employment.

What entry or entries, if any, would the Henry Smith Company make on its books during the first year of employment?

20XX		($ in dollars)	
December 31	Wages Expense	4,000	
	Vacation Wages Payable		4,000

Each employee receives $400 gross wages per week, and there are five employees, so this is $2,000 gross wages per week that the employer must pay (5 employees × $400 per week each = $2,000 per week). Vacation pay is two weeks per year, beginning the second year of employment, so vacation pay is $4,000 ($2,000 gross wages per week × 2 weeks' vacation = $4,000).

Therefore, there are no paid vacations during the first year, since the contract does not allow paid vacations the first year. However, the first year's work determines the vacations for the second year. Therefore, accrued (built-up) monies for vacations at the end of the first year amount to $4,000 (two weeks' pay at first year's wages). Thus, on December 31 of the first year, an adjusting entry is made on the books of the Henry Smith Company debiting Wages Expense for $4,000. This is an expense of the first year, since the employees' work in that year builds up to pay for their vacations the following year. The Liability account entitled Vacation Wages Payable is credited for $4,000 to show that at the end of the first year the company has a liability built up during the first year to pay the employees vacation pay during the second year.

At the beginning of the second year, the Henry Smith Company raises each employee's pay from $400 per week to $410 per week.

What entry will the company make on its books at the end of the second year to show payment for vacations, assuming that each employee takes a two-week vacation during the second year?

20XX		($ in dollars)	
December 31	Vacation Wages Payable	4,000	
	Wages Expense	100	
	Cash		4,100

The adjusting entry at the end of the first year credited Vacation Wages Payable for $4,000 showing the accrued wages for vacations at the end of that year. Now debit Vacation Wages Payable for $4,000 to close out that account. Cash is credited because that amount is paid the employees for their two weeks' vacation at the new higher wage rates for the second year (5 employees × $410 per week new wages × 2 weeks' vacation = $4,100). The difference between the old two weeks' wage of $4,000 and the new two weeks' wage of $4,100 ($100) is debited to Wages Expense and is an expense of the second year.

Also on December 31 of the second year, another accrual entry needs to be made to accrue the vacations earned by the employees during the second year but not paid to them until the next year. This entry will be as follows:

20XX		($ in dollars)	
December 31	Wages Expense	4,100	
	Vacation Wages Payable		4,100

The figure $4,100 is the total wages for the two-week period at the new wage rate for the second year. This amount is debited to Wages Expense and is an expense for the second year that the employees have built up during that year but that will not be used until the third year. Vacation Wages Payable is a Liability account and credited for the $4,100 since it is owed to the employees who will use it next year.

At the same time, an employer incurs liabilities for certain payroll taxes. These include FICA tax (figured at the same rate and on the same amount of earnings as the employees), federal unemployment tax, and state unemployment tax. The journal entry to record the employer's tax expense and liabilities is reflected in Example 13.4.2.

EXAMPLE 13.4.2

The Sample Company
General Journal

Date	Description	Debit	Credit
20XX Jan. 15	Payroll Tax Expense FICA Tax Payable State Unemployment Tax Payable Federal Unemployment Tax Payable	2,790	1,050 810 930

Problem Solving Example:

The William Smith Company is beginning business. William Smith, the owner, works full time and has just employed Mary Harmon to be his office secretary at a gross wage of $500 per month, as of the first of January. She gets paid once a month.

Assume that the William Smith Company is located in a place where there are no state and local withholding taxes. William Smith debits Wages and Salary Expense for the total gross pay of $500. He credits Withholding Taxes Payable for $75, a figure which he gets from a federal withholding table. He credits FICA Taxes Payable for $38.25 ($500 gross pay × 7.65% = $38.25). He also credits United Way Payable for $10 and credits Cash for the take-home pay of $376.75.

What entry will the William Smith Company need to make on its books on January 31, for employer payroll taxes, and why?

20XX		($ in dollars)
January 31	Payroll Tax Expense	70.75
	FICA Taxes Payable	38.25
	FUTA Taxes Payable	4.00
	SUTA Taxes Payable	28.50

For the Federal Insurance Contributions Act, the employer is required to match the amount that he withheld from the employee. In this case it is $38.25 ($500 gross pay × 7.65% = $38.25). Therefore, FICA Taxes Payable is credited for $38.25. The Federal Unemployment Tax Act requires employers to withhold 0.8% of the employee's gross pay up to a ceiling of $7,000 at the present time. Since this is the first month of the year and the employee, Mary Harmon, has not yet earned the ceiling amount, all of her gross pay is subject to the 0.8% tax which is just on the employer ($500 gross pay × 0.8% = $4). Thus, the employer credits FUTA Taxes Payable for $4.

Most states force employers to pay 5.7% of the employee's gross pay. Assume that this state has the 5.7% rate. The employer then credits SUTA Taxes Payable for $28.50 ($500 gross pay × 5.7% = $28.50).

The total of the three taxes is $70.75 ($38.25 Federal Insurance Contributions Act + $4 Federal Unemployment Tax Act + $28.50 State Unemployment Tax Act = $70.75). Thus, the account Payroll Tax Expense is debited for $70.75. This is a regular expense of the business and is deductible in the Income Statement of the William Smith Company.

These four entries are also made on the last day of February and the last day of March.

How will the Withholding Taxes Payable account and the FICA Taxes Payable account appear on the books of the William Smith Company on March 31?

Withholding Taxes Payable

(employee withholding)	1/31/20XX	75.00
(employee withholding)	2/29/20XX	75.00
(employee withholding)	3/31/20XX	75.00
		225.00

FICA Taxes Payable

(employee withholding)	1/31/20XX	38.25
(employer taxes)	1/31/20XX	38.25
(employee withholding)	2/29/20XX	38.25
(employer taxes)	2/29/20XX	38.25
(employee withholding)	3/31/20XX	38.25
(employer taxes)	3/31/20XX	38.25
		229.50

Each quarter the William Smith Company is to mail in the withholding tax and the FUTA tax to the federal government.

How much will this be, and what entry will be made on the books of the William Smith Company?

20XX			($ in dollars)
March 31	Withholding Taxes Payable	225.00	
	FICA Taxes Payable	229.50	
	Cash		454.50

At March 31, the Withholding Taxes Payable account has a credit balance of $225 ($75 per month times three months = $225). At March 31, the FICA Taxes Payable account has a credit balance of $229.50 ($38.25 deducted twice each month for three months = $38.25 × 6 = $229.50).

Therefore, on March 31, at the time the William Smith Company remits its taxes to the federal government, the Withholding Taxes Payable account is debited for $225.00 to close out this account. Also, the FICA Taxes Payable account is debited for $229.50 to close out this account. Cash is credited for the total of $454.50 which is remitted by check to the federal government ($225.00 + $229.50 = $454.50).

13.5 Warranties

A business may have liabilities that, while quite real, can only be estimated. A company that sells appliances with warranties can incur this kind of liability. In such situations, the company guarantees free repair within a specified period of time in the event of a problem with their product.

The estimate of the probable expense of such repairs may be based on prior experience. In such a case, the liability for warranties might be a percentage of total sales in a given period. For example, assume the Sample Company sells 200 refrigerators in a year with one-year warranties. Based on past experience, the company expects five percent of its refrigerators to be defective within the one-year warranty period. The average service call is estimated at $25. During the year, three refrigerators are repaired at a total cost of $70. In the next year, six refrigerators are repaired at a cost of $130. Example 13.5.1 reflects the entries necessary to record expenditures for repairs as well as the entry to estimate warranty liability. Note that warranty **expense** is incurred in the accounting period when the refrigerators are sold, not when the repairs are made.

EXAMPLE 13.5.1

To Record $70 Repair Costs

Date	Description	Debit	Credit
20XX Various	Warranty Expense	70	
	Cash, Parts, Labor		70

To Record Estimated Liability Under Warranties for Repairs to Be Performed on Refrigerators Sold

Date	Description	Debit	Credit
Dec 31	Warranty Expense	175	
	Estimated Liability Under Warranty Obligations		175

Two hundred (200) refrigerators sold × .05 = 10 estimated to need repair. Ten minus three repaired in 20XX = 7 estimated to be repaired in the following year at $25 each for estimated liability of $175.

Example 13.5.2 illustrates the entries to record the cost of warranty repairs during the following year.

EXAMPLE 13.5.2

To Record Expenditures Related to Sales in the Following Year

Date	Description	Debit	Credit
20XX Various	Estimated Liability Under Warranty Obligations Cash, Parts, Labor	130	130

At the end of the following year, the Estimated Liability Under Warranty Obligations account will show a $45 credit balance. Ideally, the balance in this account would be zero if the company's estimate had been perfect. Since the estimating process is an ongoing one, there is no need to adjust the liability account unless it becomes obvious that the estimates are continually too high or too low. In such cases, a revision of the firm's estimating process is warranted.

13.6 Returnable Deposits

Businesses may sometimes require customers to put up cash deposits as part of a business transaction. For example, an apartment owner may require a renter to put up a deposit equivalent to two months' rent. This deposit is usually refundable to the renter under certain conditions specified in the rental contract. Since the apartment owner is obligated to return the deposit if the contract terms are met, this amount is a liability of the company. Example 13.6.1 illustrates such a situation.

Assume that a renter is required to put up a $500 deposit upon renting an apartment on May 1. On May 1 of the next year, the renter moves out after meeting all provisions of the rental contract. The entries to record those events are shown as follows:

EXAMPLE 13.6.1

To Record Receipt of $500 Apartment Deposit

Date	Description	Debit	Credit
Year 1 May 1	Cash Returnable Deposits	500	 500

To Record Refund of $500 Apartment Deposit

Year 2 May 1	Returnable Deposits Cash	500	 500

Problem Solving Example:

 The Northern Electric Company requires a $20 returnable fee from each potential customer before the electric lights are turned on. At present they have 150,000 customers, and therefore, hold $3,000,000 in returnable fees. There is a 10% turnover of customers, on the average, each year.

What entry will be made on the books when a new customer pays his/her fee; what entry will be made on the books when a customer leaves town; and how will these fees be placed in the Balance Sheet of the Northern Electric Company at year's end?

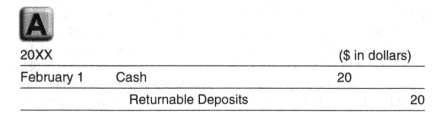

20XX		($ in dollars)	
February 1	Cash	20	
	Returnable Deposits		20

A new customer has arrived in town, and he advances the Northern Electric Company $20 before his lights will be turned on. The company debits Cash for $20 since it is receiving this amount of money. It credits the Liability account Returnable Deposits since it now owes the customer this amount of money.

20XX		($ in dollars)
April 1	Returnable Deposits	20
	Cash	20

On April 1, a customer moves away from town and asks for his $20 deposit. This is given to him. The company debits the Liability account Returnable Deposits since this cuts down the company's debt to the customer. The company credits Cash, because $20 is leaving the company's coffers and going to the customer.

Northern Electric Company
Partial Balance Sheet
December 31, 20XX

Liabilities:

Current Liabilities:	
Returnable Deposits (Current Portion)	300,000
Long-Term Liabilities:	
Returnable Deposits (Long-Term Portion)	2,700,000

Returnable deposits are definitely a liability to the Northern Electric Company, because the company must pay the customers their $20 when they leave town. But should these be current liabilities or long-term liabilities?

At present there are 150,000 customers, so the total amount of money in the Returnable Deposits account is $3,000,000 (150,000 customers × $20 fee = $3,000,000).

From past experience it is determined that there is a 10% turnover of customers during the average year, so 10% of the $3,000,000 needs to be on hand to pay customers leaving town (10% × $3,000,000 = $300,000). Thus, $300,000 should be placed in the company's Balance Sheet as a Current Liability. The remaining $2,700,000 should be placed in the company's Balance Sheet as a Long-Term Liability ($3,000,000 − $300,000 = $2,700,000).

CHAPTER 14

Long-Term Liabilities

14.1 Definitions

Long-term liabilities are liabilities that have an expected life of more than one year. Usually a long-term liability will be reclassified as current near the end of its life. In other cases, the life of the liability may not be clearly known. In these cases, the classification is done on the best estimate of the expected life; current if less than one year and long-term if more than one year.

Three types of liabilities that could conceivably be long-term are notes payable, product warranties, and returnable deposits. These items were covered in Chapter 13. It should be noted that often notes payable will be long-term upon the signing of the notes.

The topic that takes up the majority of discussion about long-term liabilities is **bonds payable**. This topic is covered in Chapter 15 along with the asset side of bonds.

14.2 Pensions

During recent years, **pensions** have become a much more involved and debated topic. This is a result of numerous factors. In 1974, Congress passed the Employee Retirement Income Security Act (**ERISA**) which set up special rules for protecting employee benefits. Under these guidelines, a pension plan can be either **contributory** or **noncontributory, qualified** or **unqualified**, and **funded** or **unfunded**. Each of these distinctions will be examined individually.

It has become increasingly difficult for organizations to set up quali-fied plans and follow all of the law's requirements. Most companies now get expert legal and accounting assistance to assure compliance.

Problem Solving Example:

The Johnson Construction Company has five employees. For several years they have been clamoring for the corporation to set up a retirement pension plan for them. The accountant for the company determines that if the plan is set up properly so that it is actuarially sound, following the general requirements of the Employee Retirement Income Security Act of 1974, corporation payments into the plan can be deducted as business expenses in determining corpo-rate net income for tax purposes.

After determining the soundness of the corporate finances over the past several years, the Board of Directors of the Johnson Construction Company decides on a defined contribution plan. This means that the company will guarantee to place with a trustee a certain percent of the employees' incomes regularly at the end of each year. The contribution each year will be guaranteed, not the future benefits. The board de-cides that the corporation can afford five percent of the employees' incomes as a defined contribution.

During the year, all five employees earn combined incomes of $300,000. Five percent of this figure is $15,000 ($300,000 total in-comes × 5% determined percent figure = $15,000). What entry will be made on the books of the Johnson Construction Company and why?

A

20XX		($ in dollars)
December 31 Pension Expense	15,000	
Cash		15,000

The Board of Directors of the Johnson Construction Company appoints the Trust Department of the First National Bank to be the pension agent. At the end of the year, the Johnson Construction

Company sends a check for $15,000 to the Trust Department of the First National Bank and makes the preceding entry on its books—that is, on the books of the Johnson Company.

Pension Expense is debited for $15,000, and because this is a plan set up according to the guidelines of the ERISA (Employee Retirement Income Security Act of 1974), this pension expense is fully deductible as a corporation business expense for income tax purposes, legally cutting down the corporate net income by this amount. The asset account Cash is credited for $15,000, because this amount of money is leaving the Johnson Construction Company and being paid to the Trust Department of the First National Bank.

14.2.1 Contributory and Noncontributory

A **contributory plan** provides that the employer withholds a portion of the employee's earnings as a contribution to the pension. The employer also contributes a portion as specified in the plan.

Under a **noncontributory plan**, the employer incurs the entire burden of the plan. The employees do not make a contribution.

14.2.2 Qualified and Unqualified

A **qualified plan** is one that complies with the federal income tax requirements which allow the deduction of the pension contributions on the income tax returns of the employer. Most plans are qualified. It would be much to the disadvantage for all concerned if an unqualified plan were set up. To the employer, the contributions would not be a tax expense. As a result of that, the employer will be likely to pass this cost on to the employees in the form of lower compensation.

14.2.3 Funded and Unfunded

A **funded plan** is one in which the employer makes pension payments to an independent funding agency. This agency is then responsible for accounting for all contributions to and disbursements from the fund. The most common independent funding agencies are insurance companies. An **unfunded plan** is managed completely by the employer rather than an independent agency.

14.2.4 Net Periodic Pension Cost

For any given year, the employer's cost of an employee's pension plan is called the **net periodic pension cost**. This cost is charged to the operating expense account called Pension Expense. The credit will be totally to Cash if it is a fully funded plan. If it is partially funded, any unfunded portion will be credited to an account called Unfunded Pension Cost. A sample entry is given in Example 14.2.1.

EXAMPLE 14.2.1

To Record the 20XX Funding of Pension Plan

The Sample Company
General Journal

Date	Acct. No.	Description	Debit	Credit
20XX Dec. 31	27	Pension Expense	12,000	
	1	Cash		5,000
	12	Unfunded Pension – Accrued Costs		7,000

Depending on when the unfunded portion is to be paid, this account can be either a current liability or a long-term liability.

The employer's financial statements should very clearly state all pertinent details of the pension plan. These would include who is covered, how the plan is funded, what sort of accounting is done for the plan, and other details deemed essential to understanding the plan.

14.3 Contingent Liabilities

Potential obligations that will result only if certain future events occur are called **contingent liabilities**. If the amount is definite, then it should be noted. More likely, a contingent liability is for an indefinite amount.

Examples would be lawsuits that are being settled in court and notes that are guaranteed by the company. The company would only have to pay if the originator of the notes did not pay them.

Contingent liabilities can be shown in the balance sheet between long-term liabilities and stockholders' equity. However, they do not need to be detailed in the body of the balance sheet. Instead, they can be disclosed in footnotes to the financial statements. In the increasingly litigation-happy mood of the United States, contingent liabilities have taken on an increasingly important role in financial statements.

Problem Solving Example:

 Where in the balance sheet is it incorrect to place contingent liabilities?

(A) Between the asset section and the liability section
(B) Between the liability section and the owner's equity section
(C) As a footnote at the bottom of the balance sheet

 The answer is choice (A).

14.4 Unearned Revenue (Deferrals)

Revenue that is collected in advance of earning it is called **unearned revenue**. It is also sometimes referred to as **revenue collected in advance**. When the revenue is first collected, the entry would be as in Example 14.4.1.

EXAMPLE 14.4.1

To Record Revenue Collected in Advance from the Smith Company

The Sample Company
General Journal

Date	Acct. No.	Description	Debit	Credit
20XX Jan 1	4	Accounts Receivable: Smith Company	3,000	
	17	Unearned Sales Revenue		3,000

Examples of such collections in advance might be airline tickets paid for in advance, advertising, or insurance premiums. Another large category would be repairs paid for in advance such as service contracts. As the revenue is earned, the journal entry would be made as in Example 14.4.2.

EXAMPLE 14.4.2

To Record Sales of Merchandise that was Paid For in Advance.

The Sample Company
General Journal

Date	Acct. No.	Description	Debit	Credit
20XX Jan 1	17	Unearned Sales Revenue	1,000	
	60	Sales Revenue		1,000

Unearned revenue is usually shown on the balance sheet as a current liability. This placement would, however, depend on the length of time involved. It is very likely that this would be a long-term liability.

Problem Solving Examples:

Q Give the journal entry for a newspaper upon receiving advertising income, in advance, of $400.

A

	Debit	Credit
Cash	400	
Unearned Revenue		400

Q On the day the advertising in the problem above comes out in the newspaper, what entry would be made in the newspaper's journal, using general journal form?

A

Unearned Revenue	400	
Advertising Revenue		400

Quiz: Current Liabilities – Long-Term Liabilities

1. Current liabilities are

   (A) assets that change in value within a year.

   (B) liabilities that must be paid off within a year.

   (C) liabilities that do not need to be paid off within a year.

   (D) owner's equity.

2. How do accounts payable differ from notes payable?

   (A) There is no difference.

   (B) The notes payable are current liabilities whereas accounts payable are long-term liabilities.

   (C) Notes payable are oral debts whereas accounts payable are written debts.

(D) Notes payable are written debts whereas accounts payable are oral debts.

3. A firm borrows $500 for 30 days at 6% and writes a promissory note. What entry is made on the books of the firm?

    (A) Debit Cash and credit Notes Payable $500

    (B) Debit Cash and credit Notes Receivable $500

    (C) Debit Notes Payable and credit Cash $500

    (D) Debit Notes Receivable and credit Cash $500

4. Warranties are guarantees

    (A) that the article sold will continue to be useful permanently.

    (B) that the article sold will continue to be useful for a period of time.

    (C) that the article sold will continue to be useful given certain conditions.

    (D) None of the above

5. Let us say that when a tenant moves in, he deposits $150 with the landlord guaranteeing that the apartment will remain in good shape while this person is a tenant. This deposit is

    (A) an asset to the landlord.

    (B) a liability to the landlord.

    (C) immaterial to the landlord.

    (D) None of the above

6. Long-term liabilities differ from current liabilities in that

    (A) long-term liabilities must be paid off within a year while this is not true of short-term liabilities.

    (B)   short-term liabilities must be paid off within a year while this is not true of long-term liabilities.

    (C)   the amount of a long-term liability is used by readers of balance sheets to determine the liquidity of a business.

    (D)   short-term liabilities are usually bonds and mortgages, while long-term liabilities include interest and taxes.

7.   Which one of the following is NOT usually a long-term liability?

    (A)   Accounts payable

    (B)   Mortgages payable

    (C)   Notes payable

    (D)   None of these

8.   It is important for employers to set up pension plans for their employees because

    (A)   employees are greedy and want all they can get.

    (B)   employers have happier and more long-serving employees if there is a pension program.

    (C)   high pensions are passed on in high costs.

    (D)   None of these

9.   Contingent liabilities are placed

    (A)   in the Income Statement under Cost of Goods Sold.

    (B)   in the Asset Section of the Balance Sheet.

    (C)   in the Liabilities Section of the Balance Sheet.

    (D)   as a footnote in the Balance Sheet.

10. What are unearned revenues?

   (A) Unearned revenues are the opposite of deferrals.

   (B) Unearned revenues are monies paid in advance, like prepaid insurance.

   (C) Unearned revenues are monies collected in advance like airline ticket income.

   (D) None of these

ANSWER KEY

1.	(B)	6.	(B)
2.	(D)	7.	(B)
3.	(A)	8.	(B)
4.	(B)	9.	(D)
5.	(B)	10.	(C)

CHAPTER 15

Bonds

15.1 Bonds Defined

A corporation may seek long-term financing through the issuance of **bonds**. Bonds are similar to notes payable in that the corporation is obligated to repay a stated amount at a specific time and to pay interest at regular intervals to investors. There is, however, an important difference. Notes payable are usually owed to one investor, but bonds can be subdivided and sold to many investors through securities brokers. This allows a corporation to raise larger amounts of money than might be obtainable from any single lender. While bonds are traded as marketable securities, they differ from stock in that bonds are debt instruments only. Ownership of a bond does not provide an ownership interest in the issuing entity.

15.2 Purchase of Bonds

A corporation may purchase bonds of another entity as an investment. The journal entry to record the purchase of a bond may involve accounting for accrued interest if the purchase date is between bond interest payment dates. Assume, for example, on August 1, an investor purchases a $100,000 Smith Corporation bond at face value. The bond pays 12% interest semiannually on June 1 and December 1. The journal entry to record this purchase is shown in Example 15.2.1.

EXAMPLE 15.2.1

Date	Description	Debit	Credit
20XX Aug 1	Marketable Securities	100,000	
	Bond Interest Receivable	2,000	
	Cash		102,000

The $2,000 debit to Bond Interest Receivable consists of interest accrued during the 60-day period between the last interest date (June 1) and the purchase date (August 1). This amount (calculated as $100,000 \times .12 \times 60/360$) is added to the purchase price of the bonds ($100,000) for a total cash outlay of $102,000. The investor will recover the $2,000 when the regular interest payment is received at the next interest date.

Problem Solving Example:

 Harry Smith decides on a long-term investment and buys a $1,000 American Telephone and Telegraph bond and another $1,000 Ameritech bond. This is done on June 1, at which time the American Telephone and Telegraph bond is selling at par, or $1,000, and the Ameritech bond is selling at a $200 premium, or $1,200. What entry will he make on his books? Let us say the broker charges $150 for the purchase of these two bonds.

A

20XX		($ in dollars)
June 1 Investment in Bonds	2,350	
Cash		2,350

Since Harry Smith decides this is a long-term investment and that he will hold the bonds for a longer period than a year, he debits the long-term asset account Investment in Bonds. This is recorded under

Investments under Assets in the Balance Sheet and not as a Current Asset.

The $2,350 debit to Investment in Bonds account is computed as follows: $1,000 paid for the American Telephone and Telegraph bond, $1,200 paid for the Ameritech bond, and $150 brokerage fee ($1,000 + $1,200 + $150 = $2,350). The broker has added his commission to the purchase price of the two bonds, and this commission cannot legally be deducted as an expense but must be added to the cost of the bond.

15.3 Income on Bonds Receivable

Using the Example 15.2.1, on December 1, the investor will receive interest of $6,000 (calculated as $100,000 × .12 × 180/360) for the six months ending December 1. The journal entry to record this transaction is shown in Example 15.3.1.

EXAMPLE 15.3.1

Date	Description	Debit	Credit
20XX Dec 1	Cash Bond Interest Receivable Bond Interest Revenue	6,000	 2,000 4,000

Only the portion earned since the purchase of the bonds on August 1 is recognized as revenue.

Again using the same example, if the investor maintains calendar year records, bond interest accrued from the December 1 payment date should be accounted for as shown in Example 15.3.2.

EXAMPLE 15.3.2

Date	Description	Debit	Credit
20XX Dec 31	Bond Interest Receivable Bond Interest Revenue	1,000	1,000

This journal entry recognizes that interest revenue has been earned since the last payment date (December 1), but has not yet been received. Example 15.3.3 reflects the journal entry to record the receipt of the next regular interest payment of $6,000 on June 1, six months later. In this example, the revenue earned during this period (January 1 to June 1) is recognized as revenue and the Bond Interest Receivable account created at year-end is paid off.

EXAMPLE 15.3.3

Date	Description	Debit	Credit
20XX June 1	Cash Bond Interest Receivable Bond Interest Revenue	6,000	1,000 5,000

Problem Solving Examples:

Q Let us say that interest payment dates on the bond that Harry Smith has purchased are July 1 and January 1. Smith purchased the bond on an interest payment date. Let us say that Harry Smith purchases a Ford Motor Company bond on an interest payment date. The interest payment dates are July 1 and January 1. Six months later, on January 1, Smith receives a check for $225 to cover the interest for a half a year ($5,000 × 9% × 1/2 year = $225). What entry does Smith make on his books on January 1?

A

20XX		$ (in dollars)
January 1	Cash	225
	Bond Interest Revenue	225

Smith debits Cash for $225 because he receives a check for that amount. He credits the revenue account entitled Bond Interest Revenue for $225 because he has been giving the Ford Motor Company the use of his money. This revenue must be reported as income for income tax purposes.

 Harry Smith has sold his General Motors stock and wishes to invest this money in a safe place that will bring him decent returns. He turns to the Corporate Bond Market. His broker suggests Ford Motor Company bonds that pay 9% and are selling at a small discount. On July 1, the date of purchase, the bonds are quoted on the market at 98% ($5,000 × .98 = $4,900). This means that a $5,000 bond can now be purchased for only $4,900. However, the broker's commission of $80 is added to this, making a total payment of $4,980. What entry does Harry Smith make on his books on the date he purchases this $5,000 bond?

A

20XX		$ (in dollars)
July 1	Marketable Debt Securities	4,980
	Cash	4,980

The current asset account Marketable Debt Securities is debited for $4,980, the amount Smith remits to his broker. This is considered the purchase price of the bond. The Financial Accounting Standards Board recommends that bonds be kept at cost, and this is being done here. Some purchasers of bonds keep their records at Lower of Cost or

Market. In this case the entry would be the same, since at this time the cost price is the same as the market price.

15.4 Bonds Payable

A corporation may choose to raise funds through the issuance of bonds which become long-term liabilities of the business. As an example, assume a corporation intends to raise $1,000,000 by selling bonds that carry a 12% interest rate, payable semiannually on July 1 and January 1. If these bonds can be sold at face value on July 1, the journal entry is shown in Example 15.4.1.

EXAMPLE 15.4.1

Date	Description	Debit	Credit
20XX July 1	Cash	1,000,000	
	Bonds Payable		1,000,000

The journal entry to record the semiannual interest payments each January 1 and July 1 is shown in Example 15.4.2. The semiannual interest payment of $60,000 is calculated as $1,000,000 × .12 × 180/360.

EXAMPLE 15.4.2

Date	Description	Debit	Credit
	Bond Interest Expense	60,000	
	Cash		60,000

At maturity, the necessary entry to record redemption of the bonds is shown in Example 15.4.3.

EXAMPLE 15.4.3

Date	Description	Debit	Credit
	Bonds Payable Cash	1,000,000	1,000,000

If the bonds were issued between interest dates, for example on April 1, the purchase cost would include the interest accrued during the 90-day period between the last interest payment date (January 1) and the purchase date (April 1). This accrued interest, $30,000, calculated as $1,000,000 \times .12 \times 90/360$, is reflected as a liability account called Bond Interest Payable. Example 15.4.4 shows the entry needed in such an event.

EXAMPLE 15.4.4

Date	Description	Debit	Credit
20XX Apr 1	Cash Bonds Payable Bond Interest Payable	1,030,000	1,000,000 30,000

At the next regular payment date (July 1), the corporation will pay bondholders the full amount of interest earned since the last payment date (January 1). As shown in Example 15.4.5, only the amount of interest accruing from the issue date of April 1 is recognized as an expense.

EXAMPLE 15.4.5

Date	Description	Debit	Credit
20XX July 1	Bond Interest Payable Bond Interest Expense Cash	30,000 30,000	60,000

15.5 Bond Issue Price

Previous examples have assumed issue of bonds at face (par) value. The issue price of bonds often differs from face value due to two factors: (1) The relationship between the bond interest rate and the market rate required by investors; and (2) The perceived ability of the issuing entity to pay the interest and principal required by the bond terms.

15.6 Bonds Sold at a Discount

If a corporation issues bonds paying 8 percent, but investors require a 10 percent return, the bond issue price will be less than the face amount. Investors are thus discounting the bonds' value to a point where the combined yield of interest income plus the difference in purchase price and the face amount is equivalent to a 10 percent yield over the life of the bond. Example 15.6.1 reflects a situation where a $1,000,000 bond issue with a 10-year maturity is sold for $950,000. The difference between the face value and the actual sales price is the discount.

EXAMPLE 15.6.1

Date	Description	Debit	Credit
	Cash	950,000	
	Discounts on Bonds Payable	50,000	
	Bonds Payable		1,000,000

The discount must be amortized over the life of the bond. The simplest method of amortization is the straight-line method, allocating an equal portion of the discount to bond interest expense at each interest payment date. Amortization of the $50,000 discount ($50,000/10 years = $5,000 annually or $2,500 semiannually) and payment of interest ($1,000,000 × .08 × 180/360 = $40,000 semiannually) are shown in Example 15.6.2.

EXAMPLE 15.6.2

Date	Description	Debit	Credit
	Bond Interest Expense Cash	40,000	40,000
	Bond Interest Expense Bond Discount	2,500	2,500

Problem Solving Example:

Q Let us say that the $5,000 bond that Harry Smith purchased was a 10-year bond with a maturity date of July 1. Smith bought the bond for only $4,900, so he bought it at a $100 discount ($5,000 – $4,900 = $100). This discount should be amortized (written off) over the life of the bond. Since it is a 10-year bond, it will be amortized over a period of 20 half-years (10 years times 2 half-years per year = 20 half years). The amortization period is 20 half-years because the amortization entry is usually made at the same time as the interest entry, and the interest is received every half-year. What entry will be made on January 1, to amortize the discount at the end of the first half-year of the life of the bond?

A

20XX		($ in dollars)
January 1	Marketable Debt Securities	5
	Bond Interest Expense	5

The current asset account Market Debt Securities is debited for $5 ($100 discount divided by 20 half-years = $5). This will be done every half-year for 20 half-years, thus bringing the Marketable Debt Securities account up to $5,000 from $4,900 by the maturity date of July 1. The $80 additional brokerage fee will still be part of this account.

Bond Interest Expense is credited for $5 because the process of accruing discount deducts from this expense account. As a rule, both amortization of premium and amortization of discount are carried on through the Bond Interest Expense account.

How will the Marketable Debt Securities current asset account appear on the books of Harry Smith after the first amortization entry on January 1?

Marketable Debt Securities	
4,980	
5	
4,985	

On July 1, the day the bond was purchased, the Marketable Debt Securities' current asset account was debited for $4,980, which includes the $4,900 paid for the bond plus the $80 brokerage fee. On January 1, after Harry Smith had held the bond for six months, the amortization entry debited the account for another $5, bringing it up to a balance of $4,985.

Let us say that on January 2, the first business day of the new year, Harry Smith decides to sell the bond. At that time the market price of the bond had risen to $5,100, and the broker's fee was another $80. What entry will Harry Smith make on his books to record the sale of the bond on January 2?

20XX		($ in dollars)	
January 2	Cash	5,020	
	Marketable Debt Securities		4,985
	Gain on Sale of Bond		35

The bond was sold for $5,100, but the broker deducted his brokerage fee of $80, remitting the remainder of $5,020 to Harry Smith. So Harry Smith debits Cash for the $5,020. At that time on Harry Smith's books, the Marketable Debt Securities account has a debit balance of $4,985. Since Smith is mailing in his bond to his broker and giving up the legal possession of his bond, he credits Marketable Debt Securities for this amount, $4,985, to close out the account.

Smith also credits the revenue account Gain on Sale of Bond for $35 to balance the books ($5,020 – $4,985 = $35). This gain account is a revenue and must be reported as income for income tax purposes.

Let us say that by January 2, the first business day of the new year, Harry Smith decides to sell the bond. However, in this case, let us say that the market price of the bond had dropped to $4,800, and still the broker's fee was another $80. What entry will Harry Smith make on his books to record the sale of the bond on January 2?

20XX			($ in dollars)
January 2	Cash	4,720	
	Loss on Sale of Bond	265	
	Marketable Debt Securities		4,985

The bond was sold for $4,800, but the broker deducted his brokerage fee of $80, remitting the remainder of $4,720 to Harry Smith. So Harry Smith debits Cash for $4,720. At that time on Harry Smith's books, the Marketable Debt Securities account has a debit balance of $4,985. Since Smith is mailing in his bond to his broker and giving up the legal possession of this bond, he credits Marketable Debt Securities for this amount, $4,985, to close out the account.

Smith also debits an expense account, Loss on Sale of Bond, for $265, the difference between the $4,985 and the $4,720 ($4,985 – $4,720 = $265). This loss account is an expense and can be deducted from income for income tax purposes.

On March 1, two years and eight months after he bought the original bond, Harry Smith buys a $1,000 Smith-Corona bond at par (for $1,000). This bond pays 10% interest annually and the interest payment dates are January 1 and July 1. Four months after purchasing the bond is July 1, the interest payment date mentioned in the fine print on the face of the bond.

On November 1, three years and eight months after he bought the $1,000 Smith-Corona bond, Harry Smith decides to sell the $1,000 Smith-Corona bond, and can sell it at par for $1,000. The brokerage fee is $50. What entry does Harry make on the date of sale?

20XX		($ in dollars)	
November 1	Cash	950.00	
	Loss on Sale of Bond	83.32	
	Bond Interest Revenue		33.32
	Marketable Debt Securities		1,000.00

Since the bond is being sold at par, $1,000 is paid to Smith's broker, who takes his $50 brokerage fee and remits the remaining $950 to Harry Smith. Thus, Smith debits the Cash account for the $950.00. The last interest payment date on the bond was July 1, so between that date and the date of sale, November 1, the four months of July, August, September, and October had elapsed. The interest on the bond is $100 per year ($1,000 × 10% = $100). The interest per month is $8.33 ($100 divided by 12 months = $8.33). Since interest has accrued for four months since the last interest payment date, four months' interest is $33.32 ($8.33 × 4 = $33.32). So Harry Smith credits the account Bond Interest Revenue for $33.32.

When Smith originally bought the $1,000 Smith-Corona bond, he debited Marketable Debt Securities for $1,000. Now that he is selling the bond, he must get rid of this account: so he credits Marketable Debt Securities for $1,000. The plug figure to make the debits equal the credits in this entry is to debit the expense account Loss on Sale of Bond for $83.32. The reasons for the loss were, first, because of the broker's fee of $50 and second because of the bond interest revenue. If we subtract the bond interest revenue of $33.32 from the loss on sale of bond of $83.32, we get the $50 broker's fee ($83.32 − $33.32 = $50). In this case, then, the $50 broker's fee can be deducted from income for income tax purposes, as a business expense.

15.7 Bonds Sold at a Premium

If the rate of interest paid on a bond exceeds the market rate, investors will pay a premium over the face amount. Using the previous example in section 15.6 of a $1,000,000 bond issue, but changing the bond interest rate to 12% (the market rate remains 10%), the bonds may sell for $1,050,000. Example 15.7.1 reflects the effect of this transaction.

EXAMPLE 15.7.1

Date	Description	Debit	Credit
	Cash	1,050,000	
	Bonds Payable		1,000,000
	Premium on Bonds		
	Payable		50,000

Like the bond discount, the bond premium must be amortized over the life of the bond. The semiannual journal entry to record the required interest payment plus the premium amortization is shown in Example 15.7.2.

EXAMPLE 15.7.2

Date	Description	Debit	Credit
	Bond Interest Expense	60,000	
	Cash		60,000
	Premium on Bonds Payable	2,500	
	Bond Interest Expense		2,500

Should interest payment dates not coincide with period-end, the interest accrued since the last payment date must be recognized. Using the above example, but changing the interest payment dates to June 1 and December 1, the entry required at year-end is shown in Example 15.7.3. One month's interest ($1,000,000 × 0.12 × 30/360) is $10,000 while one month's premium amortization is $417 ($50,000/10 = $5,000 annually or $417 per month).

EXAMPLE 15.7.3

Date	Description	Debit	Credit
Dec 31	Bond Interest Expense	10,000	
	Bond Interest Payable		10,000
	Premium on Bonds Payable	417	
	Bond Interest Expense		417

The entry then required at the next regular interest payment date of June 1 is shown in Example 15.7.4.

This properly recognizes only the expenses incurred during this accounting period.

EXAMPLE 15.7.4

Date	Description	Debit	Credit
June 1	Bond Interest Payable	10,000	
	Bond Interest Expense	47,917	
	Premium on Bonds Payable	2,083	
	Cash		60,000

Problem Solving Examples:

On August 1, Mary Henshaw purchases a $1,000 American Telephone and Telegraph Corporation bond for $1,200, since the bond is selling at a $200 premium. The reason for this is not only because American Telephone and Telegraph is a safe investment, but also that the bond is paying 16% interest, which is higher than what most other bonds happen to be paying at this time. The fine print on the bond indenture mentions that interest payment dates are March 1 and September 1. What entry will Mary Henshaw make on her books when she purchases this bond? Let us say that Mary's future plans at this time are to hold the bond for more than a year. Let us also assume that this is a new bond issue and there are no brokerage fees at this time.

A

20XX		($ in dollars)
August 1	Investment in American Telephone and Telegraph 16% Bonds	1,200.00
	Bond Interest Receivable	66.67
	Cash	1,266.67

Since Mary Henshaw plans to hold the bonds for more than a year, she debits the long-term asset account Investment in American Telephone and Telegraph 16% Bonds. She debits this account for $1,200, which is the total of the $1,000 face value of the bond and the $200 premium.

The last interest payment date was March 1, and she purchases the bond on August 1, five months later. Therefore, she debits the current asset account Bond Interest Receivable for $66.67, five months' accrued interest ($1,000 × 0.16 × 5/12 = $66.67). This is a current asset account, because on the next interest payment date, in this case, September 1, after holding the bond only one month, she will be paid six months' interest. She credits Cash for $1,266.67, which includes the $1,000 face value of the bond plus $200 premium, plus $66.67 accrued interest.

On September 1, Mary Henshaw receives a check for six months' interest on the American Telephone and Telegraph Corporation bond, which she bought on August 1, for $1,000 at $200 premium. This bond pays 16% interest on March 1 and September 1 for each year and runs until March 1, the maturity date. What entry does she make on her books on September 1?

20XX		($ in dollars)
September 1	Cash	80.00
	Bond Interest Receivable	66.67
	Bond Interest Revenue	13.33

Because the bond indenture mentions that the holders of the bond on March 1 and September 1 of each year receive six months' interest, Mary Henshaw receives a check for six months' interest even though she has held the check only one month. So she debits Cash for $80 ($1,000 × 0.16 × 1/2 = $80).

On August 1, when she bought the bond, she debited the current asset account Bond Interest Receivable for $66.67, which represented five months' accrued interest. Now she must cancel out this account, so she credits Bond Interest Receivable for that amount. She also credits Bond Interest Revenue for $13.33, the interest she has earned for the month of August. This $13.33 is taxable interest income.

On August 1, Mary Henshaw bought a $1,000 AT&T 16% bond at a $200 premium. She has decided to amortize this premium over the life of the bond and to make this amortization entry each December 31, the last day of the calendar year. What entry will Mary Henshaw make on December 31?

20XX		($ in dollars)	
December 31	Bond Interest Expense	8.70	
	Investment in AT&T 16% Bonds		8.70

This is a 10-year bond, and 10 years is 120 months (10 × 12 months in a year = 120 months). The bond was originally ready to sell on March 1, but Mary Henshaw didn't buy the bond until five months later, on August 1. Therefore, her bond runs only 115 months (120 months − 5 months = 115 months). The premium was $200 so this is divided by 115 months running to discover the monthly amortization ($200 premium divided by 115 months running = $1.74 monthly amortization). Since the bond was purchased on August 1, and it is now December 31, five months have elapsed since the bond was purchased. The amortization for five months is therefore $8.70 ($1.74 monthly amortization × 5 months = $8.70).

On March 1 of the following year, Mary Henshaw receives an interest income check from AT&T Corporation. She had purchased this $1,000 bond for $1,200, since the bond was selling at a $200 premium. It pays 16% interest. The fine print on the bond indenture mentions that interest payment dates are March 1 and September 1. What entry will Mary Henshaw make on her books to record this interest?

20XX		($ in dollars)
March 1	Cash	80
	Bond Interest Revenue	80

Mary Henshaw receives a check for $80 interest on her $1,000 bond at 16 ($1,000 × 0.16 × 1/2 = $80). She debits Cash for $80. She credits Bond Interest Revenue for $80 since she is giving the AT&T Corporation the use of her money. This is fully taxable interest income.

On December 31, Mary Henshaw sells her $1,000 AT&T 16% bond for $1,300, which includes the $1,000 face value plus $300 premium on that date. She had originally purchased this bond on August 1 for $1,200, which included the $1,000 face value of the bond plus $200 premium. It is a 10-year bond with a maturity date of March 1. What entry will she make on her books when she sells this bond? (The broker also charged a $50 brokerage fee.)

It will take two entries: The first is an amortization entry to bring the amortization up to date, as follows:

20XX		($ in dollars)
December 31	Bond Interest Expense	20.88
	Investment in AT&T 16% Bonds	20.88

Mary Henshaw had chosen to amortize the bond premium on December 31 of each year. Her last amortization entry was in the year she purchased the bond, on December 31, so this amortization will be for the following year. The bond was purchased originally for a $200 premium to be written off over 115 months ($200 divided by 115 months = $1.74 per month). This amortization entry is for all 12 months of the following year. So we multiply the monthly amortization amount of $1.74 by 12 months to get the whole year's amortization figure of $20.88 ($1.74 × 12 = $20.88).

Bond Interest Expense is debited because amortization is written off through that account. Investment in AT&T 16% bonds is credited to help eventually bring this account down by maturity date to the face value of the bond: $1,000.

Let us now take a look at the Investment in AT&T 16% Bonds account:

Investment in AT&T 16% Bonds

1,200.00	8.70
	20.88
	29.58
1,170.42	

As can be seen, the value of the Investment in AT&T 16% Bonds account has dropped from $1,200 to $1,170.42 during the period in which Mary Henshaw owned the bond.

The next step is to record Mary Henshaw's sale of the bond:

20XX		($ in dollars)
December 31 Cash	1,250.00	
Investment in AT&T 16% Bonds		1,170.42
Gain on Sale of Bonds		79.58

Cash was debited for $1,250, which was the $1,300 price for the sale of the bond, after subtracting the broker's $50 fee ($1,300 – $50 = $1,250). The Investment account in AT&T 16% Bonds was credited for $1,170.42 to close that long-term asset account. The difference of $79.58 was credited to a revenue account entitled Gain on Sale of Bonds. This gain is fully taxable for income tax purposes, due to the rise in the price of the bonds during the period in which Mary Henshaw held her bond.

The Sioux Indian Tribe was granted federal permission to build a gambling casino on their land. It was going to cost $700,000 and the financial consultants advised that 10% interest should be paid. By the time the bonds were sold, the national effective interest rate was somewhat lower than that figure. Also, the prospective bondholders believed the gambling casino would be a "gold mine" and wanted to buy the bonds. So the bonds were sold for $800,000, of which $100,000 was premium ($800,000 cash received – $700,000 face value of bonds = $100,000 premium). How would this entry be shown on the books of the Sioux Tribe if the investment bankers were paid $5,000 for their work?

20XX		($ in dollars)
December 31 Cash	795,000	
Bond Selling Expense	5,000	
Premium on Bonds Payable		100,000
Bonds Payable		700,000

The amount of cash that the investment bankers received from the bondholders was actually $800,000, but the investment bankers took $5,000 of this for their work of selling the bonds and actually remitted only the difference of $795,000 to the Sioux Tribe ($800,000 – $5,000 = $795,000). Thus, the Cash account was debited for $795,000 on the tribe's books, and this amount was used to build the casino.

The Bond Selling Expense was debited for $5,000 because the tribe received $5,000 of services from the investment bankers in selling the bonds through brokers all over the world. The long-term liability account entitled Bonds Payable was credited for $700,000, because bond certificates totaling this amount were mailed to the new bondholders everywhere. The First National Bank in Sioux Falls, South Dakota, was appointed trustee, and they kept the names and addresses of the bondholders and the dollar amounts that each bondholder held.

Finally, the liability account entitled Premium on Bonds Payable was credited for $100,000. This is the difference between the money the investment bankers received from the bondholders ($800,000) and the face value of the bonds ($700,000) ($800,000 – $700,000 = $100,000).

Around May 1, when the weather became warm enough, construction began on the casino, and it opened on July 4. Give the amortization entry and the interest payment entry at the end of the bonds' first year, on December 31.

20XX		($ in dollars)	
December 31	Bond Interest Expense	70,000	
	Cash		70,000
	Premium on Bonds Payable	10,000	
	Bond Interest Expense		10,000

These are 10-year bonds, sold on December 31, and maturing 10 years later, on December 31. The yearly interest is $70,000, because the face value of the bonds was $700,000 and the interest rate printed on the face of the bonds was 10% ($700,000 × 10% = $70,000).

Thus, the Bond Interest Expense was debited for $70,000, because the tribe received the use of the borrowed money ($700,000) during the entire year. Cash was credited for $70,000 because the trustee sent $70,000 out as interest checks to the bondholders worldwide on December 31, at the end of the first year.

The amount of $10,000 was amortized at the year's end. The liability account entitled Premium on Bonds Payable had been credited for $100,000 on December 31, and this amount is to be written off each year of the 10-year life of the bonds (1/10 × $100,000 = $10,000). So Premium on Bonds Payable is debited for $10,000 to begin to write off this premium of $100,000, and Bond Interest Expense is credited for $10,000. This credit to Bond Interest Expense effectively cuts down the amount of this expense account. Both bond premiums and bond discounts are amortized through Bond Interest Expense.

What entries will be made on the books of the tribe on December 31, the maturity date of the bonds?

20XX		($ in dollars)	
December 31	Bond Interest Expense	70,000	
	Cash		70,000
31	Premium on Bonds Payable	10,000	
	Bond Interest Expense		10,000
31	Bonds Payable	700,000	
	Cash		700,000

The yearly interest on the bonds is $70,000, because the face value of the bonds was $700,000 and the interest rate printed on the face of the bonds was 10% ($700,000 \times 10\% = 70,000$).

Bond Interest Expense was debited for $70,000, because the tribe received the use of the borrowed money ($700,000) during the entire year. Cash was credited for $70,000, because the trustee sent $70,000 out as interest checks to the bondholders worldwide on December 31, the maturity date of the bond.

The amount of $10,000 was amortized at the end of the year the bonds mature, as had been done at the year-ends of all the nine years preceding. The liability account entitled Premium on Bonds Payable had been credited for $100,000 on December 31, and this amount was to be written off each year for the 10-year life of the bonds ($1/10 \times \$100,000 = 10,000$). Premium on Bonds Payable is debited for $10,000 as the final write-off of this premium of $100,000, and Bond Interest Expense is credited for $10,000. This credit to Bond Interest Expense effectively cuts down the amount of this expense account. Both bond premiums and bond discounts are amortized through Bond Interest Expense.

After making the final amortization entry on December 31, the Premium on Bonds Payable account is written off and has a zero balance, as follows:

Premium on Bonds Payable

12/31/(Year 1)	10,000	12/31/20XX	100,000
12/31/(Year 2)	10,000		
12/31/(Year 3)	10,000		
12/31/(Year 4)	10,000		
12/31/(Year 5)	10,000		
12/31/(Year 6)	10,000		
12/31/(Year 7)	10,000		
12/31/(Year 8)	10.000		
12/31/(Year 9)	10,000		
12/31/(Year 10)	10,000		
	100,000		100,000

Let us say that the casino has done very well, and during the 10 years since it was built it has put aside enough money to pay off the bondholders. (Even if this had not been true, the bondholders are due their principal on maturity date, and if they do not get their money, they could force the casino into bankruptcy.)

The entry to pay the principal to the bondholders on the maturity date (in this case, December 31) debits Bonds Payable because the trustee bank receives all the bond certificates from all the bondholders in the total amount of $700,000. Cash is credited for $700,000 because the trustee bank at this time mails checks in this amount to the bondholders worldwide, and the debt is canceled.

15.8 Effective Interest Method

Previous examples have assumed the use of straight-line amortization of bond discount or premium. While simple to calculate, the Accounting Principles Board has ruled that the straight-line method should be used only if its use does not result in a material difference from the **effective interest method**. The weakness in the straight-line method is the fact that bond interest expense is the same each period, while the carrying value of the bond increases (if amortizing a discount) or decreases (if amortizing a premium) each period. In such cases, the **effective interest rate** for the bonds varies each period.

EXAMPLE 15.8.1

Face value of bonds = $1,000,000
Stated rate of interest = 0.12
Market rate of interest = 0.10
Life of bonds = 5 years

Semi-annual Interest Period	Carrying Value at Beginning of Period	Semi-annual Interest Expense	Semi-annual Interest Paid	Amortization of Premium	Unamortized Bond Premium at End of Period	Carrying Value at End of Period
0					77,217	1,077,217
1	1,077,217	53,861	60,000	6,139	71,078	1,071,078
2	1,071,078	53,554	60,000	6,446	64,632	1,064,632
3	1,064,632	53,232	60,000	6,768	57,864	1,057,864
4	1,057,864	52,893	60,000	7,107	50,757	1,050,757
5	1,050,757	52,538	60,000	7,462	43,295	1,043,295
6	1,043,295	52,165	60,000	7,835	35,460	1,035,460
7	1,035,460	51,773	60,000	8,227	27,233	1,027,233
8	1,027,233	51,362	60,000	8,638	18,594	1,018,594
9	1,018,594	50,930	60,000	9,070	9,524	1,009,524
10	1,009,524	50,476	60,000	9,524	0	1,000,000

Use of the effective interest method provides a steady rate of interest expense over the life of the bond. Interest expense each period is calculated as the **market rate** at the time of issue multiplied by the carrying value of the bonds (defined as face value minus unamortized discount or plus unamortized premium).

Like the previous example 15.7.1, in which the market rate of interest was 10% (compared to an actual interest of 12% on the bonds), assume bonds with a face value of $1,000,000 were sold for $1,077,217 creating a premium of $77,217 to be amortized over the life of the bonds (five years in this example). As shown in Example 15.8.1, semiannual interest expense is calculated based on the **market rate**, not the face rate. Carrying value at the end of the period is calculated as carrying value at the beginning of the period less premium amortization for that period. Note that the carrying value is equal to the face value at the end of semiannual period 10 (maturity of the bonds).

15.9 Retirement of Bonds Payable

Bonds may include provision for redemption at the issuer's option for a specified price. In any event, a corporation may redeem its bonds by purchasing them in the open market. If the purchase price is less than the carrying value, a gain is realized on retirement of the debt. If the price is higher than the carrying value, a loss is realized. For example, assume a corporation intends to purchase $500,000 of its own bonds at a price of 102 (102% of face value), or $510,000. Also assume the bonds have an unamortized premium of $5,000. The journal entry to record this transaction is shown in Example 15.9.1.

EXAMPLE 15.9.1

Date	Description	Debit	Credit
	Bonds Payable	500,000	
	Premium on Bonds Payable	5,000	
	Loss on Redemption of Bonds	5,000	
	Cash		510,000

Conversely, if the bonds can be purchased at 98 (98% of face value), or $490,000, the necessary journal entry is shown in Example 15.9.2.

EXAMPLE 15.9.2

Date	Description	Debit	Credit
	Bonds Payable Premium on Bonds Payable Gain on Redemption of Bonds Cash	500,000 5,000	 15,000 490,000

CHAPTER 16

Partnerships

16.1 Partnerships

16.1.1 Characteristics of Partnerships

As defined by the Uniform Partnership Act, a **partnership** is the combination of two or more people for the purpose of co-owning a business for profit. A partnership is basically a form of business between the sole proprietorship and a corporation.

There are a number of distinctive characteristics about partnerships. They include life of partnership, mutual agency, participation in income, as well as many others. We will look at a number of these in the following sections of this chapter.

16.1.2 Limited Life

The **life of a partnership** is limited. This is because a partnership is dissolved if any of the partners leave the firm. Possible reasons include death of a partner, withdrawal of a partner, and bankruptcy. A new partnership must also be started if a new partner is admitted.

16.1.3 Unlimited Liability

The usual form of a partnership is a **general partnership** where all partners have **unlimited liability**. That is, when a partnership is found to be insolvent, for whatever reason, the partners must contribute enough of their own personal assets to resolve the insolvency.

There is a form of partnership, **limited partnership**, where the limited partners are liable only to the level of investment in the partnership. However, all partnerships must have at least one general partner who will have unlimited liability.

16.1.4 Co-ownership of Property

All property in a partnership is owned by all partners. In the case of a dissolution, partners' claims to assets will be determined by their capital account balances.

16.1.5 Mutual Agency

Mutual agency means that any one partner can make a deal on behalf of the partnership. All other partners are then legally bound by such agreements.

16.1.6 Participation in Income

All partners have **participation of income** in the partnership. Losses and income are both distributed according to the partnership agreement. If the agreement is silent to the level of participation, then all partners share equally.

If the partnership agreement does not speak to the issue of losses, they are distributed on the same basis as income.

16.1.7 Nontaxable Entity

A partnership is a **nontaxable entity**. It is, therefore, not required to pay taxes. It does, nevertheless, file forms with the IRS that give details about partnership operations. These are called **information forms**.

16.2 Advantages and Disadvantages of a Partnership

A partnership is very **easy to set up** and begin. It also provides for **increased managerial skills** — those of the additional partners. It is easier to raise capital than in a sole proprietorship. Often the partners will be **taxed at a lower rate** than if the organization was a corporation and was a taxed entity.

At the same time, there can be major disadvantages to a partnership. These include most of the characteristics of a partnership; co-ownership of property, mutual agency, limited life, and unlimited liability. It is also usually more difficult to raise capital with a partnership than a corporation.

16.3 Accounting for Partnerships

Most of the accounting for partnerships will be identical with that for businesses run by individuals that we have discussed in earlier chapters. The chart of accounts can be identical except for **drawing** and **capital** accounts for each partner.

The main areas of differences in accounting for partnerships is formation, liquidation, and income distribution. We will look next at many of these unique accounting techniques.

16.4 Accounting for Investments in a Partnership

An individual entry will be made for each partner's contribution to the partnership. Any assets and liabilities turned over to the partnership will be debited and credited as they normally would. The partner's Capital account is credited for the net amount.

For instance, assume that two sole proprietorships involved in servicing microcomputers are going to be merged into a partnership. Each of the partners is to contribute various assets (including some cash from both) and liabilities to the partnership. The entry for recording the contributions of Jimmie Techie is illustrated in Example 16.4.1.

EXAMPLE 16.4.1

To Record the Investment of Jimmie Techie in the Partnership

The Sample Partnership
General Journal

Date	Acct. No.	Description	Debit	Credit
20XX Jan 15	1	Cash	2,000	
	3	Accounts Receivable	4,000	
	11	Merchandise Inventory	4,500	
	15	Office Equipment	3,500	
	4	Allowance for Doubtful Accounts Receivable		800
	23	Accounts Payable		2,500
	31	Jimmie Techie – Capital		10,700

Note that all the assets contributed by Jimmie equaled a total of $14,000. When taking into account the Allowance for Doubtful Accounts Receivable and the Accounts Payable, the net contribution for Jimmie will be $10,700:

$$\$2,000 + \$4,000 + \$4,500 + \$3,500 - \$800 - \$2,500 = \$10,700$$

A similar entry would be done for each partner admitted to the partnership. In each case, the partner would have a Capital account with his or her name.

16.5 Partnership Income Division

There are three basic ways to divide income of a partnership. One is to do a simple division of income (or loss) on the **basis of a percentage to each partner**. Another method would be to recognize **service of partners**. The last method would be to recognize the **service and investment of partners**. Of course, any combination of these three could also be used.

The important point to remember is that the division of income (or loss) is on the basis of the partnership agreement. If the agreement does not speak to the issue of division, then we assume it is an equal amount for each partner.

For purposes of demonstrating the various methods, assume the information in Table 16.5.1 was provided.

TABLE 16.5.1

THE SAMPLE PARTNERSHIP
Accounting Information on Partners

Explanation	Techie	Softie	Total
Capital Account	30,000	40,000	70,000
Salary	30,000	20,000	50,000

16.5.1 Straight Division of Income

The most common basis for splitting income and loss in a partnership is by a **percentage formula** laid out in the partnership agreement. If the agreement specified that income is to be split in equal amounts for each partner, and there was net income of $35,000, the journal entry to record the division of income would be as in Example 16.5.1.

EXAMPLE 16.5.1

To Record the Division of Yearly Income

The Sample Partnership
General Journal

Date	Acct. No.	Description	Debit	Credit
20XX Dec 31	40	Revenue and Expense Summary	35,000	
	31	Techie – Capital		17,500
	15	Softie – Capital		17,500

If there had been a loss instead of income, the Revenue and Expense Summary would have been credited for the amount of the loss, and each partner's Capital account would be debited for one-half of the loss.

16.5.2 Recognizing Service of Partners

Often, a partnership agreement will call for a certain salary level for one or more of the partners. Let's assume the salary levels as given in Table 16.5.1. Also assume that there was an income of $40,000 for the year. Finally, we will assume that the agreement calls for equal division of income and is silent with respect to losses. The calculations of each partner's share is given in Table 16.5.2.

TABLE 16.5.2

Techie Salary	$30,000
Softie Salary	20,000
Total Salary	50,000
Yearly Income	40,000
Excess of Allowances over Income	$10,000

This means that effectively, the partnership has a loss of $10,000 after salaries are paid. Each partner will then have a $5,000 loss. The income division is shown in Example 16.5.2.

EXAMPLE 16.5.2

To Record the Division of Yearly Income.

The Sample Partnership
General Journal

Date	Acct. No.	Description	Debit	Credit
20XX Dec 31	40	Revenue and Expense Summary	40,000	
	31	Techie – Capital		25,000
	15	Softie – Capital		15,000

If either of the partners had taken their money out in cash, the credit for their portion would have been to the Cash in Bank account.

Problem Solving Examples:

 Jim and Joe are partners who share profits and losses equally. Last year, their firm's net profit was $28,400. What is each partner's profit?

 A partnership is a business organization owned by two or more individuals. In a partnership, the profits and losses are shared in a manner to which all the partners have agreed. Here they are shared equally. Since there are two partners, each receives a 1/2 share of the profits or losses. In this case, each partner receives 1/2 of $28,400, or $14,200.

 Matthews and Green are partners in a delicatessen. They have agreed that Matthews should receive 60% of the profits or losses, and that Green should receive 40%. If the profits for a year were $10,200, what was each partner's share?

 Matthews received 60% of $10,200 = 0.60 × $10,200 = $6,120. Green received 40% of $10,200 = 0.40 × $10,200 = $4,080.

To check, add the two shares together, to see if the sum is the annual profit.

$ 6,120   (Matthew's share)
+   4,080   (Green's share)

$10,200   (annual profit)

 Frank Lee and Steve Barnes are partners. Barnes receives a weekly salary of $300, and 1/3 of the remaining net income. The other 2/3 of the remaining income goes to Lee. If the profits are $28,269, how much does each partner receive?

Barnes' annual salary = $300/week × 52 weeks = $15,600. The balance of the profits is $28,269 – $15,600 = $12,669. Barnes' share of this is 1/3 × $12,669 = $4,223, giving him a total of $15,600 + $4,223 = $19,823. Lee's share of the profits is 2/3 × $12,669 = $8,446. To check:

$$
\begin{array}{ll}
\$\ 8,446 & \text{(Lee's share)} \\
+\ \ 19,823 & \text{(Barnes' share)} \\
\hline
\$28,269 & \text{(total profits)}
\end{array}
$$

Schaeffer, Brown, and Smith invested $10,000, $15,000, and $25,000, respectively, in a partnership. They share profits and losses in proportion to their investments. Last year, their profit was $42,000. What was each partner's share of the profit?

Each partner's share, when profits and losses are shared proportionally, is computed by the formula:

$$\frac{\text{partner's investment}}{\text{total investment}} \times \text{profit or loss.}$$

Total investment = $10,000 + $15,000 + $25,000 = $50,000.

Schaeffer's share = $\dfrac{\$10,000}{\$50,000} \times \$42,000 = \dfrac{1}{5} \times \$42,000 = \$8,400.$

Brown's share = $\dfrac{\$15,000}{\$50,000} \times \$42,000 = \dfrac{3}{10} \times \$42,000 = \$12,600.$

Smith's share = $\dfrac{\$25,000}{\$50,000} \times \$42,000 = \dfrac{1}{2} \times \$42,000 = \$21,000.$

Mr. Joseph Miles and Mr. Gary Rose are partners in a manufacturing company. Mr. Miles receives a salary of $600 a month, and the balance of the profits is to be divided equally. During their first year, profits were $6,000. How much did each receive?

A Since there are 12 months in a year, Mr. Miles' salary for the year was $12 \times \$600 = \$7,200$. The profits are not large enough to pay his salary.

$7,200 (salary)
– $6,000 (profits)
—————————————
$1,200 (loss)

Since both partners share the balance of the profits and losses, they each lost $1,200 ÷ 2 = $600.

Thus, Mr. Miles received $7,200 (salary) – $800 (deficit) = $6,600. Mr. Rose lost $600.

16.5.3 Recognizing Service of Partners and Investment

Often, a partnership agreement will call for recognition of the partners' investment, in addition to the salary allowances. This is usually done on an agreed upon interest rate, which should be included in the partnership agreement.

Let's assume the salary levels as given in Table 16.5.1. Also, assume that there was an income of $90,000 for the year, and that the agreement calls for equal division of income and is silent with respect to losses. Finally, assume that the agreement calls for an interest rate of 20 percent on investment. Table 16.5.3 shows the calculation of each partner's share.

TABLE 16.5.3

Techie Salary	$30,000
Softie Salary	20,000
Techie Investment (30,000 × 20%)	6,000
Softie Investment (40,000 × 20%)	8,000
Total Allowances	$64,000
Yearly Income	90,000
Excess of Income over Allowances	$26,000

This means that effectively, the partnership has a gain of $26,000 after salaries and investments are allowed for. Each partner will then share equally, or have a $13,000 gain. Example 16.5.3 gives the journal entry for this division of income.

EXAMPLE 16.5.3

To Record the Division of Yearly Income

The Sample Partnership
General Journal

Date	Acct. No.	Description	Debit	Credit
20XX Dec. 31	40	Revenue and Expense Summary	90,000	
	31	Techie – Capital		49,000
	15	Softie – Capital		41,000

If either of the partners had taken their money out in cash, the credit for their portion would have been to the Cash in Bank account. The calculations for each partner's share is shown in Table 16.5.4 below.

TABLE 16.5.4

Explanation	Techie	Softie	Total
Salary	$30,000	$20,000	$50,000
Investment	6,000	8,000	14,000
Equal Parts Income	13,000	13,000	26,000
Totals	$49,000	$41,000	$90,000

As can be seen, the sum of the two totals for Techie and Softie is equal to the total income of $90,000.

16.6 Partnership Statements

At the end of an accounting period, a statement of the partners' equity can be prepared. This statement would show the beginning balance of each partner's Capital account and any withdrawals they may have had for the period. This statement would also show any additional investments for any of the partners.

It would, of course, include any entries for salaries, investments, and division of profits and losses. The final number for each partner would be the ending balance in that partner's Capital account.

16.7 Other Considerations

We have covered the most common accounting problems encountered when working with partnerships. There are a number of other considerations that are beyond the scope of this review. Some of these are the dissolution of a partnership, whether it be because of admission of new partners, death of a partner, or withdrawal of a partner.

A situation where one or more of the partners bring goodwill to the partnership is often encountered. Accounting for this can become very involved, and experts should be contacted.

Lastly, there is the very real possibility of a liquidation of a partnership. This could be for any of a number of reasons. There could be gains on the liquidation, or losses. It would also be possible to have deficiencies in capital in the case of losses on a liquidation. In this case, the personal assets of the partners would be at risk.

CHAPTER 17

Corporations

17.1 Corporation Defined

A corporation is a legal entity with an existence separate and distinct from its owners. A corporation has many of the powers accorded to individuals. A corporation can own property and enter into contracts in its own name. Since it has legal status, a corporation can sue and be sued. Corporations do not possess an individual's right to vote or hold public office.

17.2 Advantages of a Corporation

Corporations provide several advantages over other forms of business organizations. These are: (1) Stockholders have no personal liability for corporate debts. Creditors have a claim against the assets of a corporation, not those of its owners. The personal risk of each owner is limited to the amount of the investment; (2) Capital can be accumulated easily through the sale of shares of stock in the corporation. These shares represent ownership in the corporation and may be widely held; (3) Ownership interest in the corporation can be easily transferred. Shares of stock of a corporation may be bought and sold without dissolving or disrupting company operations; (4) A corporation is a legal entity with a perpetual existence; (5) Professional management can be hired and supervised by a board of directors elected by stockholders.

17.3 Disadvantages of a Corporation

Disadvantages of a corporate organization are: (1) Corporate income is subject to "double taxation." Operating income of a corporation is subject to federal (and sometimes state and municipal) income taxes. Income after taxes is then distributed to stockholders through dividends, which are then taxed again as income to individual stockholders; (2) Corporations are subject to a greater degree of state and federal regulation than other forms of business organization; (3) The separation of ownership and control may contribute to a situation where management may not act in the stockholders' best interests.

17.4 Par Value Stock

A corporation's articles of incorporation will provide for **authorization** for a specific number of shares of stock and the par value (if any) of that stock. Shares of stock that have been issued are said to be **outstanding**. The number of shares of stock outstanding must be less than or equal to the number of shares authorized. The **par value** represents the legal capital per share. Stockholders' equity cannot be reduced below this amount except by losses from business operations or legal action taken by a majority vote of shareholders. Dividends that would reduce stockholders' equity below the par value of outstanding shares are prohibited in many states.

When par value stock is **issued**, the Capital Stock account is credited with the par value of the stock issued, regardless of whether the issue price is above or below par. For example, assume that a corporation issues 50,000 shares of $10 par value stock at a price of $20 per share. Example 17.4.1 shows the journal entry necessary to record this transaction.

EXAMPLE 17.4.1

The Sample Company
General Journal

Date	Description	Debit	Credit
	Cash	1,000,000	
	Capital Stock		500,000
	Paid-in Capital in Excess		
	of Par		500,000

Paid-in capital represents the excess of the issue price over the par value of the stock.

Problem Solving Example:

Crimson Company issues 400 shares of $10 par common stock and 50 shares of $100 par preferred stock for a lump sum of $110,000. Prepare the journal entry for issuance when the market value of the common shares is $180 each and the market value of the preferred stock is $200 each.

Par Value Computations:

Common Stock   400 shares @ $10 Par = $4,000
Preferred Stock   50 shares @ $100 Par = $5,000

Market Value Computations:

Common Stock   400 shares @ $180 market = $72,000
Preferred Stock   50 shares @ $200 market = $10,000
    Total $82,000

$$\frac{72,000}{82,000} \times \$110,000 = \$96,585.37$$

$$\frac{10,000}{82,000} \times \$110,000 = \underline{\$13,414.63}$$

$$\overline{\$110,000.00}$$

Using the computations, we can make the following entry:

	$ (in dollars)	
Cash (Given)	110,000.00	
Common Stock (400 shares @ $10 Par)		4,000.00
Paid-in Capital, Common ($96,585.37 – $4,000)		92,585.37
Preferred Stock (50 shares @ $100)		5,000.00
Paid-in Capital, Preferred ($13,414.63 – $5,000)		8,414.63

17.5 No-Par Stock

In some instances, stock may be issued without a par value. In such cases, it is customary for the corporation to indicate a **stated value**, which for accounting purposes serves the same purpose as par value. Using the previous example, assume it is no-par stock with a stated value of $5 per share. Example 17.5.1 shows the entry necessary to record this transaction.

EXAMPLE 17.5.1

The Sample Company
General Journal

Date	Description	Debit	Credit
	Cash	1,000,000	
	Capital Stock		250,000
	Paid-in Capital in Excess		
	of Stated Value		750,000

Without a stated value, the entire $1,000,000 would be considered capital stock and subject to the limitations on withdrawal described previously.

Problem Solving Example:

During its first year of operations, the Jones Company had several transactions involving its common stock. (a) Prepare the journal entries assuming that the common stock has a par value of $10 per share. (b) Prepare the journal entries assuming that the common stock is no-par with a stated value of $1 per share.

January 20 — Issued 10,000 shares for cash at $10 per share.
March 5 — Issued 1,000 shares to attorneys in payment for their services. The bill was $30,000.
July 1 — Issued 30,000 shares for cash at $12 per share.
September 1 — Issued 60,000 shares for cash at $15 per share.

Part (a) $ (in dollars)

January 20	Cash (10,000 shares @ $10)	100,000	
	Common Stock (10,000 shares @ $10)		100,000
March 5	Organization Costs	30,000	
	Common Stock (1,000 shares @ $10)		10,000
	Paid-in Capital		20,000
July 1	Cash (30,000 shares @ $12)	360,000	
	Common Stock (30,000 shares @ $10)		300,000
	Paid-in Capital		60,000
September 1	Cash (60,000 shares @ $15)	900,000	
	Common Stock (60,000 shares @ $10)		600,000
	Paid-in Capital		300,000

Part (b) $ (in dollars)

January 20	Cash (10,000 shares @ $10)	100,000	
	Common Stock (10,000 shares @ $1)		10,000
	Paid-In Capital		90,000

March 5	Organization Costs	30,000	
	Common Stock (1,000 shares @ $1)		1,000
	Paid-in Capital		29,000
July 1	Cash (30,000 shares @ $12)	360,000	
	Common Stock (30,000 shares @ $1)		30,000
	Paid-in Capital		330,000
September 1	Cash (60,000 shares @ $15)	900,000	
	Common Stock (60,000 shares @ $1)		60,000
	Paid-in Capital		840,000

17.6 Common Stock

There are two general classes of stocks: common stock and preferred stock. **Common stock** is the most basic form of capital stock. Common stockholders have several basic rights. These include: (1) The right to be represented in the management of a corporation through election of a board of directors. Approval of major actions, such as a merger or acquisition, selection of independent auditors, or establishment of a stock option plan, may require a majority vote of stockholders. Stockholders receive one vote for each share of stock held in their name, although this vote may be transferred to another through proxy; (2) The right to share in the profits of a corporation by receiving dividends declared by the board of directors; (3) The right to share in the distribution of assets if the corporation is liquidated. Creditors have first claim on corporate assets in such a situation, followed by preferred shareholders, but any remaining assets are divided between common stockholders based on percentage of shares owned; (4) The right of first refusal if a corporation decides to increase the number of shares of stock outstanding. This allows stockholders to maintain their ownership percentage in the company. In practice, this right is often waived to provide management with flexibility in issuing new stock.

Problem Solving Example:

 Mr. Darnell purchased 20 shares of American Telephone and Telegraph common stock at $182.50 per share. Two months later, he sold the stock at $168.75 per share. What was his loss per share? Total loss?

A Since Mr. Darnell purchased the stock at $182.50 per share and sold it at $168.75 per share, his loss per share was

$182.50 – $168.75 = $13.75.

He had 20 shares, so his total loss was

20 × $13.75 = $275.00

17.7 Preferred Stock

Another class of capital stock is **preferred stock**. Here the basic rights of common stockholders are modified to some extent. The characteristics of preferred stock include: (1) Preferred stock usually provides for a stated dividend rate that must be paid before any dividends are distributed to common stockholders; (2) In the event of liquidation of the corporation, the claims of preferred stockholders have preference over those of common stockholders. These claims are, however, secondary to those of the corporation's creditors; (3) Preferred stock is usually callable at the option of the corporation; (4) Preferred stockholders have no voting power at stockholders' meetings.

Problem Solving Example:

 Jonesville Corporation was organized early in the year. It is authorized to issue 20,000 shares of 8%, $100 par preferred stock, and 500,000 shares of no-par common stock with a stated value of $1 per share. It has already issued all its authorized common stock.

March 10	Issued 10,000 shares of preferred stock for cash at $104.
April 10	Issued 200 shares of preferred stock for

land. The land is worth $80,000.

May 1   Issued 8,000 shares of preferred stock for cash at $115.

Nov. 10   Issued 1,000 shares of preferred stock for cash at $105.

Record the journal entries.

20XX			$ (in dollars)
March 10	Cash (10,000 shares @ $104)	1,040,000	
	Preferred Stock (10,000 shares @ $100)		1,000,000
	Paid-in Capital		40,000
April 10	Land (Fair Market Value)	80,000	
	Preferred Stock (200 shares @ $100)		20,000
	Paid-in Capital		60,000
May 1	Cash (8,000 shares @ $115)	920,000	
	Preferred Stock (8,000 shares @ $100)		800,000
	Paid-in Capital		120,000
November 10	Cash (1,000 shares @ $105)	105,000	
	Preferred Stock (1,000 shares @ $100)		100,000
	Paid-in Capital		5,000

17.8 Convertible Preferred Stock

A corporation may offer a conversion privilege which allows owners of preferred stock to convert their shares for common stock according to a specified formula. As an example, assume that a corporation's preferred stock is convertible in a ratio of three $10 par common shares for each share of $50 par preferred stock. Example 17.8.1 shows the entry needed to record conversion of 1,000 preferred shares to common stock.

EXAMPLE 17.8.1

Date	Description	Debit	Credit
	Convertible Preferred Stock Common Stock Paid-in Capital in Excess of Par Value	50,000	 30,000 20,000

In this example, 1,000 shares of $50 par value preferred stock were converted into 3,000 shares of $10 par value common stock. The $20,000 difference is paid-in capital in excess of par value.

17.9 Treasury Stock

When a company purchases its own stock, that stock is said to be placed in the treasury of the company as **treasury stock**. Treasury shares are not retired, but can be held indefinitely and reissued at any time. Shares held as treasury stock are not entitled to vote, receive dividends, or share in assets upon dissolution of the company. Treasury shares are not considered outstanding shares of stock for computation of earnings per share. Example 17.9.1 illustrates the purchase of 1,000 shares of Sample Company common stock by that company for $5,000.

EXAMPLE 17.9.1

**To Record the Purchase of 1,000 Shares of
Sample Company Stock at $5 Per Share**

Date	Description	Debit	Credit
	Treasury Stock Cash	5,000	 5,000

Example 17.9.2 illustrates the entry needed for reissuance of the stock at $6 per share.

EXAMPLE 17.9.2

To Record the Reissuance of 1,000 Shares of Treasury Stock, with Cost of $5 Per Share, at $6 Per Share

Date	Description	Debit	Credit
	Cash	6,000	
	Treasury Stock		5,000
	Paid-in-Capital from		
	Treasury Stock Sales		1,000

No gain or loss is recognized on treasury stock transactions. Treasury stock is shown on the balance sheet as a **deduction** from capital. The Common Stock account is unaffected by treasury stock transactions.

Problem Solving Example:

 The James Company originally sold its common stock at $35 per share. Later they repurchased 50,000 shares at the regular market price of $40 per share. The par value is $2 per share. Give the general journal entry to record the purchase of this treasury stock by the cost method.

	($ in dollars)
Treasury Stock	2,000,000
Cash	2,000,000

Several years after the James Company had purchased the 50,000 shares of its own treasury stock at $40 per share, they sold 20,000 shares of this treasury stock for the present market price of $51 per share.

Give the general journal entry for this transaction according to the cost method.

	($ in dollars)	
Cash (20,000 shares @ $51)	1,020,000	
Treasury Stock (20,000 shares @ $40)		800,000
Retained Earnings ($1,020,000 – $800,000)		220,000

Fifteen thousand shares of treasury stock were exchanged by the James Company for undeveloped land. Since the land had not been bought or sold for a number of years prior to that time, it was difficult to determine its value. At the time of the exchange, the common stock of the James Company was trading on the market at $50 per share. Record the journal entry using the cost method. The treasury stock had been purchased by the company at $45 per share.

	($ in dollars)	
Land (15,000 shares @ $50)	750,000	
Treasury Stock (15,000 shares @ $45)		675,000
Paid-in Capital ($750,000 – $675,000)		75,000

Quiz: Bonds – Corporations

1. Bonds are

   (A) debt instruments of a corporation similar to accounts payable.

   (B) debt instruments of a corporation similar to current assets.

   (C) debt instruments of a corporation similar to common stocks.

   (D) debt instruments of a corporation similar to notes payable.

2. When an investor receives a check for interest on his bond investment, what entry should he make on his/her books?

    (A) Debit Investment in Bonds and credit Cash

    (B) Debit Cash and credit Bonds Payable

    (C) Debit Cash and credit Bond Interest Income

    (D) Debit Notes Payable and credit Cash

3. A corporation borrowed $500,000 through the sale of bonds. They are 10% bonds. What entry will be made a half-year later when the corporation has to mail out interest checks to the bondholders?

    (A) Debit Bond Interest Expense $25,000 and credit Cash $25,000

    (B) Debit Bond Interest Expense $50,000 and credit Cash $50,000

    (C) Debit Cash $50,000 and credit Bond Interest Income $50,000

    (D) Debit Cash $25,000 and credit Bond Interest Income $25,000

4. Why are bonds sometimes sold above or below face value?

    (A) Because prices rise and fall on the stock market

    (B) Because of the detention

    (C) Because of the financial ability of the corporation issuing the bonds

    (D) None of these

5. The life of a partnership is

    (A) limited.   (C) periodic.

    (B) unlimited.   (D) None of the above

6. Which one of the following statements is true concerning corporations?

    (A) Corporations are legal entities separate from their owners.

    (B) Corporations are true partnerships.

    (C) Corporations do not sue single individuals.

    (D) Corporations usually become single proprietorships.

7. Which one of the following is NOT a disadvantage of a corporation?

    (A) Separation of management from ownership

    (B) Double taxation

    (C) Increased governmental regulation

    (D) Separate entity

8. Which one of the following is the best definition of no-par stock?

    (A) No-par stock has no value on the stock exchange.

    (B) No-par stock has no par value stated on the face of the stock certificate.

    (C) No-par stock has no preferred stock outstanding.

    (D) No-par stock is not traded on the stock exchange.

9. Which one of the following is NOT a benefit that common stockholders of a corporation enjoy?

    (A) Common stockholders take a direct part in the day-to-day management of a corporation.

    (B) If a corporation is liquidated, common stockholders will usually get a share of that distribution.

(C) Common stockholders have a right to receive dividends if these are declared by the board of directors.

(D) Common stockholders have the right to vote for the board of directors of the corporation.

10. All of the following are basic rights for common stockholders except

(A) the right to be represented in the management of a corporation through election of a board of directors.

(B) the right to hire and fire senior-level management of a corporation such as the president or CEO.

(C) the right to share in the profits of a corporation by receiving dividends declared by the board of directors.

(D) the right to share in the distribution of assets if the corporation is liquidated.

ANSWER KEY

1.	(D)	6.	(A)
2.	(C)	7.	(D)
3.	(A)	8.	(B)
4.	(C)	9.	(A)
5.	(A)	10.	(B)

CHAPTER 18

Corporations: Earnings and Dividends

18.1 Equity Section Structures

Although there is not an absolute correct structure for the order of accounts listed in the balance sheet equity section, there are a few guidelines that most preparers of financial statements follow. There is also a fair amount of diversity of terms that really mean the same thing. We will look at a few of these items in this chapter as well as consider dividends and **earnings per share** (EPS).

The major section in a balance sheet dealing with the investment of the owners is likely to be titled many different ways. Some of the more common are **Stockholders' Equity, Owners' Equity**, and **Shareholders' Equity**. In all three of those titles, the word "equity" might very well be replaced with "investment."

Normally the various classes of stock (Common, Preferred, etc.) and the amounts of each are listed first. Then all additional premiums or discounts on stock transactions are listed. These are then followed by the remaining paid-in capital accounts, which are often lumped into one title on the balance sheet.

18.2 Corporate Income Taxes

Corporations differ from sole proprietorships and partnerships in that they are a separate legal entity. As such they are subject to income taxes of the federal government as well as states and municipalities. The usual procedure for paying taxes is to pay a quarterly estimate which should be equal to one-fourth of the estimated total for the year.

Assume, for instance, that the Sample Company estimated their taxes for the year to be $200,000. The entry for each of the first three quarters would be as in Example 18.2.1.

EXAMPLE 18.2.1

To Record First Quarter Federal Income Tax

The Sample Company
General Journal

Date	Acct. No.	Description	Debit	Credit
20XX Mar 31	39	Income Tax	50,000	
	1	Cash		50,000

At the end of the year, any adjustment needed to bring the income tax to the correct total would have to be made. Assume for instance that in the example above, that at the end of the year, the Sample Company discovered upon doing their tax returns that they really only owed $185,000. The adjusting entry would be as in Example 18.2.2.

EXAMPLE 18.2.2

To Record Adjustment to Yearly Income Taxes

The Sample Company
General Journal

Date	Acct. No.	Description	Debit	Credit
20XX Dec. 31	2	Accounts Receivable: Income Tax	15,000	
	39	Income Tax		15,000

If instead of less taxes, the company had more than the amount paid in the four quarters, the entry would have included an additional debit to Income Tax and a credit to a liability account called **Income Tax Payable**.

When working with income taxes, there are two times when the income tax paid will differ from what normally would be determined from the accounts. The first of these is **permanent differences**. In this case, the tax law provides for special consideration of classes of expenses or revenues. These differences are no problem for financial accounting as the amount reported on the financial statements will be the amount determined using the tax laws.

A more involved process evolves when the difference is a **timing difference**. In this case, the amount reported on the financial statements will be different than the amount paid to the taxing authority during the period. Usually the amount paid is less than the amount reported on the financial statements. This difference will usually be reversed in later years.

There are usually one of two reasons that such differences develop. In many cases, GAAP allows for one method of accounting to be used for tax purposes and another for financial statement purposes. This is the most likely reason for a timing difference. The other would be when the company uses an accounting technique that is not generally accepted. In that case the procedure would normally not be acceptable for calculating income tax liability.

Problem Solving Example:

 On December 31, the John Brown Construction Company estimates its income tax liability to the federal government for the year is $23,000.

What entry will it make on its books at this time?

20XX		($ in dollars)
December 31 Income Tax Expense	23,000	
Income Tax Payable		23,000

Income Tax Expense is an expense of a corporation, but not of a partnership or single proprietorship. Partnerships and single proprietorships, as such, pay no income taxes, but these are paid through the personal income taxes of the partners or of the proprietor. Assume that the John Brown Construction Company is a corporation. The Income Tax Expense is the next-to-last line in a corporation's Income Statement and is the last deduction prior to the Net Income—the last line of the Income Statement. Income Tax Payable is credited for $23,000, and it is a current liability account which will be closed out a couple of months later when the corporation pays its income tax. Of course, the corporation could pay an estimated tax earlier than this to avoid extra interest or penalties from the government for not paying its taxes earlier.

18.3 Deferred Income Taxes

When timing differences occur, there will be a deferral of income taxes to a later period. This will usually entail setting up an account called **Deferred Income Taxes Payable** and crediting it for the difference between current taxes to be paid and the amount shown on the financial statements as income tax expense. In later periods, the deferral should be reduced.

To illustrate, let us assume that all the information in Table 18.3.1 was provided on the Sample Company.

TABLE 18.3.1

THE SAMPLE COMPANY
Selected Data

Taxable income per company financial records	$500,000	
Income tax calculated on $500,000 at 40%		$200,000
Taxable income per company tax return	$300,000	
Income tax based on $300,000 at 40%		$120,000
Income tax to be deferred to later years		$ 80,000

Example 18.3.1 gives the journal entry to formally recognize this timing difference.

EXAMPLE 18.3.1

To Recognize Income Tax Expense for the Year and Set Up Deferral

The Sample Company
General Journal

Date	Acct. No.	Description	Debit	Credit
20XX Dec. 31	39	Income Tax	200,000	
	65	Income Tax Payable		120,000
	43	Deferred Income Tax		
		Payable		80,000

The income tax payable will be a current liability. The deferred income tax payable may be in two groupings. That amount that will be due in one year will be a current liability. The rest will go after long-term liabilities on the balance sheet. In later years the reverse situation should come about. At that point an entry will need to be made to reduce the deferred income tax account. Assume that in a year, $40,000 of the deferred income tax payable was to be paid. The entry for this reduction is shown in Example 18.3.2.

EXAMPLE 18.3.2

To Reclassify Deferred Taxes Payable to a Current Account

The Sample Company
General Journal

Date	Acct. No.	Description	Debit	Credit
20XX Dec 31	43	Deferred Income Tax Payable	40,000	
	65	Income Tax Payable		40,000

Problem Solving Example:

On December 31, the John Brown Construction Company estimates its income tax liability to the federal government for the year is $23,000. It debits Income Tax Expense and credits Income Tax Payable for $23,000 on that date. On January 15, after completing its income tax forms in more detail, it determines that it only owes the government $22,500, so it sends in the forms and a check for $22,500 on that date.

What entry will the John Brown Construction Company make on its books?

A

20XX		($ in dollars)	
January 15	Income Tax Payable	23,000	
	Deferred Tax Liability		500
	Cash		22,500

Income Tax Payable is debited for $23,000 to close out this account. Cash is credited to show that $22,500 was sent to the government. The difference of $500 is credited to Deferred Tax Liability, a long-term liability account which may or may not need to be paid in the future.

18.4 Unusual Items

In attempting to give as much information as possible in the financial statements of a company, accountants have developed four categories of unusual items that require special reporting.

The first of these is **prior period adjustments**. These are changes made in net income from earlier periods. These will appear as adjustments to the beginning retained earnings balance of the period the adjustment is made. This will be done on the retained earnings statement. The adjustment will be stated net of related income tax effect. The tax effect should be stated in the adjustment.

Discontinued operations is the second category that deserves special attention. When an organization sells, closes, or in some other way disposes of a segment of the business, a gain or loss will normally result. To be sure these are not mixed in with operations that will be ongoing, this item will be shown as a **gain or loss from discontinued operations** net of related taxes. This will be done on the income statement. Footnotes to the financial statements should disclose the details of the segment that was discontinued.

Gains or losses that occur as a result of transactions that are both unusual in nature and happen infrequently are termed **extraordinary**

items. As a result of the strict guidelines established, very few items meet both criteria. Those that do will be shown on the income statement, net of related tax effect.

It is not unusual for a company to adopt a generally accepted accounting principle different from one it had been using. This will likely cause an effect on prior period income figures as well as for the current period. This adjustment will be called **change in accounting principle** and be shown on the income statement in two parts. The cumulative effect of the change on prior periods net income will be shown as a special item. The second step will be to show the effect on net income for the current period.

18.5 Earnings Per Share

As a result of difference in size of companies, it is difficult to compare multiple companies in a specific industry or region. One way to assist in this comparison is to calculate the **earnings per share of common stock** (EPS). This is the number that is most often reported in the financial press and in the news. By reducing the earnings to a number per share of common stock, comparisons are easier to make.

If there is just common stock outstanding, the EPS can be arrived at by dividing net income by the number of shares of stock outstanding. If preferred stock also exists, the amount of preferred dividends required would be subtracted from net income before dividing by the number of shares outstanding.

It is normal to show the EPS for all of the categories of unusual items discussed earlier in this chapter as separate items. If other classes of stock exist or bonds exist that could be converted into common stock, the net income would need to be **diluted** to show the effect of these other potential shares. Calculations for fully diluted earnings per share can be extremely complicated and are beyond the scope of this review.

18.6 Retained Earnings Appropriations

When a board of directors of a company wants to limit the amount of dividends paid from retained earnings, they can **appropriate** or

reserve the amount in a separate classification on the balance sheet. This may be done as a result of a contract, state law, or some other situation that requires the appropriation. The appropriated portion would appear above the unappropriated in the retained earnings section of the balance sheet.

Example 18.6.1 shows the two journal entries required to appropriate retained earnings and to eliminate the appropriation a year later.

EXAMPLE 18.6.1

To Appropriate Retained Earnings for Bond Redemption.

The Sample Company
General Journal

Date	Acct. No.	Description	Debit	Credit
Year 1 Dec 31	31	Retained Earnings	200,000	
	32	Appropriated Retained Earnings–Bonds		200,000

To Eliminate the Appropriation for Retained Earnings for Bonds

Date	Acct. No.	Description	Debit	Credit
Year 2 Dec 31	32	Appropriated Retained Earnings–Bonds	200,000	
	31	Retained Earnings		200,000

An appropriation of retained earnings **does not** mean there is actually that amount of money set aside. If money **is** set aside as cash or securities, the appropriation is said to be **funded**.

Appropriations need not be formalized in the financial statements in the form of journal entries. They can just be noted in footnotes that contain the details of the appropriation.

18.7 Cash Dividends

Cash dividends are a distribution of corporate earnings to the stock-holders in the form of cash. This is the most usual form of dividends. There are three important dates involved with cash dividends. They are:

1. Date of declaration—this is the date the formal announcement of a cash dividend was made.

2. Date of record—people owning shares on this date will receive the cash dividend.

3. Date of payment—this is the day the actual cash dividend is paid.

Cash dividends are usually declared as a percent of par or stated value. If a company had 20,000 shares of stock at a par value of $10, the entry for a 5% cash dividend would be:

$$20,000 \times \$10 \times 0.05 = \$10,000$$

Example 18.7.1 gives the journal entries for declaration of the dividend and then the payment of the dividend. The date of declaration was November 30. The date of payment was February 10 of the following year.

EXAMPLE 18.7.1

To Record the Declaration of a 5% Cash Dividend

The Sample Company
General Journal

Date	Acct. No.	Description	Debit	Credit
20XX Nov 30	93	Cash Dividends	10,000	
		Cash Dividends Payable		
	62			10,000

To Record Payment of Cash Dividend Declared
on November 30

20XX Feb 10	62	Cash Dividends Payable	10,000	
	1	Cash		10,000

The cash dividends will be closed to retained earnings at the end of the accounting period.

Problem Solving Example:

 The Swift Eagle Corporation has 1,000,000 shares of common stock outstanding. On December 25, the board voted a $1 per share cash dividend to stockholders of record on January 10 and payable on January 20. (a) What are the entries if the dividend represents a distribution of earnings? (b) What are the entries if the dividend represents a distribution of treasury stock? (c) What are the entries if the distribution is a liquidating dividend?

Part (a)

20XX			$ (in dollars)	
December 25	Retained Earnings	1,000,000	
	Dividends Payable		1,000,000

20XX				
January 10	(No entry)		
20	Dividends Payable	1,000,000	
	Cash		1,000,000

On the date of declaration the Retained Earnings account is debited because dividends are taken out of retained earnings. The Retained

Earnings account usually has a credit balance, so a debit to Retained Earnings cuts down the value of this account, in this case by the amount of the dividend. As soon as the dividend is declared by the board, the corporation owes the $1,000,000 to the stockholders; so the current liability account Dividends Payable is credited for the $1,000,000. On January 20, the dividend is mailed to the stockholders, so Cash is credited for $1,000,000. Dividends Payable is debited for $1,000,000 to close out this temporary account.

Part (b)

20XX		$ (in dollars)	
December 25	Retained Earnings	1,000,000	
	Stock Dividends Distributable		1,000,000

20XX			
January 10	(No entry)		
20	Stock Dividends Distributable	1,000,000	
	Treasury Stock		1,000,000

On the date of declaration the Retained Earnings account is debited because dividends are taken out of retained earnings. Since this is a stock dividend (rather than a cash dividend), the account Stock Dividends Distributable is credited. Stock Dividends Distributable is an owner's equity account, and this account will appear on the balance sheet at the end of the year. Let us assume that when the treasury stock was originally purchased by the corporation, it was purchased for $1 per share. Since the board has voted a dividend of $1 per share, on the date of the stock distribution (in this case January 20) Treasury Stock will be credited for $1,000,000 (1,000,000 shares @ $1 per share). At the same time, the account Stock Dividends Distributable will be debited for $1,000,000 to close out the account.

Part (c)

20XX		$ (in dollars)	
December 25	Paid-in Capital	1,000,000	
	Dividends Payable		1,000,000

20XX			
January 10	(No entry)		
20	Dividends Payable	1,000,000	
	Cash		1,000,000

Liquidating dividends are not taken out of retained earnings, since these dividends come from paid-in capital, not from past profits. These dividends come from money previously paid in by the stockholders themselves; so Paid-in Capital is debited on the date of declaration. Since liquidating dividend is a cash dividend, and the money is owed by the corporation to the stockholders on the date of declaration, the current liability account Dividends Payable is credited.

On January 10, the date of record, the computer prints out the names, addresses, and number of shares owned by all the stockholders of record on that date, so that this information can be used to determine the amount of cash dividend to send to each individual shareholder. However, these are changes in subsidiary records, so no entry is made in the general journal on this date.

On January 20, the date that the dividend checks are sent out to the stockholders, Cash is credited for $1,000,000 to show the dividend checks being sent out. Dividends Payable is debited to cancel this current liability account, since the debt to the stockholders is canceled by the dividend payment.

18.8 Stock Dividends

When a corporation is not able to (or does not want to) pay cash dividends, they may issue a **stock dividend**. This is usually done when they have losses or want to retain funds for expansion. Assuming the dividend was a stock dividend rather than cash, the entry will be as in Example 18.8.1. The debit to Stock Dividends will be closed to Retained Earnings.

EXAMPLE 18.8.1

To Record the Declaration of a 5% Stock Dividend

The Sample Company
General Journal

Date	Acct. No.	Description	Debit	Credit
20XX Nov 30	94	Stock Dividends	10,000	
	63	Stock Dividends Distributable		10,000

To Record Payment of A Stock Dividend Declared on November 30

20XX Feb 10	63	Stock Dividends Distributable	10,000	
	38	Common Stock		10,000

Problem Solving Examples:

Q The James Brooks Company Board of Directors voted to issue a stock dividend of $50,000 to its stockholders. What entry would be made on the date that the Board declared the stock dividend? What entry would be made on the date that the shares of stock were mailed to the stockholders?

	Debit	Credit
Stock Dividends	50,000	
Stock Dividends Distributable		50,000
Stock Dividends Distributable	50,000	
Common Stock		50,000

Q The Jordan Company is making good profits and recording these in its Retained Earnings account. However, it is a growing company and uses most of its extra cash for expansion. The board of directors wishes to show the stockholders how well the company is doing, but it does not have the extra cash to pay a cash dividend. Therefore, it decides to issue a stock dividend. The par value of the outstanding stock is $5 per share, and the market value of the stock is $10 per share. There are at present 100,000 shares of stock outstanding, so the board declares a 5% stock dividend. How will this be recorded on the books (a) at the date of declaration, (b) at the date of record, and (c) at the date of payment?

A

20XX			$ (in dollars)
January 5	Retained Earnings	50,000	
	Stock Dividends Distributable		25,000
	Paid-in Capital		25,000
18	(No entry on date of declaration)		
25	Stock Dividends Distributable	25,000	
	Common Stock		25,000

On the date of declaration, January 18, Retained Earnings is debited for $50,000. (There are 100,000 shares of common stock outstanding times a 5% stock dividend declared or 5,000 shares to be issued as a stock dividend.) The market price of the stock at the time is $10 per share (5,000 shares @ $10 = $50,000). Stock Dividends Distributable is credited for $25,000. This is an owner's equity account and is credited for the par value of the stock (5,000 shares to be issued as a stock dividend times $5 par value per share). The remaining $25,000 is credited to Paid-in Capital, which can only be paid to stockholders eventually if a liquidating dividend is declared.

On January 18, the date of declaration, no entries are made in the general journal, because no accounts in the ledger change value at this time.

On January 25, the date the stock certificates are mailed out to the stockholders, Stock Dividends Distributable is debited for $25,000 to close out this account, showing the stock has been distributed. Common Stock is credited for $25,000, the total par value of the stock being mailed out, to show the stock certificates have left the company and are being sent to the stockholders.

Q The books of the Harrison Company have been examined and the following information has been found: treasury Stock has been purchased for $10,000; common stock with a par value of $50,000 has been sold; all the net incomes over the years that the corporation has been in existence amount to $130,000; the appropriation for contingencies is $5,000; the stock dividends distributed amount to $20,000; and the cash dividends distributed amount to $18,000. Treasury stock has been sold at a gain of $3,000. What is the balance of the Retained Earnings account?

A

Retained Earnings

(Appropriation for		(Net incomes)	130,000
Contingencies)	5,000		
(Stock Dividends declared)	20,000		
(Cash Dividends declared)	18 000		
	43,000		
		(Balance)	87,000

The purchase of treasury stock does not involve the Retained Earnings account. The sale of common stock also does not involve the Retained Earnings account. An appropriation takes money out of Retained Earnings and puts it in an Appropriations account. Declarations of cash dividends and stock dividends also take money out of the Retained Earnings account. The sale of treasury stock at a gain does not involve retained earnings.

18.9 Stock Splits

Stock splits occur when a company issues a proportionate number of additional shares to the stockholders. This will have the effect of reducing the par or stated value per share. It is usually done to reduce the market price per share to encourage more small investors to buy company shares.

The value of each stockholder's investment will remain the same, only the number of shares will change. There is no formal entry in the company's books. However, the new financial statements should reflect the new number of shares outstanding.

Problem Solving Example:

Q The Jones Company has 50,000 shares of its common stock outstanding with a par value of $1 per share (50,000 @ $1 = $50,000 total par value of the common stock). Because the corporation has been doing well financially, its stock has risen to heights previously undreamed of by the owners. As a result of this, however, very few shares are now being bought or sold. The board of directors believes that this is true because the price of the stock is high. In order to lower the price of the stock, the board has voted a 2-for-1 stock split, effective December 31. What entry should be made on the corporate books as of that date?

20XX

December 31 (Two-for-one stock split of common stock of the Jones Company. Prior to the stock split, there were 50,000 shares of stock outstanding at $1 par, for a total of $50,000 par value of common stock. Following the 2-for-1 stock split, there are now 100,000 shares of stock outstanding at $.50 par, for a total of $50,000 par value of common stock.)

It will be noted that the only entry made for a stock split is merely an explanation in parentheses. There is no formal entry made, because nothing is to be posted from the journal to the ledger. The accounts in the ledger remain with the same dollar values as previous. The only change due to the stock split is in the number of shares outstanding and in the par value per share.

18.10 Effect of Treasury Stock

If treasury stock exists, cash dividends will not be paid on the treasury stock. In the case of stock dividends, the dividend can be paid on shares outstanding, or shares issued. Both are acceptable. Treasury stock may be included in a stock split.

Quiz: Corporations: Earnings and Dividends

1. What is the difference between stockholders' equity, owners' equity, and shareholders' equity?

   (A) There is no difference. They all mean the same thing.

   (B) Stockholders' equity shows what the stockholders have in the business, and this is different from what the owners have in the business.

(C)　Shareholders' equity shows what the shareholders have in the business, and this is different from what the stockholders have in the business.

(D)　None of these.

2.　How do corporate accountants set up the Equity section of the Balance Sheet?

(A)　Common Stock, Preferred Stock, Premiums and Discounts if any, Total Paid-in Capital, Retained earnings.

(B)　Retained Earnings, Total Paid-in Capital, Premiums and/or Discounts, Preferred Stock, Paid-in Capital, Retained Earnings

(C)　Preferred Stock, Common Stock, Paid-in Capital, Retained Earnings

(D)　Earned Surplus, Retained Earnings, Premiums or Discounts, Total Paid-in Capital, Common Stock, Preferred Stock

3.　We estimate that the corporation owes the federal government $50,000, so we send the government a check for that amount. What entry do we make on the books of the corporation?

(A)　Debit Income Tax Asset $50,000 and credit Cash $50,000

(B)　Debit Cash $50,000 and credit Revenue $50,000

(C)　Debit Owners' Equity $50,000 and credit Dividends Payable $50,000

(D)　Debit Income Tax Expense $50,000 and credit Cash $50,000

4.　Why are some income taxes deferred until later periods?

(A)　Poor accounting and bookkeeping methods

(B)　Lack of facts

    (C)   Tax return liabilities are often less than tax liabilities computed for the corporation's books.

    (D)   Shady tax laws

5.   Which one of the following is NOT considered an "unusual item" on a corporate financial statement?

    (A)   Prior period adjustments

    (B)   Gain or loss from discontinued operations

    (C)   Retained earnings

    (D)   Extraordinary items that are unusual and infrequent

6.   How does one calculate earnings per share on common stock of a corporation that has issued no preferred stock?

    (A)   Look at government documents

    (B)   Divide sales by the number of common shares outstanding

    (C)   Divide gross profit by the number of common shares outstanding

    (D)   Divide net income by the number of common shares outstanding

7.   Why would a corporation's board of directors set aside (or appropriate) some of the dividends from the Retained Earnings account?

    (A)   So that this amount of money cannot be paid out as dividends to stockholders

    (B)   So that this amount of money cannot be appropriated by creditors

    (C)   To hide this money from possible corporate raiders

    (D)   None of these.

8. Which of the following is NOT one of the three important dates regarding a corporation's payment of dividends?

    (A) Date of liquidation   (C) Date of declaration

    (B) Date of payment   (D) Date of record

9. Which of the following is NOT a reason why corporations sometimes issue stock dividends rather than cash dividends?

    (A) The corporation is short of money.

    (B) The corporation has a surplus of cash.

    (C) The corporation wants to hold back extra money in order to expand the company.

    (D) The corporation board of directors wishes to invest corporate money in other corporations.

10. Are dividends paid on treasury stock?

    (A) Yes   (C) Sometimes

    (B) No   (D) None of these

ANSWER KEY

1.	(A)	6.	(D)
2.	(A)	7.	(A)
3.	(D)	8.	(A)
4.	(C)	9.	(B)
5.	(C)	10.	(B)

CHAPTER 19

Consolidations

19.1 Parent and Subsidiary Company Relationships

A corporation that owns more than 50% of the common stock of another corporation is known as a **parent company**. A company that is majority owned by another corporation is known as a **subsidiary**. The parent controls election of the subsidiary's board of directors (and therefore all company activities) through exercise of voting rights associated with its majority stock ownership. In effect, parent and subsidiary companies operate as one entity controlled by directors of the parent company.

Since a parent company and its subsidiaries are separate legal entities, separate financial statements are prepared for each company. In the separate financial statements for the parent company, subsidiaries appear only as investments. In recognition of the fact that parent and subsidiaries function as one entity, **consolidated** financial statements are also prepared. In consolidated financial statements, assets, liabilities, revenue, and expenses of two or more separate corporations are combined in a single set of financial statements.

19.2 Intercompany Eliminations

To accurately reflect the financial position of a parent and its subsidiaries on a consolidated basis, it is necessary to eliminate the effects of **intercompany transactions**. These transactions may include intercompany loans, property leases, or sales of inventory or equipment. Viewing a parent and its subsidiaries as one entity, those assets or liabilities that are simply transfers from one part of the entity to another should be eliminated.

19.3 Preparation of Consolidated Financial Statements

19.3.1 Purchase Method

One method of accounting for acquisition of one company by another is the **purchase method**. This method is used when the stock of a subsidiary is acquired by cash payment. It is also used when a parent issues bonds payable or capital stock to acquire the stock of a subsidiary company.

In preparing consolidated financial statements, a worksheet is used to determine the necessary elimination entries. These entries are used for this purpose only. They are not recorded in the financial records of the parent or its subsidiaries. As shown in Example 19.3.1, the worksheet contains the asset and liability account balances for the parent and each subsidiary. Debit and credit columns are provided for intercompany eliminations and a column is provided for the **consolidated** asset and liability account balances. In this example, assume that Smith Corporation purchased 100% of the stock of Jones Corporation for $100,000 cash on January 1. On that same date, Smith Corporation lends $50,000 to Jones Corporation for working capital purposes. Jones Corporation executes a note payable to Smith Corporation to evidence the loan.

EXAMPLE 19.3.1

SMITH CORPORATION AND SUBSIDIARY
Worksheet for Consolidated Balance Sheet
January 1 (Date of Acquisition)
(in 000's)

	Smith Corp.	Jones Corp.	Intercompany Eliminations Debit	Intercompany Eliminations Credit	Cons. Bal. Sheet
Cash	60	40			100
Receivables:					
Notes	50			50	
Accounts (net)	45	32			77
Inventories	75	50			125
Investment in Jones					
Corporation	100			100	
Property, Plant, and					
Equipment	55	50			105
Total	385	172		150	407
Notes Payable		50	50		
Accounts Payable	33	22			55
Capital Stock:					
Smith Corporation	200				200
Jones Corporation		40	40		
Retained Earnings:					
Smith Corporation	152				152
Jones Corporation		60	60		
Total	385	172	150		407

Intercompany eliminations include elimination of (1) intercompany debt, (2) intercompany stock ownership, and (3) intercompany revenue and expenses. In the preceding example, the loan from the parent Smith Corporation to its subsidiary (Jones Corporation) is eliminated from the consolidated balance sheet since the effect would be to artificially inflate the consolidated assets and liabilities. The $100,000 purchase price of Jones Corporation (carried as an investment on Smith's books and as capital stock and retained earnings for Jones) is eliminated for the same reason. The consolidated balance sheet for Smith Corporation and its subsidiary can now be prepared from the figures shown in the worksheet.

Problem Solving Examples:

 Looking at the Worksheet for Consolidated Balance Sheet in Example 19.3.1, why is there no figure for Notes Receivable in the right column?

 The $50 note receivable for the Smith Corporation is offset by the $50 note payable of the Jones Corporation.

 Looking at the Worksheet for Consolidated Balance Sheet in Example 19.3.1, how do they derive the $55 figure in the rightmost column?

 By adding the $33 accounts payable of the Smith Corporation and the $22 accounts payable of the Jones Corporation.

19.4 Purchase Price Above Book Value

There may be occasions when a parent will pay more for the stock of a subsidiary company than is reflected in the stockholders' equity accounts. A parent company may feel that the subsidiary's assets are undervalued or the prospects for future growth or profits may justify a higher purchase price. This excess of purchase price over stockholders' equity is known as **goodwill**. Using the previous example, assume that Smith Corporation pays $150,000 cash for Jones Corporation although the stockholders' equity of Jones Corporation is only $100,000. The eliminations needed in this situation are shown in Example 19.4.1.

Note that again the entire amount of Smith's investment in Jones is eliminated by crediting that account for $150,000. Debits are to Goodwill ($50,000), Jones Corporation Capital Stock ($40,000), and Jones Corporation Retained Earnings ($60,000).

EXAMPLE 19.4.1

SMITH CORPORATION AND SUBSIDIARY
Work Sheet for Consolidated Balance Sheet
January 1 (Date of Acquisition)
(in 000's)

	Smith Corp.	Jones Corp.	Intercompany Eliminations Debit	Intercompany Eliminations Credit	Cons. Bal. Sheet
Cash	60	40			100
Receivables:					
Notes	50			50	
Accounts (net)	45	32			77
Inventories	75	50			125
Investment in Jones					
Corporation	150			150	
Goodwill			50		50
Property, Plant, and					
Equipment	55	50			105
Total	435	172	50	200	457
Notes Payable		50	50		
Accounts Payable	33	22			55
Capital Stock:					
Smith Corporation	200				200
Jones Corporation		40	40		
Retained Earnings:					
Smith Corporation	202				202
Jones Corporation		60	60		
Total	435	172	150		457

EXAMPLE 19.5.1

SMITH CORPORATION AND SUBSIDIARY
Work Sheet for Consolidated Balance Sheet
January 1 (Date of Acquisition)
(in 000's)

	Smith Corp.	Jones Corp.	Intercompany Eliminations Debit	Intercompany Eliminations Credit	Cons. Bal. Sheet
Cash	160	40			100
Receivables:					
Notes	50			50	
Accounts (net)	45	32			77
Inventories	75	50			125
Investment in Jones					
Corporation	75			75	
Property, Plant, and					
Equipment	55	50			105
Total	360	172		125	407
Notes Payable		50	50		
Accounts Payable	33	22			55
Capital Stock:					
Smith Corporation	200				200
Jones Corporation		40	30[1]		
			10[2]		
Retained Earnings:					
Smith Corporation	127				127
Jones Corporation		60	45[1]		
			15[2]		
Minority Interest				25	25
Total	360	172	150	25	407

[1] To eliminate Smith Corporation's 75% interest.
[2] To classify remaining 25% as minority interest.

19.5 Purchase of Less Than 100 Percent of Subsidiary

If a parent company purchases less than 100 percent (but still a majority) of the stock of a subsidiary, a **minority interest** will appear on the consolidated balance sheet. This minority interest represents the stock held by stockholders other than the parent company. In this situation, only the portion of the subsidiary's stockholder equity owned by the parent is eliminated. Again using the previous example, assume that Smith Corporation purchases 75 percent of Jones Corporation for $75,000. Stockholders' equity for Jones Corporation is $100,000. The eliminations necessary are shown in Example 19.5.1.

19.6 Consolidated Income Statement

A consolidated income statement, like the consolidated balance sheet, is prepared by combining revenue and expense accounts for the parent and subsidiary companies. Items to be eliminated during consolidation of income statements include: (1) intercompany sales; (2) cost of goods sold resulting from intercompany sales; (3) interest expense on intercompany loans; (4) interest revenue from intercompany loans; (5) rent or income received for services to affiliated companies; and (6) rent or expenses paid for services from affiliated companies.

19.7 Pooling of Interest Method

If the stock of a subsidiary is acquired in exchange for shares of the parent company's stock, and if certain other criteria are met, a business combination may be treated as a **pooling of interest**. In this situation, stockholders of the subsidiary become stockholders of the parent company. The stockholders of the two companies are said to have pooled their interests, rather than one party selling out to the other. Since there is no real purchase or sale, the assets of the subsidiary are not revalued and no goodwill is recorded. Another difference between this method and the purchase method is that under the pooling of interest method, earnings of the subsidiary for the entire year in which the affiliation occurs are included in the consolidated income statement. Under the purchase method, earnings of the subsidiary are combined with those of the parent only from the date of acquisition.

CHAPTER 20

Statement of Cash Flows

20.1 Purpose of Statement of Cash Flows

According to the Financial Accounting Standards Board, the purpose of the **statement of cash flows** is to provide information about cash receipts and payments as well as information about the operating, investing, and financing activities of a business.

The statement of cash flows should aid users to: (1) assess the probability of positive future cash flows; (2) assess the ability to meet financial obligations; (3) assess reasons for difference between income and cash flow; and (4) assess cash and noncash aspects of financing transactions.

The statement of cash flows is composed of three major sections. **Cash flows from operating activities** consist of the cash effects of transactions that determine income. **Cash flows from investing activities** include lending activities, securities transactions, and acquisition and sale of productive assets. **Cash flows from financing activities** include transactions related to obtaining resources from owners and creditors.

20.2 Preparation of the Statement of Cash Flows

20.2.1 The Worksheet Approach

There are several approaches to the preparation of the statement of cash flows; however, for simplicity, the following example concerns only one—the work sheet approach. Using this approach, a four column spreadsheet is prepared with account balances at the beginning of the period in column one and account balances at period end in column four. Columns two and three will be used for debit and credit analysis, respectively.

Example 20.2.1 shows a worksheet prepared for Smith Corporation for the year ended December 31. Note that accounts with debit balances are listed first, followed by accounts with credit balances.

The debit and credit analysis is simple. For debit accounts that show an increased balance at year-end, the amount of the increase is entered in the debit column (column two). Net decreases in asset balances are entered in the credit column (column three). For credit accounts that show an increased balance at year-end, the amount of increase is entered in the credit column. Decreases are entered in the debit column (column two). The totals of debit and credit balances should be equal.

20.2.2 Completion of the Statement of Cash Flows

Using the transaction information from the worksheet, it is relatively simple to complete the statement of cash flows. As shown in Example 20.2.2, the statement contains the three major sections (cash flows from operating activities, investing activities, and financing activities), with detailed account transactions from the worksheet. The net change in cash shown in the statement of cash flows should be equal to the amount of change in cash shown in the worksheet.

EXAMPLE 20.2.1

SMITH CORPORATION
Worksheet for Statement of Cash Flows
For the Year Ended December 31

Summary of Yearly Entries

	Jan. 1 Balance	Debit	Credit	Dec. 31 Balance
Debits				
Cash	25,000		5,000	20,000
Accounts Receivable	40,000	10,000		50,000
Inventory	65,000	20,000		85,000
Prepaid Expenses	7,500		1,000	6,500
Land	50,000			50,000
Buildings	75,000	15,000		90,000
Equipment	35,000	20,000		55,000
Patents	9,000		2,000	7,000
Total Debits	306,500	65,000	8,000	363,500
Credits				
Accumulated Deprecation	25,000		17,000	42,000
Accounts Payable	35,000	4,000		31,000
Accrued Liabilities	28,000		8,000	36,000
Bonds Payable	100,000			100,000
Premium on Bonds Payable	6,000	500		5,500
Common Stock	20,000		20,000	40,000
Retained Earnings	92,500		16,500	109,000
Total Credits	306,500	4,500	61,500	363,500
Summary Entry Totals		69,500	69,500	

EXAMPLE 20.2.2

SMITH CORPORATION
Statement of Cash Flows
For the Year Ended December 31

Net Cash from Operating Activities:

Net Income		16,500
Noncash Expenses, Revenues, Losses, and Gains Included in Income:		
Increases:		
Decrease in Prepaid Expenses	1,000	
Increase in Accrued Liabilities	8,000	
Depreciation Expense	17,000	
Patent Amortization	2,000	28,000
Decreases:		
Increase in Accounts Receivable	10,000	
Increase in Inventory	20,000	
Decrease in Accounts Payable	4,000	
Amortization of Bond Premium	500	34,500
Net Cash Flow from Operating Activities		(6,500)
Cash Flows from Investing Activities:		
Decreases:		
Cash used in purchase equipment	20,000	
Cash used to purchase buildings	15,000	(35,000)
Cash Flows form Financing Activities:		
Increases:		
Cash from sale of common stock		20,000
Net Decrease in Cash		(5,000)

Problem Solving Example:

At the beginning of the year, the Halburton Construction Company had cash on hand of $100,000. At the end of the year, their cash on hand was $126,500. The reported net income for the year on the accrual basis was $100,000. The Depreciation Expense amounted to $10,000. Accounts Receivable at the beginning of the year was $26,000, and at the end of the year was $29,000. Accounts Payable at the beginning of the year was $45,000, and at the end of the year was $47,000. Prepaid Rent at the beginning of the year amounted to $500, and at the end of the year was $2,000.

During the year, $30,000 of land was purchased. A building was purchased for $50,000. Equipment was purchased for $10,000.

Bonds sold during the year amounted to $20,000. Cash dividends paid out were $11,000.

Prepare a Statement of Cash Flows including sections for Operating Activities, Investing Activities, and Financing Activities.

A

Accumulated Depreciation

1/1/20XX	18,000
12/31/20XX	10,000
12/31/20XX	28,000

The Accumulated Depreciation account for the Halburton Construction Company at the beginning of the year amounted to $18,000, and at the end of the year was $28,000. The difference of $10,000 was derived by an adjusting entry at year's end as follows:

20XX		($ in dollars)
December 31	Depreciation Expense	10,000
	Accumulated Depreciation	10,000

Thus, depreciation for the year was $10,000. This is a business expense that was deducted in the Income Statement from gross income to derive net income. Since depreciation expense takes no cash outflow, it must be added back in the Statement of Cash Flows to determine Cash Provided by Operating Activities.

Accounts Receivable

1/1/20XX	26,000		
12/31/20XX	3,000		
	29,000		

As of January 1, customers owed the Halburton Construction Company $26,000. As of year's end the customers owed Halburton $29,000. This means that Accounts Receivable increased $3,000 during the year. When Accounts Receivable increase during the year, this means that the Sales on Account were (in this case) $3,000 higher than the collections. This makes an outflow of cash of $3,000 for the year because of the increase in Accounts Receivable.

Accounts Payable

		1/1/20XX	45,000
		12/31/20XX	2,000
			47,000

As of January 1, the Halburton Construction Company owed creditors a total of $45,000. As of year's end, Halburton owed creditors $47,000. This means that the Halburton Construction Company owed $2,000 more at year's end than it did at the beginning of the year. By not paying this $2,000, Halburton conserved cash that it should have paid out in bills. This makes an inflow of cash of $2,000 for Halburton.

Prepaid Rent

1/1/20XX	500	12/31/20XX	500
12/31/20XX	2,000		
	2,500		
	2,000		

At January 1, the Halburton Construction Company had Prepaid Rent to the landlord of $500. During the year, the Rent Expense of $500 was deducted from Prepaid Rent and Halburton prepaid another amount of $2,000, leaving a balance in the Prepaid Rent account at year's end of $2,000. Subtracting the $500 balance of Prepaid Rent at the beginning of the year from the $2,000 balance in the account at year's end, we get an increase in Prepaid Rent during the year of $1,500. Of course, this increase in Prepaid Rent was paid with cash so it is an outflow of cash of $1,500.

In order to derive Cash Provided by Operating Activities we add the Net Income (accrual basis) of $100,000, add back the Depreciation Expense of $10,000, deduct the increase in Accounts Receivable of $3,000, add the increase in Accounts Payable of $2,000, and deduct the increase in Prepaid Rent of $1,500, giving Cash Provided by Operating Activities of $107,500. ($100,000 + $10,000 − $3,000 + $2,000 − $1,500 = $107,500 Cash Provided by Operating Activities.) We have thus turned the accrual basis figure, $100,000 Net Income, into the cash basis figure $107,500 Cash Provided by Operating Activities.

The next section of the Cash Flow Statement is entitled Cash Flows from Investing Activities, and this involves mainly the purchase and sale of such long-term assets as land, building, and equipment. During the year, a piece of land was purchased for $30,000 cash. This totaled a cash outflow of $30,000. Also during the year, a building was purchased for $50,000. This totaled a cash outflow of $50,000. Also during the year, manufacturing equipment of $10,000 was purchased for cash. This totaled a cash outflow of $10,000. No long-term assets were sold during the year. Thus, net cash used (expended) through investing activities during the year totaled $90,000 ($30,000 + $50,000 + $10,000 = $90,000).

The final section of the Cash Flow Statement is entitled Cash Flows from Financing Activities.

During the year, the Halburton Construction Company sold at par $20,000 worth of its own bonds to help purchase some long-term assets. This sale of bonds resulted in a cash inflow of $20,000.

During the year, the Halburton Construction Company declared and paid its stockholders dividends of $11,000. This dividend resulted in a cash outflow of $11,000.

The Net Cash Provided by Financing Activities was $9,000. [($20,000 cash received from selling bonds – $11,000 cash paid out in dividends = $9,000 increase in cash) (or cash provided) by financing activities.]

Let us now take a look at the Retained Earnings Statement for Halburton Construction Company for the year.

Retained Earnings

		Beginning Balance	
		1/1/20XX	500,000
		Net Income	
Dividend	11,000	12/31/20XX	100,000
12/31/20XX			600,000
			589,000

At the beginning of the year, the Retained Earnings account of the Halburton Construction Company was $500,000. The Net Income of $100,000 for the year was added to this figure, giving a total of $600,000 on the credit side of the account. On the debit side of the Retained Earnings account is the $11,000 dividends declared during the year. Subtracting the $11,000 dividends from the $600,000 credit total, we get an Ending Balance of $589,000 in the Retained Earnings account.

Halburton Construction Company
Statement of Cash Flows
For Year Ending December 31

Cash Flows from Operating Activities:

Net Income		$100,000
Adjustment to Reconcile Net Income to		
Net Cash Provided by Operating Activities:		
Depreciation Expense	10,000	
Increase in Accounts Receivable	(3,000)	
Increase in Accounts Payable	2,000	
Increase in Prepaid Rent	(1,500)	7,500
Net Cash Provided by Operating Activities		$107,500

Cash Flows from Investing Activities:

Purchase of Land	(30,000)	
Purchase of Building	(50,000)	
Purchase of Equipment	(10,000)	
Net Cash Used by Investing Activities		(90,000)

Cash Flows from Financing Activities:

Issuance of Bonds	20,000	
Payment of Cash Dividends	(11,000)	
Net Cash Provided by Financing Activities		9,000
Net Increase in Cash		26,500
Cash on Hand Balance, January 1		100,000
Cash on Hand Balance, December 31		$126,500

The Statement of Cash Flows moves the reader from the accrual basis (net income) to the cash basis. This statement has become extremely important in recent years, because firms go bankrupt from the lack of immediate cash to pay immediate debts.

The Statement of Cash Flows for the Halburton Construction Company for the year begins with the Net Income (figured on the accrual basis) of $100,000. To this is added back Depreciation Expense of $10,000 because Depreciation Expense had been subtracted in the Income Statement as an expense, when actually this expense takes no cash outflow. Accounts Receivable has increased $3,000 during the year, so the $3,000 is deducted because it takes $3,000 extra cash. Accounts Payable has increased $2,000 during the year, and this has saved the firm that much cash which should have been paid to creditors, so this results in a cash inflow of $2,000. Prepaid Rent of $1,500 more was paid out during the year than was used up, so this results in a $1,500 decrease in cash. All these added algebraically result in Net Cash Provided by Operating Activities of $107,500 ($100,000 + $10,000 − $3,000 + $2,000 − $1,500 = $107,500).

Regarding the Cash Flows from Investing Activities, during the year, the firm purchased land for cash amounting to $30,000. This resulted in a cash outflow of $30,000. During the year the firm purchased a building for cash amounting to $50,000. This resulted in a cash outflow of $50,000. During the year, the firm purchased equipment for cash amounting to $10,000. This resulted in a cash outflow of $10,000. The total cash outflow from investing activities therefore was $90,000 ($30,000 + $50,000 + $10,000 = $90,000).

Regarding the Cash Flows from Financing Activities, during the year, the Halburton Construction Company sold its own bonds at par, resulting in cash income of $20,000. Also during the year, Halburton paid out $11,000 in dividends to its stockholders. This resulted in a cash outflow of $11,000. The Net Cash Provided (incoming cash) by Financing Activities therefore amounted to $9,000 ($20,000 − $11,000 = $9,000).

In recapitulation, Net Cash Provided by Operating Activities amounted to $107,500. Net Cash Used (spent) by Investing Activities amounted to $90,000. Net Cash Provided (incoming) by Financing Activities amounted to $9,000. Adding algebraically, the Net Increase in Cash was therefore $26,500 ($107,500 − $90,000 + $9,000 = $26,500).

The Cash on Hand at the beginning of the year was reported as $100,000. This is added to the Net Increase in Cash of $26,500, to get Cash on Hand at year's end of $126,500 ($100,000 + $26,500 = $126,500).

On the cash basis, the actual cash on hand at year's end was $126,500, and the actual cash on hand at the beginning of the year was $100,000. This Statement of Cash Flows informs the reader how the cash was handled during the year.

CHAPTER 21

Financial Statement Analysis

21.1 Comparative Financial Statements

Comparative financial statement analysis involves examination of financial statements for a single company for two or more accounting periods (years, quarters, or months) and noting the change in both amount and percentage between periods. This form of analysis provides evidence of significant changes in individual accounts and can give a user valuable insight into items that should be further investigated.

21.2 Trend Analysis

Trend analysis is a form of comparative analysis, but instead of examining the entire balance sheet and income statement for two years, this form of analysis involves examination of selected financial statement information over longer periods of time (usually at least five years and as much as 10 – 20 years). Trend analysis is performed by selecting a **base year** and assigning a value of 100% to the amount of the selected financial statement item or items. Each successive year would be compared to the base year on a percentage basis. To illustrate, sales, cost of goods sold, and net income for Years 1 through 7 and the resulting trend percentages are shown in Example 21.2.1.

EXAMPLE 21.2.1

(in millions)	Year 1	Year 2	Year 3	Year 4	Year 5	Year 6	Year 7
Sales	10.0	15.0	19.0	25.0	31.0	40.0	50.0
Gross Profit	5.0	8.5	10.0	14.0	18.0	24.0	30.0
Net Income	3.5	4.5	6.5	8.0	10.0	12.5	15.0

% Analysis Based on Year 1 (Base Year)

	Year 1	Year 2	Year 3	Year 4	Year 5	Year 6	Year 7
Sales	100%	150%	190%	250%	310%	400%	500%
Gross Profit	100	170	200	280	360	480	600
Net Income	100	129	186	229	286	357	428

Using this example, the benefits of trend analysis become evident. Analysis of the actual sales, gross profit, and income data indicates continuing growth in sales and income. Trend analysis, however, shows a different picture. Income is continuing to increase, but at a slower percentage than sales. This, combined with the indication that gross profit is increasing faster than sales, may indicate that management is doing a good job of continuing to reduce material and direct labor costs, but is not controlling administrative or overhead expenses. This indicates a need for further investigation as to the cause of this trend.

21.3 Common-Size Financial Statements

Relating financial statement items to each other within a single time period is known as **vertical analysis**. Common-size financial statements show each financial statement item as a percentage of a key item in that statement. For example, a common-size income statement might present each income and expense item as a percentage of sales for that period. Example 21.3.1 shows a Common-Size Income Statement for Jade Corporation.

EXAMPLE 21.3.1

JADE CORPORATION
Common-Size Income Statement
For the Year Ended 20XX

Sales	100.0%
Cost of Goods Sold	(55.5)
Gross Profit	44.5
Operating Expenses:	
Selling	(18.9)
General and Administrative	(12.5)
Total Operating Expenses	(31.4)
Income Before Income Tax	13.1
Income Tax Expense	(6.0)
Net Income	7.1%

This form of analysis may be used in combination with a horizontal analysis method such as comparative statements to detect significant changes in financial statement components from year to year. Common-size statements are particularly useful in comparing companies of different sizes.

21.3.1 Financial Ratios

Another form of vertical analysis is the use of financial ratios. There are many ratios used by financial analysts, but 13 of the more common ratios used are outlined in Table 21.3.1.

TABLE 21.3.1

FINANCIAL RATIOS

Ratios to Gauge Earnings Performance

Rate of return on total assets =

$$\frac{\text{income before interest expense}}{\text{average total assets}}$$

Rate of return on common stockholders' equity =

$$\frac{\text{net income} - \text{preferred dividends}}{\text{average common stockholders' equity}}$$

Earnings per share =

$$\frac{\text{net income} - \text{preferred dividends}}{\text{average number of common shares outstanding}}$$

Price-earnings ratio =

$$\frac{\text{net income} - \text{preferred dividends}}{\text{earnings per share of common stock}}$$

Dividend yield rate =

$$\frac{\text{dividends per share of common stock}}{\text{current market price per share of common stock}}$$

Ratios to Gauge Debt-Paying Ability

Times interest earned =

$$\frac{\text{income before interest expense and income taxes}}{\text{annual interest expense}}$$

Debt to total assets =

$$\frac{\text{total liabilities}}{\text{total assets}}$$

Stockholders' equity to total assets =

$$\frac{\text{total stockholders' equity}}{\text{total assets}}$$

Financial Ratios to Gauge Liquidity

Current ratio =

$$\frac{\text{current assets}}{\text{current liabilities}}$$

Quick ratio =

$$\frac{\text{quick assets}}{\text{current liabilities}}$$

Inventory turnover =

$$\frac{\text{cost of goods sold}}{\text{average merchandise inventory}}$$

Accounts receivable turnover =

$$\frac{\text{credit sales}}{\text{average accounts receivable}}$$

Average age of receivables =

$$\frac{\text{365 days}}{\text{accounts receivable turnover}}$$

Ratios are most useful when compared to a standard. These standards can be obtained by analyzing financial statements of companies in the same industry or through the use of industry averages provided by trade associations and research firms. Ratios are more meaningful when the companies studied are in the same industry, approximately the same size, and use similar accounting methods.

Problem Solving Example:

 The Comparative Income Statements and Balance Sheets for the Bonner Wholesale Hardware Company for the Years 1 and 2 are shown on the following pages.

Give examples of ratios, tell how they are computed, and explain how these computations help in analyzing the financial statements.

A

LIQUIDITY RATIOS

The liquidity ratios are computed to show the ability of a firm to meet its current obligations as they come due. Here, we look mainly at Current Liabilities. Does the firm have enough cash on hand, or can it procure enough cash on hand to pay the Current Liabilities as they come due? If it can, the firm can stay solvent. If it cannot, bankruptcy may ensue. Banks and other short-term creditors are especially interested in these ratios.

Current Ratio

The current ratio for the Bonner Wholesale Hardware Corporation is computed as follows:

$$\frac{\text{Current Assets}}{\text{Current Liabilities}}$$

The Current Assets (see the Balance Sheet) for Year 1 are $515,000, and the Current Liabilities for Year 1 are $237,000. So, we divide $515,000 by $237,000 to get 2.17299578 times.

Bonner Wholesale Hardware Corporation
Comparative Income Statements
For Years Ending December 31, Years 1 and 2

	Year 1	Year 2
Revenues:		
Net Sales	$800,000	$750,000
Interest Income	3,000	2,000
Other Revenue	1,000	1,000
Total Revenue	804,000	753,000
Costs & Expenses:		
Cost of Goods Sold	600,000	500,000
Depreciation	25,000	20,000
Selling & Administrative Expenses	100,000	90,000
Interest Expense	5,000	3,000
Total Costs & Expenses	730,000	613,000
Income before Taxes	74,000	140,000
Less Income Taxes (30%)	− 22,200	− 42,000
Net Income after Taxes	$ 51,800	$ 98,000
Number of Shares Outstanding	10,000	10,000
Earnings Per Share	$5.18	$9.80

The Current Assets (see the Balance Sheet) for Year 2 are $482,000, and the Current Liabilities for Year 2 are $180,000. So, we divide $482,000 by $180,000 to get 2.677777 times.

Another way to express this ratio is as follows:

Current Ratios:

$$\text{Year 1:} \quad \frac{\$515,000}{\$237,000} = 2.17299578 \text{ times}$$

$$\text{Year 2:} \quad \frac{\$482,000}{\$180,000} = 2.677777 \text{ times}$$

Bonner Wholesale Hardware Corporation
Comparative Balance Sheets
December 31, Year 1 and December 31, Year 2

	Year 1	Year 2
Assets		
Current Assets:		
Cash	$ 20,000	$ 22,000
Marketable Securities (at Cost)	70,000	70,000
Accounts Receivable	225,000	200,000
Inventories (at lower of Cost or Market)	200,000	190,000
Total Current Assets	515,000	482,000
Investments (at Cost)	150,000	150,000
Fixed Assets:		
Property, Plant, & Equipment (at Cost)	900,000	850,000
Less Accumulated Depreciation	(100,000)	(90,000)
	800,000	760,000
Goodwill	25,000	12,500
Total Assets	$1,490,000	$1,404,500
Liabilities & Stockholders' Equity		
Current Liabilities:		
Accounts Payable	75,000	70,000
Notes Payable	150,000	100,000
Accrued Liabilities	12,000	10,000
Total Current Liabilities	237,000	180,000
Long-Term Debt		
Bonds Payable	600,000	700,000
Long-Term Notes Payable	200,000	150,000
Total Long-Term Debt	800,000	850,000
Total Liabilities	1,037,000	1,030,000
Stockholders' Equity:		
Common Stock, $10 Par	100,000	100,000
Additional Paid-in Capital	300,000	300,000
Retained Earnings	53,000	(25,500)
Total Stockholders' Equity	453,000	374,500
Total Liabilities & Stockholders' Equity	$1,490,000	$1,404,500

Many analysts believe that a current ratio of at least 2 to 1 is adequate for the average business. This means that Current Assets are twice as high as the Current Liabilities, because usually in an emergency the current assets can be turned into cash to pay the current liabilities as they come due. It is also helpful to see whether or not the current ratio is improving from year to year. Looking at the preceding current ratios for the Bonner Wholesale Hardware Corporation, one sees that in both Years 1 and 2 the ratios are higher than 2 to 1, which means that in this respect the corporation is in good shape. Also, the ratio of Current Assets to Current Liabilities has gone up from 2.17 to 1 in Year 1, to 2.677 to 1 in Year 2, which is excellent.

Acid-Test Ratio (Quick Ratio)

Sometimes a business with a satisfactory current ratio can still go bankrupt because so much of the current assets are tied up in inventory that they perhaps cannot be turned into cash rapidly enough to pay off the current creditors. In order to take this possibility into consideration, the so-called acid-test ratio has been developed. Another name for this is the quick ratio. It is computed by dividing the Quick Assets by the Current Liabilities. Quick Assets are those current assets that can easily be turned into cash if necessary to pay off current creditors. Quick Assets are determined by subtracting Merchandise Inventory and prepaid items from Total Current Assets. Since this current problem involving the Bonner Wholesale Hardware Corporation has no prepaid items (such as Prepaid Rent or Prepaid Insurance), it is only necessary here to deduct the Merchandise Inventory from the Current Assets in order to get the Quick Assets. Then, the Quick Assets are divided by the Current Liabilities to get the acid-test ratio (quick ratio).

For Year 1, the inventory is $200,000. This is subtracted from the Total Current Assets of $515,000 to get Quick Assets of $315,000. Next, the Quick Assets of $315,000 are divided by the Current Liabilities of $237,000 to get the acid-test ratio for Year 1 of 1.329113924 to 1.

For Year 2, the inventory is $190,000. This is subtracted from the Total Current Assets of $482,000 to get Quick Assets of $292,000. Next, the Quick Assets of $292,000 are divided by the Current Liabilities of $180,000 to get the acid-test ratio for Year 2 of 1.6222 to 1.

Another way of expressing these acid-test ratios follows:

Year 1: $\dfrac{(\$515,000 - \$200,000)}{\$237,000} = \dfrac{\$315,000}{\$237,000}$ 1.329113924 to 1

Year 2: $\dfrac{(\$482,000 - \$190,000)}{\$180,000} = \dfrac{\$292,000}{\$180,000}$ 1.6222 to 1

Most analysts believe that an acid-test ratio of 1 to 1 or higher is good, because this means that in an emergency the Quick Assets could be turned into cash to pay off current liabilities, and thus, stave off bankruptcy. It will be noted in the computations above that in both the Years 1 and 2 the acid-test ratios have been higher than 1 to 1.

Now we should compare the acid-test ratios for the two years. It will be noted that in Year 1 the ratio was 1.329 to 1 and in Year 2 the ratio rose to 1.622 to 1. So, not only are the ratios for both years higher than 1 to 1, but also the ratio has improved with the ratio in Year 2 being better than Year 1, showing that Bonner Wholesale Hardware Corporation is in a better financial position and better able to pay off its immediate debts in Year 2 than it was in Year 1.

Accounts Receivable Turnover

Accounts receivable turnover is computed by dividing the Net Sales by the average receivables. This shows how many times the Net Sales are greater than the average receivables, or, in other words, how many times the receivables have turned over in the form of sales during the year. In Year 1 the Net Sales were $800,000. It is not possible to exactly determine the average receivables because we do not know the receivables at the end of the previous year. So, we divide the Net Sales by the receivables at the end of Year 1, which are $225,000, to get 3.56 times. This means that the net sales are 3.56 times as high as the receivables in Year 1.

For Year 2 the Net Sales are $750,000. The receivables at the end of Year 1 are $225,000 and the receivables at the end of Year 2 are $200,000, giving average receivables as $212,500 ($225,000 + $200,000 = $425,000; $425,000 divided by 2 = $212,500). We then divide the Net Sales of $750,000 by the average receivable of $212,500 to get 3.53 times for the accounts receivable turnover for Year 2.

Another way to show this is as follows:

Year 1: $\dfrac{\$800,000}{\$225,000}$ = 3.56 times (accounts receivable turnover)

Year 2: $\dfrac{\$750,000}{\$212,500}$ = 3.53 times (accounts receivable turnover)

As seen from the computations above, the accounts receivable turnover has dropped from 3.56 times in Year 1 to 3.53 times in Year 2. This does not seem to be a significant decrease in the turnover and is probably due to the drop in sales between the two years. Whether 3.56 times or 3.53 times is a good enough ratio is not discernible here and should be compared to the turnover ratio for the entire wholesale hardware industry.

Inventory Turnover

The inventory turnover is computed by dividing the Cost of Goods Sold by the average inventory. In Year 1, the Cost of Goods Sold is $600,000. The average inventory cannot be determined because we do not have the figures for the previous year, so we will use the inventory at the end of Year 1 which is $200,000. Six hundred thousand dollars divided by $200,000 means that during Year 1 the inventory turned over three times.

In Year 2, the Cost of Goods Sold is $500,000. The average inventory is computed by adding the inventory at the end of Year 1 ($200,000) to the inventory at the end of Year 2 ($190,000) and dividing by 2 ($200,000 + $190,000 = $390,000; $390,000 divided by 2 = $195,000).

We then divide the $500,000 Cost of Goods Sold for Year 2 by the $195,000 average inventory to get 2.564 times.

This can be stated another way as follows:

Year 1: $\dfrac{\$600,000}{\$200,000}$ = 3 times

Year 2: $\dfrac{\$500,000}{\$195,000}$ = 2.564 times

It will be noted that the inventory turnover dropped from three times in Year 1 to only 2.564 times in Year 2. This is a dangerous red flag and should be more closely examined. Why is the inventory moving more slowly? It will be noted that the Cost of Goods Sold dropped greatly, from $600,000 in Year 1 to only $500,000 in Year 2. And the reason that the Cost of Goods Sold dropped was because the sales dropped. Of course, the inventory dropped too (from $200,000 in Year 1 to only $190,000 in the Year 2), but this was only a $10,000 difference ($200,000 – $190,000 = $10,000). The difference in the Cost of Goods Sold between the two years was $100,000 ($600,000 – $500,000 = $100,000). Proportionately, the Cost of Goods Sold dropped a much greater extent than the inventory. This is a danger signal in that the inventory that the firm is carrying is probably too high in proportion to the sales that are being made. How should this be corrected? Perhaps the firm should do more advertising in order to increase the sales next year. Or the firm should not buy as much new merchandise until some of the merchandise sitting in the warehouse is sold.

Is a turnover of 2.5 to 3 times satisfactory for the Bonner Wholesale Hardware Corporation? This can only be answered by comparing Bonner's inventory turnover with that of competing firms, probably through national statistics provided by the trade association.

Asset Turnover

Another method of financial analysis of the business is the computation of asset turnover. This is found by dividing the Net Sales by the average total assets, not including investments, to determine how well the assets are being used to bring in sales. The investment figures are not used in this computation because investments are extra money invested in businesses other than this business.

For Year 1 we take Total Assets of $1,490,000 and subtract investments of $150,000 to get assets used in the business of $1,340,000. We cannot get average assets as such, since we do not have the figures for the previous year. We divide the Net Sales for Year 1 ($800,000) by the assets used in the business during Year 1 ($1,340,000) to get 0.59. This means that the Net Sales during the year are only 60% of the value of the assets used in the business to make those sales.

For Year 2 we take the Total Assets of $1,404,500 and subtract investments of $150,000 to get $1,254,500 assets used in the business at the end of Year 2. The assets used in the business at the end of Year 1 have previously been computed to be $1,340,000. The average of these two figures is $1,297,250, which is found by adding these two figures together and dividing by 2 ($1,254,500 + $1,340,000 = $2,594,500; $2,594,500 divided by 2 = $1,297,250). Now we divide the Net Sales for Year 2 of $750,000 by the average total assets used in the business of $1,297,250 to get 0.57. This means that the Net Sales during the year are only 58% of the value of the average assets used in the business to make those sales.

This can be stated in another way as follows:

Year 1: $\dfrac{\$800,000}{\$1,340,000} = 0.59$

Year 2: $\dfrac{\$750,000}{\$1,297,250} = 0.57$

How should these figures be interpreted? In Year 1, the sales were only 60% of the assets used to make the sales. In Year 2, the sales were only 58% of the average assets used to make the sales. This is a slight drop, and what caused it? In the first place, there was a significant drop in sales between the Years 1 and 2. The assets used to make the sales also dropped but not as greatly percentage wise. The slight drop in asset turnover is probably not too significant, but the drop in Net Sales is certainly a red flag.

Is the 60% or 58% asset turnover proper? This can only be determined by comparing these figures with the asset turnover rate of competitors.

Profit Margin on Sales

Further analysis into the financial health of the Bonner Wholesale Hardware Corporation can be determined by computing the profit margin on sales. This can be done by dividing the Net Income for the year by the Net Sales for the year.

In Year 1, the Net Income was $51,800, and the Net Sales were $800,000. Dividing the Net Income of $51,800 by Net Sales of $800,000, we get a profit margin of .06475 or 6.475%. This means that for each dollar of sales we earn a profit of $.06475.

In Year 2, the Net Income was $98,000 and the Net Sales were $750,000. Dividing the Net Income of $98,000 by Net Sales of $750,000, we get a profit margin of .1306666 or 13.0666%. This means that for each dollar of sales we earn a profit of $.1306666.

Another way to express these computations is as follows:

Year 1: $\dfrac{\$51,800 \text{ Net Income}}{\$800,000 \text{ Net Sales}} = .06475$

Year 2: $\dfrac{\$98,000 \text{ Net Income}}{\$750,000 \text{ Net Sales}} = .130666$

This margin on Net Sales shows an excellent increase for the company. In Year 1, the firm earned only a little over 6¢ on each dollar of sales, and in Year 2 the firm earned a little over 13¢ on each dollar of sales. Why the bountiful increase? The important reason is that Net Income almost doubled. It increased from $51,800 in Year 1 to $98,000 in Year 2, and also, Net Sales decreased from $800,000 in the Year 1 to $750,000 in Year 2. Of course, it is not good to have sales decrease, but in the time of a decrease in sales the Net Profit almost doubled. How could this be? It was because cost and expenses dropped so radically, especially Cost of Goods Sold.

Rate of Return on Assets

Another analysis computation is rate of return on assets. This is found by dividing Net Income by average Total Assets used in the business.

For Year 1, the Total Assets were $1,490,000, and from this figure we deduct $150,000 investments which are assets not used in the business to get $1,340,000 assets used in the business. We then divide the Net Income of $51,800 by $1,340,000 assets used in the business to get .038656716 or 3.8656716%.

For Year 2, the Total Assets were $1,404,500, and from this figure we deduct $150,000 investments which are assets not used in the business to get $1,254,500 assets used in the business. We then divide the Net Income of $98,000 by the $1,254,500 assets used in the business to get .07811877 or 7.811877%.

Another way to express these computations follows:

Year 1: $$\frac{\$51,800 \text{ Net Income}}{\$1,340,000 \text{ Assets Used in Business}} = 3.8656716\%$$

Year 2: $$\frac{\$98,000 \text{ Net Income}}{\$1,254,500 \text{ Assets Used in Business}} = 7.811877\%$$

This means that in Year 1, the assets used in the business were bringing in a Net Income of 3.866% of the value of these assets. It also means that in Year 2, the assets used in the business were bringing in a Net Income of 7.812% of the value of these assets.

The percent increased from 3.866% of the assets in Year 1 to 7.812% of the assets in Year 2, and this is good. But the percentages themselves seem somewhat too low for a good business investment. However, to be sure, these figures would have to be compared to the rate of return on assets of competitors in the industry.

Rate of Return on Common Stockholders' Equity

Another important analysis computation is the rate of return on common stockholders' equity. Stockholders, especially, are interested in the percentage of return that their investment in the company is making. This computation is determined by dividing the Net Income minus the Preferred Stock Dividends by the average Common Stockholders' Equity.

For Year 1, the Net Income was $51,800. Since the Bonner Wholesale Hardware Corporation has no preferred stock outstanding, the computation is easier, and we merely divide the $51,800 Net Income by the total equity for Year 1 of $453,000. The total equity figure for the previous year is not available so we use the total equity figure for Year 1 and cannot get average equity. $51,800 Net Income divided by $453,000 is 11.4348785%.

For Year 2, the Net Income was $98,000. Since the Bonner Wholesale Hardware Corporation has no preferred stock outstanding, the computation is easier, and we divide the $98,000 Net Income by the average Common Stockholders' Equity. To determine the average Common Stockholder Equity, it is necessary to add the Stockholders' Equity at the end of Year 3 ($453,000) to the total Stockholders' Equity at the end of Year 4 ($374,500) and divide by 2 ($453,000 + $374,500 = $827,500; $827,500 divided by 2 = $413,750 which is the average common stockholders' equity). We now divide the Net Income of $98,000 by the average common stockholders' equity of $413,750 to get 23.6858%.

Another way of expressing this follows:

Year 1: $$\frac{\$51,800 \text{ Net Income}}{\$453,000 \text{ Stockholders' Equity}} = 11.43\%$$

Year 2: $$\frac{\$98,000 \text{ Net Income}}{\$413,750 \text{ Average Stockholders' Equity}} = 23.6858\%$$

During Year 1, the common stockholders earned 11.43% on their investment, and in Year 2, the common stockholders earned 23.6858%

on their investment. This is an excellent increase in return which should greatly please the stockholders. These rates of return also seem extremely high but must be compared with those returns of competitors also. Why did the rate of return on common stock equity jump so greatly between the two years? It was mainly due to the increase in Net Income, which is good, but it is also due to the decrease in Stockholders' Equity, which is bad, and which needs more looking into.

Earnings Per Share

Stockholders and potential stockholders are interested in a corporation's earnings per share—that is, the amount that a person would earn who holds only one share of the corporation's stock. This is determined by dividing the Net Income for the year by the Weighted Average of shares outstanding.

For Year 1, the Net Income is $51,800. The Weighted Average of shares outstanding is computed for firms buying or selling their own stock during the year. However, the Bonner Wholesale Hardware Corporation had the same number of shares outstanding at the beginning of the year as they did at the end of the year (in this case 10,000 shares), so no Weighted Average needs to be computed in this case. We divide the $51,800 Net Income by the 10,000 shares outstanding to get $5.18 earnings per share for Year 1.

For Year 2, the Net Income is $98,000. We divide this by the 10,000 shares outstanding to get $9.80 earnings per share for Year 2.

In comparing the $5.18 earnings per share for Year 1 with the $9.80 earnings per share for Year 2, we notice a large increase. Since the number of shares outstanding did not increase, this increase in earnings per share is completely due to the increase in Net Income.

Price-Earnings Ratio

Investors and potential investors are interested in the price-earnings ratio. This is the number of times that the market price of the stock is higher than the earnings per share for the year. It gives investors and potential investors a benchmark whereby they can compare this stock with other stocks to determine which stocks are the best buy at the time. The ratio is determined by dividing the market price by the earnings per share.

Let us say that as of December 31, in Year 1, the market price of Bonner Wholesale Hardware Corporation stock is $50 per share. The earnings per share for Year 3 have been determined to be $5.18. We then divide the $50 by the $5.18 to get 9.6525. This means that the market price is over nine times as much as the earnings per share. Let us say that as of December 31, in Year 2, the market price of Bonner Wholesale Hardware Corporation stock has increased to $52 per share. The earnings per share for Year 2 have been determined to be $9.80. We then divide the $52 by the $9.80 to get 5.3. This means that the market price is over five times as much as the earnings per share.

In comparing the price-earnings ratio between the two years, we note that the ratio was 9.6 times in Year 1 and that it had dropped to only 5.3 times in Year 2. Is this drop good or bad? Many times investors noting lower price-earnings ratios will believe that this denotes a good time for them to be buying the stock; so, in this respect, it is good. But why did the ratio drop? There are two reasons. In the first place, the price of the stock only increased $2 per share ($52 − $50 = $2). This is a very small increase. Between these two years the earnings per share increased by $4.62 ($9.80 − $5.18 = $4.62). This is a great increase.

Another way to express this price-earnings ratio is as follows:

Year 1: $\dfrac{\$50 \text{ per share price}}{\$5.18 \text{ earnings per share}} = 9.6525 \text{ times}$

Year 2: $\dfrac{\$52 \text{ per share price}}{\$9.80 \text{ earnings per share}} = 5.3 \text{ times}$

The main reason for the drop in the price-earnings ratio in this case is the great increase in the earnings per share between the two years.

Payout Ratio

Some investors are interested in buying growth stocks that perhaps pay little or no dividends. Other investors are more interested in "milk cow" types of stocks that pay higher dividends but that may not increase so much in market value. This second type of investor who wants high dividends is especially interested in stocks that have a high payout ratio.

The payout ratio is determined by dividing the Cash Dividends by the Net Income less Preferred Dividends. Since the Bonner Wholesale Hardware Corporation has no preferred stock, the payout ratio is computed by dividing the Cash Dividends by the Net Income.

Let us assume that Bonner Wholesale Hardware Corporation paid out $25,000 in dividends in Year 1 and paid out $30,000 in dividends in Year 2.

For Year 1, we divide the Cash Dividends paid out that year ($25,000) by the Net Income for that year ($51,800), to get a 48.2625% payout ratio. This means that during Year 1, over 48% of the earnings were paid out to the stockholders in dividends.

For Year 2, we divide the Cash Dividends paid out that year ($30,000) by the Net Income for that year ($98,000), to get a 30.6122% payout ratio. This means that during Year 2, over 30% of the earnings were paid out to the stockholders in dividends.

Another way of expressing this ratio follows:

$$\text{Year 1:} \quad \frac{\$25,000 \text{ Dividends Paid Out}}{\$51,800 \text{ Net Income}} = 48.2625\% \text{ payout ratio}$$

$$\text{Year 2:} \quad \frac{\$30,000 \text{ Dividends Paid Out}}{\$98,000 \text{ Net Income}} = 30.6122\% \text{ payout ratio}$$

As seen from the figure above, the dividend payout ratio has greatly decreased, from over 48% in Year 1, to over 30% in Year 2. This might not be good news to investors wanting higher dividend payout ratios, but let us examine this further and see why the payout ratio has decreased.

Actually, the dividends themselves have increased from $25,000 in Year 1, to $30,000 in Year 2. This means that the corporation has been more generous with its stockholders. The real answer is that the Net Income has increased so greatly—from only $51,800 in Year 1 to $98,000 in Year 2. Both the dividends and the Net Income have increased; but the Net Income has increased at a much faster clip than the dividends, and this accounts for the decrease in the payout ratio.

Debt to Total Assets

A long-term solvency computation of importance to creditors is the debt to total assets computation. The creditors feel safer if the ratio of debt to total assets is decreasing or is already low. This computation is found by dividing debt (Total Liabilities) by Total Assets.

In Year 1, the Total Liabilities of the Bonner Wholesale Hardware Corporation were $1,037,000 and the Total Assets were $1,490,000. If we divide $1,037,000 by $1,490,000, we get 69.597%. This means that at the end of Year 1, the Liabilities were over 69% of the Assets.

In Year 2, the Total Liabilities of the Bonner Wholesale Hardware Corporation were $1,030,000 and the Total Assets were $1,404,500. If we divide $1,030,000 by $1,404,500, we get 73.3357%. This means that at the end of Year 2, the Liabilities were over 73% of the Assets. Another way of showing these computations follows:

Year 1: $\dfrac{\$1,037,000 \text{ Total Liabilities}}{\$1,490,000 \text{ Total Assets}}$ = 69.597% debt to asset ratio

Year 2: $\dfrac{\$1,030,000 \text{ Total Liabilities}}{\$1,404,500 \text{ Total Assets}}$ = 73.3357 debt to asset ratio

As can be seen from the above figures, the debt to asset ratio has increased from over 69% in Year 1 to over 73% in Year 2. This is scary to creditors, because creditors want to see this ratio decrease. Why is this ratio going the wrong way? Liabilities of the corporation have actually decreased from $1,037,000 in Year 1 to $1,030,000 in Year 2, so the Liabilities are not the culprit. Let's look at Total Assets. They have decreased even more than Liabilities, with the Total Assets going down from $1,490,000 in Year 1 to $1,404,500 in Year 2. Thus, the Assets are decreasing much faster than the Liabilities. But why is this? Which assets are decreasing? Looking at the Comparative Balance Sheets for the Bonner Wholesale Hardware Corporation near the first part of this chapter, we see that Cash is increasing, and Marketable Securities are increasing, so they are not the culprits.

Accounts Receivable has decreased by $25,000 (from $225,000 in Year 1 to only $200,000 in Year 2). Also, Inventories have decreased $10,000 (from $200,000 in Year 1 to only $190,000 in Year 2). The Assets have decreased at a much greater clip than the Liabilities, and this accounts for the increase in the debt to asset ratio.

Times Interest Earned

The times interest earned computation is of great interest to bond-holders who want to make sure that the corporation has enough money to pay the interest on each interest payment date. It is computed by taking the income before taxes and interest charges, and dividing this by the interest charges. To do this, the easiest way is to work backwards up the Income Statement. Looking at the Comparative Income Statement for the Bonner Wholesale Hardware Corporation for Year 1, we see that the Net Income after Taxes is $51,800. To this, add back the Income Taxes of $22,200 to get Income before Taxes of $74,000. To this, add back Interest Expense of $5,000 to derive $79,000, which can be called Income before Taxes and Interest Charges. This figure of $79,000 is then divided by the $5,000 interest charges to get 15.8 times. This means that the Bonner Wholesale Hardware Corporation has enough money to pay interest on the bonds 15.8 times over.

Looking at the Comparative Income Statement for the Bonner Wholesale Hardware Corporation for Year 2, we see that the Net Income after Taxes is $98,000. To this, add back Income Taxes of $42,000 to get Income before Taxes of $140,000. To this, add back interest expense of $3,000 to get $143,000, which can be called Income before Taxes and Interest Charges. This figure of $143,000 is then divided by the $3,000 interest charges to get 47.667 times. This means that the Bonner Wholesale Hardware Corporation has enough money to pay interest on the bonds 47.667 times over.

Another way of expressing this is as follows:

Year 1:	$ 51,800	Net Income after Income Taxes
	+ 22,200	Income Taxes
	74,000	Net Income before Income Taxes
	+ 5,000	Interest Expense
	$ 79,000	Income before Taxes and Interest Charges

$79,000 divided by $5,000 Interest Charges = 15.8 times

Year 2:	$ 98,000	Net Income after Income Taxes
	+ 42,000	Income Taxes
	140,000	Net Income before Income Taxes
	+ 3,000	Interest Expense
	$143,000	Income before Taxes and Interest Charges

$143,000 divided by $3,000 Interest charges = 47.667 times

As can be seen from the above computations, the protection for the bondholders has increased from 15.8 times to 47.667 times. Usually, in the computation of times interest earned, 10 times protection would be good, but these figures are higher than that and seem to be increasing by leaps and bounds. Why is this?

There are two reasons. In the first place, the Income before Taxes and Interest Charges has increased greatly (from only $79,000 in Year 1 to $143,000 in Year 2). Also, the Interest Expense has decreased from $5,000 in Year 1 to only $3,000 in Year 2. Both these changes are good for the company and make the company stronger financially; therefore, they are also good for the company's bondholders.

Book Value Per Share

Investors and potential investors are interested in computing book value per share. This is the amount that an owner of one share of stock would get if the corporation broke up and liquidated immediately, sold all assets, paid off all liabilities, then paid the stockholders. Investors like to compare this book value per share to market value per share to see whether it is a good time to buy, or perhaps, to sell the stock. Book value per share is computed by dividing the Common Stockholders' Equity by the number of shares outstanding.

In Year 1, the Total Stockholders' Equity at year's end is $453,000. Since there are no preferred stockholders to pay off, the Common Stockholders' Equity is the same as the Total Stockholders' Equity. The number of outstanding shares at year's end is 10,000. We divide $453,000 by 10,000 shares to derive $45.30 book value per share. The market price of the stock as of December 31, in Year 1, is $50 per share. This means the underlying book value of $45.30 is not quite so high, and perhaps the stock is overpriced on the market.

In Year 2, the Total Stockholders' Equity at year's end is $374,500. Since there are no preferred stockholders to pay off, the Common Stockholders' Equity is the same as the Total Stockholders' Equity. The number of outstanding shares at year's end is 10,000. We divide $374,500 by 10,000 shares to get a book value per share of $37.45. As of December 31, in Year 2, the market price of the stock is $52 per share, whereas the underlying book value is only $37.45, so perhaps the stock is overpriced on the market.

Another "red flag" revealed by the Comparative Balance Sheets of the Bonner Wholesale Hardware Corporation is the Retained Earnings account. At the end of Year 1, the Retained Earnings account had a credit balance of $53,000, and at the end of Year 2 this had dropped to a deficit (debit balance) of $25,500. A closer look at the Retained Earnings account is in order. Also, reasons should be found for the decrease in Accounts Receivable and Inventories and in Property, Plant, and Equipment.

21.4 Other Sources of Financial Information

Thorough analysis of financial statements should include a review of the **auditor's report,** where the auditor expresses an opinion as to whether the financial information being presented conforms to generally accepted accounting principles. Any significant deviation from such principles will be noted.

Another source of information is the notes to the financial statements, which outline the various accounting methods used in those statements. Also contained in the financial statement notes is information as to **contingent liabilities** facing the company. These are liabilities that the company may suffer under certain circumstances. The notes should contain information about such contingencies, including the probability of loss to the company involved. Contingencies that are probable in nature and can be reasonably estimated must be shown on the balance sheet as a liability. Other descriptive notes may include information on pension plans, income taxes, and long-term debts.

Quiz: Consolidations – Financial Statement Analysis

1. Why do consolidated companies often have combined balance sheets?

    (A) Although they are two different legal entities, they are really one economic entity.

    (B) Although they are two different economic entities, they are really one legal entity.

    (C) Consolidated never have combined balance sheets.

    (D) None of these.

2. Which one of the following is NOT one of the subsections of a Statement of Cash Flows?

    (A) Operating Activities   (C) Investing Activities

    (B) Divesting Activities   (D) Financing Activities

3. What is the purpose of a Statement of Cash Flows?

    (A) To provide information on a corporation's cash receipts and payments

    (B) To provide information on a corporation's revenue and expenses

    (C) To provide information for the corporate balance sheet

    (D) None of these.

4. What is probably the easiest method of preparing a Statement of Cash Flows?

    (A) Balance Sheet approach

    (B) Work Sheet approach

    (C) Income Statement approach

    (D) Equity approach

5. What are two important methods of Financial Statement analysis?

    (A) Balance Sheet and Income Statement approaches

    (B) Trial Balance and Adjusted Trial Balance approaches

    (C) Temporary and Permanent approaches

    (D) Trend Analysis and Common-Size Analysis approaches

6. What are Comparative Financial Statements?

    (A) The process of comparing or examining financial statements of two companies for a single year

    (B) The process of comparing or examining the financial statements of a single company for two or more years

    (C) Either of the above.

    (D) Neither of the above.

7. What type of financial analysis is used with Common-Size analysis?

   (A) Vertical analysis   (C) Diagonal analysis

   (B) Horizontal analysis   (D) None of the above.

8. In comparing corporations of different sizes, is it better to use percentages or dollar values?

   (A) Dollar values   (C) Neither of these.

   (B) Percentages   (D) Both of these.

9. Where might the reader of financial statements discover other sources of financial information?

   (A) Dictionary   (C) Fiction

   (B) Atlas   (D) Footnotes of statements

10. Which one of the following is NOT a question that can be answered by a cost system in a jobbing plant?

   (A) What wages should be paid to employees?

   (B) At what price should the product be sold?

   (C) How profitable is the product now at present prices?

   (D) Should production be expanded?

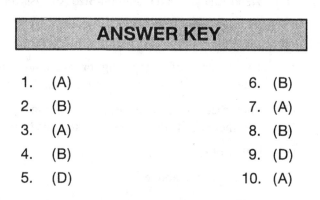

ANSWER KEY

1.	(A)		6.	(B)
2.	(B)		7.	(A)
3.	(A)		8.	(B)
4.	(B)		9.	(D)
5.	(D)		10.	(A)